"This book offers thought-provoking assessments of foundational Christian doctrines from close engagement with Asian circumstances and Asian Christian teachers. As it examines the Trinity, the church, the person and work of Christ, and the Holy Spirit, insights from Western Protestants, Catholics and the Orthodox are put to good use, but always with the aim of articulating genuinely Asian theologies. Much of the future of Christian theology worldwide is outlined in this helpful study."
Mark A. Noll, Francis McAnaney Professor of History, University of Notre Dame

"A resourceful, perceptive and much-needed work in the complex landscape of Asian theology."
K.-K. Yeo, Harry R. Kendall Professor of New Testament, Garrett-Evangelical Theological Seminary

"This is a groundbreaking work in privileging the lived experience of the Christian majority in Asia in the process of theological construction. More surprising and admirable is the author's grounding Asian grassroots theology in historic Christian theological traditions, opening a wide horizon for Asian theology to engage with and contribute to the global theological movement."
Wonsuk Ma, executive director, Oxford Centre for Mission Studies

"Here is a thoughtful and ecumenically sensitive contribution to Asian theology from one of the most respected Pentecostal theologians in Asia. Particularly striking is the careful integration of Asian traditions—both grassroots and elite, with contemporary Western reflection. With this work we are seeing the emergence of a mature Asian evangelical voice that is certain to change the dynamics of the global theological conversation. The book will be useful in both theology courses and church education classes."
William A. Dyrness, professor of theology and culture, Fuller Theological Seminary

"Simon Chan's latest work is certainly a challenge to how 'Asian theology' has been perceived in the academic world. Lavishly referenced, conservative and scholarly, this is a most welcome addition to his notable works, which challenge readers to recover the spiritual and truly 'theological' essentials of Christianity."
Allan H. Anderson, University of Birmingham, United Kingdom

"Only Simon Chan can register Pentecostal perspectives in substantive conversation with Catholic and Orthodox traditions amidst Asian religio-cultural realities with surprising results about not only the retrieval of classical or historic Christian teachings but also with new points of contact and invited adjustments to established categories and frameworks of thinking. *Grassroots Asian Theology* is methodologically exemplary in suggesting a theology that is both fully Asian and ecumenical in the biblical sense."

Amos Yong, J. Rodman Williams Professor of Theology and dean of the School of Divinity, Regent University, Virginia Beach, Virginia

GRASSROOTS
ASIAN THEOLOGY

THINKING THE FAITH FROM THE GROUND UP

SIMON CHAN

IVP Academic

An imprint of InterVarsity Press
Downers Grove, Illinois

In memory of Joseph P. Frary
(1940–2013)

InterVarsity Press
P.O. Box 1400, Downers Grove, IL 60515-1426
ivpress.com
email@ivpress.com

InterVarsity Press® is the book-publishing division of InterVarsity Christian Fellowship/USA®, a movement of students and faculty active on campus at hundreds of universities, colleges and schools of nursing in the United States of America, and a member movement of the International Fellowship of Evangelical Students. For information about local and regional activities, visit intervarsity.org.

All Scripture quotations marked NIV are taken from the Holy Bible, New International Version®. NIV®. Copyright ©1973, 1978, 1984 by International Bible Society. Used by permission of Zondervan Publishing House. All rights reserved.

While all stories in this book are true, some names and identifying information in this book have been changed to protect the privacy of the individuals involved.

Cover design: Cindy Kiple
Interior design: Beth McGill
Images: elderly Asian woman: Karl Johaentges/Getty Images
        Asian pedestrians: © Billy Hustace/Getty Images

ISBN 978-0-8308-4048-9 (print)
ISBN 978-0-8308-9544-1 (digital)

Printed in the United States of America ∞

InterVarsity Press is committed to ecological stewardship and to the conservation of natural resources in all our operations. This book was printed using sustainably sourced paper.

Library of Congress Cataloging-in-Publication Data

Chan, Simon.
  Grassroots Asian theology: thinking the faith from the ground up /
  Simon Chan.
     pages cm
  Includes bibliographical references and index.
  ISBN 978-0-8308-4048-9 (pbk. : alk. paper)
  1. Theology, Doctrinal--Asia. I. Title.
  BT75.3.C4245 2014
  230.095--dc23

                                 2014011060

| P | 21 | 20 | 19 | 18 | 17 | 16 | 15 | 14 | 13 | 12 | 11 | 10 | 9 | 8 | 7 | 6 | 5 | 4 | 3 |
| Y | 35 | 34 | 33 | 32 | 31 | 30 | 29 | 28 | 27 | 26 | 25 | 24 | 23 | 22 | 21 | 20 | 19 | | |

CONTENTS

PREFACE

Much of what the West knows as Asian theology consists largely of elitist accounts of what Asian theologians are saying, and elitist theologians seldom take grassroots Christianity seriously. Yet it is at the grassroots level that we encounter a vibrant, albeit implicit, theology. It is this theology that I wish to highlight. If we accept Prosper of Aquitaine's dictum that the rule of faith should be based on the rule of prayer (*ut legem credendi lex statuat supplicandi*), then a study of the lived theology of the people of God in Asia will yield a better theology for the Asian church and perhaps for the global church as well.

Such a theology, however, cannot be derived solely from Asian cultural resources. Any authentic theology must be developed in light of the larger Christian tradition. The appeal to Christian tradition is not simply a matter of preference but essential to our theological quest. If the Asian church is truly a part of the church catholic, the accumulated contributions of the past and present are essential to moving the church forward wherever it is found. This point has been strongly argued by the Japanese theologian Anri Morimoto against postmodern attempts to deconstruct tradition.[1] A theology developed in this way would not only be a theology for Asia but also from Asia to the universal body of Christ.

In light of this imperative I have drawn freely from Catholic and Orthodox sources. I believe they offer a broader and more solid basis for

---

[1] Anri Morimoto, "Contextualized and Cumulative: Tradition, Orthodoxy and Identity from the Perspective of Asian Theology," *Studies in World Christianity* 15 (Jan. 1, 2009): 65-80.

contextual theologies compared with what goes on in much of mainline Protestantism and evangelicalism today. Putting it another way, any healthy theological development requires holding together two processes in a healthy tension: *ressourcement* and *aggiornamento*. *Ressourcement* is not merely a return to the past; rather it is a creative engagement with earlier sources, the fountainhead of spiritual life. Only in this way can we begin to engage in the work of *aggiornamento*, or adaptation and updating in light of the new situations in which the church finds itself. Without the prerequisite of *ressourcement, aggiornamento* could easily end up with the church capitulating to the spirit of the age.[2]

I have not adopted any standardized format in the development of each theological locus but have sought to let the grassroots dictate shape and direction. Generally, however, I will present a brief sketch of elitist theologies followed by an exploration of theologies found in sermons, devotional works, testimonies and other popular writings by Asian Christians. Sometimes we will look at case studies; at other times we will examine the works of historians, sociologists and anthropologists for what light they can shed on popular thought and practices. I will use whatever resources are available within my limited competence in a highly complex situation to understand grassroots Christian experiences theologically. There is admittedly some unevenness in such an approach, but it allows for ideas to be elucidated from a number of perspectives.

This is not a systematic theology. My main focus is on how theology ought to be done. This book is as much concerned with the processes as the content of theology. Only the content that has a particular bearing on the Asian context is highlighted in each theological locus. My aim is to force a rethink on the way Asian theology is currently undertaken and in so doing show the distinctive contributions of Asian grassroots Christianity to the wider church's theological endeavors.

Traditional Chinese and Korean names are normally written with surname first, followed by given names. This is the form I have adopted.

---

[2]Marcellino D'Ambrosio, "Ressourcement Theology, Aggiornamento, and the Hermeneutics of Tradition," *Communio* 18 (Winter 1991): 530-55.

1

METHODOLOGICAL QUESTIONS

IT IS NOT UNUSUAL FOR discussions on Asian contextual theology to begin with a distinction between Eastern and Western ways of thinking. The Western way, we are told, is abstract, rationalistic and dualistic both metaphysically (for example, spiritual-material, God-creation) and epistemologically (subject-object), while the Eastern way is concrete, holistic and nondualistic; Western thought presents issues in either/or terms while Eastern thought encompasses both/and; Western thought is linear while Eastern thought is non-linear; and so on.[1]

That there are basic differences arising from different cultural experiences cannot be denied, but whether these distinctions should be demarcated as Eastern and Western is another matter. What is sometimes called the Western way of thinking should more accurately be called Cartesian and Enlightenment thought, which does not exclusively define Western epistemology and philosophy. Some postcritical, postmodern ways of thinking that are considered part of the Western philosophical tradition, such as the personalist philosophy of Michael Polanyi, have perhaps more in common with what is characteristically described as the Eastern way of thinking. Similarly, as we shall see, some Asian theologians have adopted theological presuppositions and methods derived directly from

---

[1]For example, Lee Young Jung, "The Yin-Yang Way of Thinking," in *What Asian Christians Are Thinking*, ed. Douglas Elwood (Manila: New Day, 1976); Peter Chang, "Steak, Potatoes and Chopsuey: Linear and Non-Linear Thinking in Theological Education," *Evangelical Review of Theology* (October 1981): 279-86.

Enlightenment thought.[2] Can their theologies be called Asian?

Sometimes the antithesis between East and West is no more than a way of expressing certain value judgments. In some circles, "Western" theology is theology one does not particularly like, while one's preferred theology is regarded as more authentically "Asian." For instance, some Asian theologians of a more liberal persuasion equate "the Western model of theology" with colonial domination and oppressive capitalism.[3] A similar impulse runs in some conservative Asian theologians.[4]

Perhaps it is time to get rid of the habit of describing different patterns of thought in terms of Eastern and Western ways of thinking. In a postmodern, globalized world, such descriptions are neither helpful nor accurate. Rather, a more pertinent question we need to ask in order to develop a contextual or local theology in an Asian context is: what spiritual and intellectual resources of the Christian faith can we bring to bear on the Asian context such that an authentic Christian faith can be effectively communicated and received? Implied in this question is a fundamental theological presupposition: an Asian theology is about the Christian faith in Asia. This presupposition may be phrased in different ways, but it runs through diverse Christian traditions, including Catholicism, Orthodoxy, evangelicalism and Pentecostalism.[5] Some see the common spiritual heritage binding these four traditions together as holding promise for a new ecumenism that goes beyond the currently deadlocked World Council of Churches.[6]

The evangelical mission theologian Paul Hiebert refers to this common

---

[2]For example, the theologies of C. S. Song and others to be discussed below.

[3]See the document from the seventh international conference (1986) of the Ecumenical Association of Third World Theologians (EATWOT) in K. C. Abraham, ed., *Third World Theologies: Commonalities and Divergences* (Maryknoll, NY: Orbis, 1990), p. 196.

[4]For example, Han Chul-Ha, "The Crisis in the Doctrine of God the Creator in Modern Western Theology," in *God in Asian Contexts,* ed. Bong Rin Ro and Mark C. Albrecht (Taichung, Taiwan: Asia Theological Association, 1988), pp. 62-77, accuses "modern western theology" of producing a number of faulty concepts of God—namely, concepts derived from Enlightenment rationalism.

[5]The possible exceptions are liberal Protestantism and the liberal wing of Catholicism (see below).

[6]See *In One Body Through the Cross: The Princeton Proposal for Christian Unity,* ed. Carl E. Braaten and Robert W. Jenson (Grand Rapids: Eerdmans, 2003).

spiritual heritage in terms of the givenness of the gospel, which cannot be compromised even at the cost of appearing scandalous. In language reminiscent of Barth, Hiebert declares:

> The foreignness of the culture we add to the gospel offends and must be eliminated. But the gospel itself offends. It is supposed to offend, and we dare not weaken its offense. The gospel must be contextualized, but it must remain prophetic. It must stand in judgment of what is evil in all cultures as well as in all persons.[7]

The contextualizer of the gospel therefore must have "a metacultural framework that enables him or her to translate the biblical message into the cognitive, affective, and evaluative dimensions of another culture." Hiebert speaks of the need to "clearly grasp the biblical message as originally intended"; otherwise the gospel will be distorted.[8] Discovering metacultural and metatheological frameworks requires the cooperation of the whole body of Christ in all cultures and through time: "the international community of churches and the church down through the ages." Hiebert sees this "internationalizing theology" as the way to a "supracultural theology."[9]

Hiebert's description of the gospel in context using the language of cultural anthropology would be called, in older churches, the Christian tradition. It is in terms of this tradition that I would like to consider the contextualization of the gospel in Asia. As a tradition, the Christian faith is something given and received, and in the process of being historically transmitted it finds new cultural expressions. But it is not something we create according to our cultural experience. Local cultures do shape the way the faith is received and expressed, but for a local theology to be authentically Christian, it must have substantial continuity with the larger Christian tradition.

Tradition implies a community with a history. For Christianity, the history of the church is a continuation of the history of Jesus Christ.

---

[7]Paul Hiebert, *Anthropological Reflections on Missiological Issues* (Grand Rapids: Baker, 1994), p. 86.
[8]Ibid., p. 89.
[9]Ibid., pp. 91-92, 103.

Christianity cannot be reduced to a set of principles that could be replicated in any context without reference to their historical origins. Christianity exists in historical continuity with the story of Jesus Christ's life, death, resurrection, ascension, sending of the Spirit and parousia. Theologically, the story of the church is part of the larger story of the triune God. This is seen in the fact that between the ascension and parousia, Jesus promised to send the Holy Spirit, the third person of the Trinity, to bring into being the church. The church is the result of the Pentecost event, which is the event of the Spirit and therefore part of the story of the triune God.[10] The very being of the church cannot be understood apart from the narrative of the God who reveals himself by sending Jesus Christ and the Holy Spirit. The church therefore proclaims this particular story because it is "the power of God unto salvation" (Rom 1:16 KJV).

This point needs to be reiterated in our postmodern context. The problem is particularly acute for postmodern theologians who, having quite rightly done away with a positivistic view of doctrines as universal timeless truth, end up without any particular truth claims to make. They either become trapped in their respective contexts,[11] or they attempt to universalize a particular cultural experience, such as the experience of women (feminist theology) or the poor (liberation theology).

Church and tradition, therefore, need to play a more critical role in the development of local theologies. We can no longer speak in terms of *sola scriptura*, at least not without qualification. The roles that Scripture and dogma play need to be more carefully spelled out in relation to the church and tradition. Church doctrines are not the result of Scripture alone. This is the mistake of conservative Christians who think truth is only a matter of rightly interpreting the objective meaning of Scripture and applying it to a different context. But neither are church doctrines a matter of the church's internal decision on how its texts are to be used.

---

[10]I have explored this more fully in my book *Pentecostal Ecclesiology: An Essay on the Development of Doctrine* (Blandford Forum, Dorset, UK: Deo, 2011).

[11]This is the conclusion of Max Stackhouse when he analyzes the theological proposals of Robert Schreiter, George Lindbeck and Edward Farley. See his *Apologia: Contextualization, Globalization and Mission in Theological Education* (Grand Rapids: Eerdmans, 1988), pp. 106-22.

The latter view, commonly associated with the cultural-linguistic idea of doctrine advocated by George Lindbeck, effectively reduces the intra-textual meaning of the text to its use in the community, making the latter solely determinative of doctrine.[12] According to this account church doctrines are only about the internal conversation of the church concerning its faith (a rather perverse understanding of *sola fide*).[13]

Perhaps Kevin Vanhoozer's idea of doctrine as drama provides a better way of understanding the relationship between the scriptural text and the ecclesial community that uses the text. According to Vanhoozer, "Doctrine is not merely a proposition, or an expression, but a prompt: a spiritual direction for one's fitting performance of the script."[14] Scripture can be considered the given script for the drama whose director is the Holy Spirit, who prompts the church in acting out the gospel drama. The church enacts this drama especially in its liturgy, which holds together its various "core practices." This is why the core practices, which include word and sacrament, can be regarded as the works of the Spirit.[15]

If Scripture is a kind of dramatic script, translating the gospel into new contexts is not a matter of translating "concepts" but more like interpreting a drama, which is a more fluid process. The Bible is the redemptive drama, which is not reducible to abstract, fixed concepts. When we attempt to do local theologies we are not merely trying to explain the meaning of a script; rather, we are interpreting the gospel drama by indwelling the text, enacting it and improvising as we go, much like how good actors act out the script of a play.[16] In this process of improvisation, new understandings emerge. This can be seen in the way the early church fathers developed their rule of faith from Scripture. As Vanhoozer puts

---

[12]George Lindbeck, *The Nature of Doctrine: Religion and Theology in a Postliberal Age* (Philadelphia: Westminster Press, 1984).

[13]See Stackhouse's critique: *Apologia*, p. 121.

[14]Kevin J. Vanhoozer, *The Drama of Doctrine: A Canonical Linguistic Approach to Christian Theology* (Louisville: Westminster John Knox, 2005), p. 107.

[15]See Reinhard Hütter, *Suffering Divine Things: Theology as Church Practice* (Grand Rapids: Eerdmans, 2000). Vanhoozer seems to favor this idea (*Drama of Doctrine*, p. 98) but would go even further to suggest that not only are church doctrines the Spirit's work, but the "Scriptures themselves [are] spirited practices" (p. 99).

[16]Vanhoozer, *Drama*, pp. 128-33.

it, the rule of faith was strictly not an invention of the church but "a 'construal' of Scripture as a unified narrative."[17] It "is nothing less than a summary of Scripture's own storyline."[18] It is drawn from Scripture and then applied to Scripture as its interpretive key and the norm by which the church lives out her faith.

To use a different analogy, Scripture sets the initial trajectory for the subsequent development of doctrine in the Christian tradition. There is no separation between Scripture and tradition since Scripture is apostolic tradition.[19] A genuine development in new contexts must be faithful to the historical trajectory set by Scripture. There are two reasons why the relation of Scripture and tradition should be understood in this way. First, to create a new trajectory, even one that purports to be derived directly from Scripture, is to create a new church—in fact, a gnostic church and not the church founded on the apostles and prophets. This was how Irenaeus argued against the Gnostics who claimed to have direct access to the truth apart from the apostolic tradition.[20] Modern attempts at contextual theologies based on general ethical principles Christians share with people of other faiths are no less an engagement in a gnostic quest since they dilute and make redundant the ecclesial community's particularities identifying it as the historic church of Jesus Christ.

Second, a gnostic church, while appearing tolerant and open to other religious communities, is, ironically, incapable of engaging in deep interreligious dialogue. This is because implicit in this form of engagement is the belief that the church and other religious communities are only "subcultures" of a larger public square. Dialogue, then, can be conducted on some supposedly neutral ground after each community has shed its own particularities. But the neutral ground turns out to be the secular public square, which imposes its own rules for dialogue. The way toward a genuine dialogue is to recognize that each community is a "culture" in its own right. This does not mean there is no common ground or that Chris-

---

[17]Ibid., p. 204.
[18]Ibid., p. 206.
[19]See John Breck, *Scripture in Tradition: The Bible and Its Interpretation in the Orthodox Church* (Crestwood, NY: St. Vladimir's Seminary Press, 2001).
[20]Irenaeus, *Against Heresies*, 3.24.1.

tians should not engage in common quests with non-Christians on matters concerning the common good—for example, as citizens of a nation. But that is not the primary basis for interreligious dialogue, nor is it the most meaningful since it is based on terms set by the secular public. The church as the "public" of the Spirit is itself a culture. The church, as Hauerwas is fond of saying, does not have a social ethic but *is* a social ethic.[21] In the words of Yeago,

> The question about "church and culture" must therefore be reformulated: it is rightly a question about an encounter of cultures, the meeting of the culture of the church with the cultures of the nations. The issue is not how Christian beliefs and Christian experience might function within some larger cultural context, but how the distinctive culture of the *ekklesia* is to live and grow in the midst of the alien cultures of the Gentiles, and what it means that men and women are called out by the gospel from their own indigenous ethnic cultures to the new culture of the people of God.[22]

There are, in fact, more important ways in which religious cultures overlap,[23] and this, as we shall see, entails a different approach to social engagement.

THE NATURE OF ECCLESIAL EXPERIENCE

Contextual theologies emerge as the church lives out its given script in new situations. In other words, theology is first a lived experience of the church before it is a set of ideas formulated by church theologians. This basic order is famously encapsulated in the statement of Prosper of Aquitaine, a disciple of Augustine: *ut legem credendi lex statuat supplicandi* (the rule of prayer should determine the rule of faith). Ecclesial experience

---

[21]Stanley Hauerwas, *A Community of Character: Toward a Constructive Christian Social Ethic* (Notre Dame, IN: University of Notre Dame Press, 1981), pp. 40-44; *The Peaceable Kingdom: A Primer of Christian Ethics* (Notre Dame, IN: University of Notre Dame Press, 1983), pp. 99-102.

[22]David S. Yeago, "Messiah's People: The Culture of the Church in the Midst of the Nations," *Pro Ecclesia* 6 (Spring 1997): 146-71. Theologians such as Yeago working within the Hauerwasian tradition tend to take a rather negative stance toward the highly secularized culture of the West, whereas in Asia the church shares certain spiritual affinities with primal religions.

[23]See chapter five.

constitutes the primary theology (*theologia prima*) of the church. Ecclesial experience as truth is analogous to Jesus Christ as the Truth: it is not truth as an idea "out there" or truth as subjectivity, as in Schleiermacher's "sense of absolute dependence," but truth as a living person. Further, ecclesial experience is not just the experience of the present-day church but the experience of the church through space and time. In this comprehensive sense, even the Scripture could be regarded as a part of ecclesial experience, that is, the normative experience of the first-century church.

Ecclesial experience takes as its starting point the givenness of revelation finding its end in the church's supernatural life—supernatural because it is the life of the indwelling Spirit of truth. The importance of ecclesial experience for theology is recognized in both Catholicism and Orthodoxy. The Vatican II document *Lumen Gentium* speaks of "a supernatural sense of the faith [*sensus fidei*] which characterizes the People [of God] as a whole," and this gives the whole church an unerring sense of truth. This sense of faith of the whole people of God (*sensus fidelium*) is the direct outcome of the whole body of the faithful being anointed by the Holy Spirit "from the bishops down to the last member of the laity."[24]

Eastern Orthodoxy has a similar view but links the *sensus fidelium* more closely to the Pentecost event, which is the coming of the Spirit of truth in his own person to indwell the church. This makes the church the primary locus of the Spirit's work and gives the church its unique identity as the Spirit-indwelled community.[25] Theology, then, may be further qualified as the experience of the church living by and under the power of the Spirit. Another name for ecclesial experience is the living tradition. If the Spirit of truth indwells the church, then the church is the primary locus of the Spirit's work of revealing the truth concerning the gospel of Jesus Christ. Thus Lossky describes the living tradition as "the life of the Church in the Holy Spirit."[26]

---

[24]Vatican Council, *Dogmatic Constitution on the Church: Lumen Gentium, Solemnly Promulgated by His Holiness, Pope Paul VI, on November 21, 1964* (Boston: St. Paul, 1965), p. 12.

[25]See, for example, Alexander Schmemann, *Church, World, Mission* (Crestwood, NY: St. Vladimir's Seminary Press, 1979), pp. 133-34.

[26]Vladimir Lossky, *The Mystical Theology of the Eastern Church* (London: James Clarke, 1957), p. 188.

Speaking of ecclesial experience in this way helps us avoid two major pitfalls. First, it avoids conceiving theology as purely objective facts or propositions (as in fundamentalism) or as primarily subjective experience ("faith" in Schleiermacher's sense). Second, it does not consider individuals as the primary agents of doing theology. Doing theology is essentially an ecclesial endeavor requiring cooperation between the people of God and the theologian. We could even speak of it as a relationship of mutual dependence analogous to the liturgical event as a relationship of mutual dependence between the bishop and the laity. According to Orthodox theologians, the place of the bishop is confirmed by the liturgical "amen" just as the place of the people of God (the *laos*) is affirmed by the proclamation of the bishop.[27] Theology comes as much from the laity (*laos*) as it does from the theologian. True theology occurs when the faithful respond with "amazed recognition"[28] to the theologian: "You said for us what we had wanted to say all along but could not find the words to say it." In other words, theology is ratified in the church by the laity's "amen"; without it, theology is merely the imposition of the theologian's own ideas. The work of theology, *theologia secunda*, grows out of the liturgical event. The liturgical event itself expresses a primary theology (*theologia prima*). As Schmemann puts it, the liturgy is "the epiphany of the church's faith" since in the liturgy the saving events of Jesus Christ are embodied and manifested.[29] Similarly for Vigen Guroian, an Armenian Orthodox theologian, the living tradition is not found in theological texts, creeds or liturgical forms but "is a product of the eucharistic anamnesis of the gathered worshiping community," that is, in the liturgical event.[30]

This is why we speak of the liturgy as the primary practice of the

---

[27]John D. Zizioulas, *Being as Communion* (Crestwood, NY: St. Vladimir's Seminary Press, 1985), p. 218; Alexander Schmemann, "Clergy and Laity in the Orthodox Church," Protopresbyter Alexander Schmemann (website), 1959, www.schmemann.org/byhim/clergyand laityinthechurch.html.
[28]The phrase is C. S. Lewis's.
[29]Schmemann, *Church, World, Mission*, pp. 135, 142-43.
[30]Vigen Guroian, *Ethics After Christendom: Toward an Ecclesial Christian Ethic* (Grand Rapids: Eerdmans, 1994), p. 47.

church, which is also the work of the Spirit.[31] Theologians therefore must endeavor with utmost seriousness to listen to what God by his Spirit is saying through the laity. If they speak, they must speak from within the church, as fellow worshipers with the whole people of God, before being able to speak to the church and for the church to the world. Unfortunately, much of the theologies undertaken by contextual theologians have generally failed to take ecclesial experience into serious consideration. This becomes apparent when ecclesial experience is distinguished from other kinds of experiences.

ECCLESIAL EXPERIENCE VERSUS CULTURAL EXPERIENCE

Ecclesial experience is to be distinguished from human or cultural experience in general. The latter is frequently encountered in various forms of liberationist theology. Dalit and Minjung theologians seek to articulate their theology from the experience of the poor; feminists from women's experience. A theology of human experience may at first sight seem to offer a more comprehensive vision of reality compared to a theology grounded in ecclesial experience. But there are a number of basic problems with this approach.

Fallenness of humanity. Cultural experiences may provide an important context for theology by posing questions that theology must address. But cultural experiences cannot be the source of theology since they belong to the realm of fallen humanity rather than the humanity renewed by the Spirit in the church. A theology constructed from such sources usually serves to reinforce what is culturally acceptable rather than challenge it. Take the matter of women's experience. Feminist theologians sometimes speak of the sin of pride as a male sin since it is associated with male dominance. But for women who are often the victims of male dominance, pride, according to them, cannot be their sin. The basic sin of women, so they argue, is "the failure to take responsibilities for self-actualization."[32] The path for women's liberation, therefore, is not

---

[31]See Simon Chan, *Liturgical Theology: The Church as Worshiping Community* (Downers Grove, IL: IVP Academic, 2006), chap. 6.
[32]Judith Plaskow, *Sex, Sin and Grace: Women's Experience and the Theologies of Reinhold Niebuhr*

self-denial but self-assertion. But according to Kathryn Greene-McCreight, such a view of sin based on "women's experience" not only fails to understand sin as "radical rebellion against God" by reducing sin to "a character flaw in need of amelioration," it also leaves women with a sense of chronic guilt for failing to be sufficiently self-assertive.[33] That is to say, it reduces the relational nature of sin to a psychological condition brought on by women's acquiescence to their being sinned against. What is noteworthy is how similar feminist ideals and analysis have shaped the Asian feminist project.[34]

Cultural bondage. A second problem with a theology based on cultural experience is that it tends to end up privileging some aspect of culture and making it determinative for theology. The consequence is no less debilitating than Schleiermacher's method of commending Christianity to its cultured despisers. As Barth has shown in his study of nineteenth-century Protestant theology in Europe, this produced a string of disastrous compromises with culture culminating in the uncritical acceptance of the policies of Welhelm II, which led to World War I and the hearty endorsement of Hitler's Third Reich.[35] This is the basic problem of liberal theology. Liberal theologians, according to Barth, are so preoccupied with what the world thinks that they lose "a certain carefree and joyful confidence in the self-validation of the basic concerns of theology. . . . It did not enter their minds that respectable dogmatics could be good apologetics."[36]

The story of nineteenth-century Protestant theology might have come

---

and *Paul Tillich* (Washington, D.C.: University Press of America, 1980), p. 3. Cited by Kathryn Greene-McCreight, "Gender, Sin and Grace: Feminist Theologies Meet Karl Barth's Hamartiology," *Scottish Journal of Theology* 50, no. 4 (1997): 417.

[33]Greene-McCreight, "Gender, Sin and Grace," pp. 431-32.

[34]For example, Aruna Gnanadason, "Women's Oppression: A Sinful Situation," in *With Passion and Compassion: Third World Women Doing Theology,* ed. Virginia Fabella and Mercy Amba Oduyoye (Maryknoll, NY: Orbis, 1988), pp. 69-76; Nam-Soon Kang, "Creating 'Dangerous Memory': Challenges for Asian and Korean Feminist Theology," *Ecumenical Review* 47 (January 1995): 21-31.

[35]Karl Barth, *The Humanity of God,* trans. Thomas Wieser (Atlanta: John Knox, 1976), p. 14. A fuller account can be found in Barth's *Protestant Theology in the Nineteenth Century: Its Background and History,* new ed., ed. Colin E. Gunton (Grand Rapids: Eerdmans, 2002).

[36]Barth, *The Humanity of God,* p. 20.

to an end with Barth's devastating critique, but surprisingly it continues to survive in mainline Protestantism and, in more recent times, in the liberal wing of Catholicism. For these entities, the church must continue to get its cues from the world. As has been pointed out by many observers, the Uppsala Assembly in 1968 made a decisive turn by conceiving of the world as setting the agenda for the church. No longer is the faith of the church decisive for understanding the world; rather, the reverse is the case. This new paradigm, as George Lindbeck has observed, continues to the present day.[37]

The situation is very much the same in Asia. Two examples may be cited in this connection. In 1998 the aging Bishop K. H. Ting, head of the China Christian Council, launched his "Reconstruction of Theological Thinking" (*shenxue sixiang jianshi*, or RTT) campaign. This campaign was supposedly designed to bring theological thinking up to date without changing the essentials of the faith, but it is quite misleading to suggest that all the theological reconstructions did not affect the essentials of the faith, as is clear from an observer's description of some of its "achievements":

> Some important propositions have already been established and will be the guidelines for later RTT as follows: God is Love is primary, and the other attributes such as righteousness and benevolence are secondary. Jesus is the cosmic Christ; the revelation of God is unfolding, and God's creation is still evolving. The human being is semi-finished in the creation; the doctrine of justification by faith should be watered down; beauty, goodness and truth may also be found outside the church, etc.[38]

RTT was not quite like the churchly work of *aggiornamento* seen in Vatican II, but more an attempt to return the church to the old liberal Protestant paradigm, which would ensure the church's compliance with state policy and rid the church of what Ting regarded as its excessive

---

[37]See George Lindbeck, "The Unity We Seek: Setting the Agenda for Ecumenism," *Christian Century* 122 (Aug. 9, 2005): 28-31.

[38]Zhu Xiaohong, "Call for Dialogue and Cooperation: Reflections on the *Jianshe* or the Reconstruction of Theological Thinking," in *Christianity and Chinese Culture*, ed. Miikka Ruokanen and Paulos Huang (Grand Rapids: Eerdmans, 2010), p. 324. Many of these ideas can be found in the writings of K. H. Ting himself—for example, "Christian Theism: A Theology of Society," in *What Asian Christians Are Thinking*, pp. 425-37.

pietism or devotionism. In many ways RTT was much like the Cultural Revolution. Ting's writings became required reading, just as Mao's Red Book was during the Cultural Revolution. A number of key lecturers at Nanjing Seminary, some of whom were Ting's own protégés, were dismissed because they were considered "too conservative." The irony was that when the seminary was deprived of some of its best minds, Ting brought in two American replacements. Thus American liberal theologians were thought more appropriate than homegrown theologians to promote the reconstruction of Chinese theology.[39]

My second example is C. S. Song. Song is frequently cited in Western theological texts as an example of an Asian theologian. But in point of fact, his theology hardly qualifies as Asian. The one unchanging feature of Song's theology over the years is his repudiation of any normative revelation in Israel and the church. In an early essay Song maintains that God's special dealing with Israel and the church (salvation history) provides only a "pattern" of his dealings with all other nations, such that any historical event that "manifests God's characteristic action as Creator and Redeemer" is a sign of God's action.[40] A quick comparison of this early essay with his more recent works shows the same unswerving commitment to this assumption.[41] From this premise, Song in 1974 produced a glowing report of the Cultural Revolution, insisting that "the socialist movement pressing for the right of the oppressed, the poor and the powerless will go on, and China will continue to be a major physical and spiritual force behind the movement." The sign of God at work in China

---

[39]The campaign has been carefully chronicled by Jason Kindopp of the Brookings Institution in "The Politics of Protestantism in Contemporary China: State Control, Civil Society, and Social Movement in a Single Party-State" (PhD diss., George Washington University, 2004), chap. 7. See also Kindopp's "Fragmented yet Defiant: Protestant Resilience Under Chinese Communist Party Rule," in *God and Caesar in China: Policy Implications for Church-State Tension*, ed. Jason Kindopp and Carol Hamrin (Washington, D.C.: Brookings Institution Press, 2004), pp. 131-32. Kindopp notes that the whole campaign was so unpopular with the pastors and grassroots that even the then Religious Affairs Bureau was reluctant to promote it for fear of social unrest ("The Politics," pp. 334-35).

[40]C. S. Song, "New China and Salvation History: A Methodological Enquiry," *Southeast Asian Journal of Theology* 15, no. 2 (1974): 57, 59.

[41]For example, C. S. Song, *The Believing Heart: An Invitation to Story Theology* (Minneapolis: Fortress, 1999).

is found in "the transition of the old China to the New China and in the continuing effort of the Chinese Communist Party to transform man and his society."[42]

It boggles the imagination to hear Song extolling China's "social, economic and political achievements . . . in which the suffering of the masses is largely eliminated"[43]—this at the height of the Cultural Revolution, which even by the most conservative estimates led directly to the death of at least two million Chinese![44] One might ask what led Song to speak of the "New China" in such glowing terms. Song's failure reflects the general failure of liberal Christianity as a whole. The liberal program is one of accommodation to culture and of commending Christianity to its cultured despisers. When culture sets the agenda for theologians, it is only a small step for culture to set the norms for theology as well. In the words of another Chinese theologian, Archie Lee, the context should become "the texts to be read and interpreted theologically."[45] Such a contextual theology lacks the critical distance from culture to discern its shortcomings and sins.

Selective approach to culture. The third problem is that a theology of cultural experience is actually quite limited in scope and reductionistic. Often a multidimensional theological theme is reduced to a single referent. For instance, one gets the distinct impression from an Ecumenical Association of Third World Theologians (EATWOT) publication like *Asian Christian Spirituality: Reclaiming Traditions* that spirituality is nothing but the spirituality of social and political liberation.[46] Similarly,

---

[42]Song, "New China," p. 61.

[43]Ibid., p. 65.

[44]Two million is a conservative estimate. An accurate figure may never be known. See Lucian W. Pye, "Reassessing the Cultural Revolution," *The China Quarterly* 108 (December 1986): 597-612. Estimates have ranged from two to twenty million. See "Source List and Detailed Death Tolls for the Primary Megadeaths of the Twentieth Century," Necrometrics, www.necrometrics.com/20c5m.htm#Mao.

[45]Archie Chi Chung Lee, "Contextual Theology in East Asia," *The Modern Theologians: An Introduction to Christian Theology Since 1918*, 3rd ed., ed. David F. Ford (Oxford, UK: Blackwell, 2007), p. 531.

[46]Virginia Fabella, David Suh and Peter Lee, eds., *Asian Christian Spirituality: Reclaiming Traditions* (Maryknoll, NY: Orbis, 1992). See also K. C. Abraham and Bernadette Mbuy-Beya, eds., *Spirituality of the Third World* (Maryknoll, NY: Orbis, 1994). This book containing papers from the third general assembly of EATWOT shares a similar ethos, but there are excep-

in a survey of Asian christologies in the *Dictionary of Third World Theologies*, only christologies considered socially relevant are included; excluded are "popular christologies" focusing on "the spiritual dimension of salvation" and "personal needs."[47] The article focuses predominantly on the sociopolitical context while largely ignoring the ethnographic. It sees its kind of theology as the only valid kind. Thus what passes as Asian theology tends to be confined to a limited number of themes and theologians. Although there are some refreshing exceptions in recent years,[48] the old perception of Asian theology is so deeply entrenched that it has become virtually the received view in the West.

One needs only to look at some recent works by Western scholars on Asian theology to see that for them Asian theology means Dalit in India, Minjung in Korea, liberation in the Philippines, and the theologies of Kazoh Kitamori, C. S. Song, Kosuke Koyama, M. M. Thomas and Stanley Samartha.[49] One cannot blame Western theologians for this highly selective approach, for it is a view that continues to be perpetuated by so-called "ecumenical" Asian theologians. For example, the survey of theologies in South Asia by Felix Wilfred highlights only liberal Catholic and Protestant theologians (Aloysius Pieris, Raimon Panikkar and M. M. Thomas).[50] Pandita Ramabai is noted for her "feminist" concerns, but no mention is made of the vibrant Pentecostal faith that informed her social concern. Concepts associated with a pluralist theory of religions (à la John Hick), such as universal salvation and the presence of the Spirit in all religions, are set forth as "basic truths." Mission is no longer to be thought of "in terms of salvation or damnation" but of dialogue.[51] The survey of East Asian theologies in the same work by Archie Lee is,

---

tions like Bernadette Mbuy-Beya's "African Spirituality: A Cry for Life," pp. 64-76.

[47]Monica J. Melanchthon, "Christologies: Asian," in *Dictionary of Third World Theologies*, ed. Virginia Fabella and R. S. Sugirtharajah (Maryknoll, NY: Orbis, 2000), pp. 48-49.

[48]See, for example, the wider range of theological contexts in the collection of essays edited by Sebastian C. H. Kim, *Christian Theology in Asia* (Cambridge, UK: Cambridge University Press, 2008).

[49]For example, Hans Schwarz, *Theology in A Global Context: The Last Two Hundred Years* (Grand Rapids: Eerdmans, 2005), pp. 510-39; Veli-Matti Kärkkäinnen, *The Doctrine of God: A Global Introduction* (Grand Rapids: Baker, 2004).

[50]Felix Wilfred, "Theologies of South Asia," in *The Modern Theologians*, pp. 502-17.

[51]Ibid., pp. 506, 508.

mutatis mutandis, not very different.[52] The theologians cited are, pre-
dictably, C. S. Song and Kosuke Koyama. Japanese theology is represented by Kazoh Kitamori; Korea by Minjung theology; China by T. C.
Chao, Y. T. Wu, Bishop K. T. Ting and others of similar persuasion;
Asian theological trends are exemplified by Asian feminism and by C. S.
Song's version of Schleiermacherian theology. Lee, in fact, considers
"Song's willingness to grant revelatory status to East Asian culture" as
"not only something to be desired . . . but . . . also . . . an essential step"
for doing theology in Asia.[53]

   This highly selective understanding of what constitutes Asian theology
must be challenged, not only for its uncritical assimilation of Enlightenment epistemology and the resultant lack of theological discernment,
but also for the way it totally ignores vast swaths of Christian movements
in Asia: the evangelical and Pentecostal movements in much of Asia and,
more specifically, the indigenous Christian movements in India, Japan
and China.[54] The creative theologies of men like Watchman Nee and
Wang Ming Dao are bypassed because their works do not conform to
what elitist theologians regard as theology.[55] It is not surprising that, by
ignoring the lived theologies from the grassroots, the so-called ecumenical theologians of Asia can only offer rehashes of old ideas.[56] Take,

---

[52]Archie Chi Chung Lee, "Contextual Theology," pp. 518-34. The coverage of East Asian theology by Edmund Tang is not very different from Lee's. Edmond Tang, "East Asia," in *An
Introduction to Third World Theology*, ed. John Parratt (Cambridge, UK: Cambridge University Press, 2004), pp. 74-104.

[53]Lee, "Contextual Theology," p. 530. Wilfred is Catholic and Lee is Protestant. Together, they
could be said to represent the more liberal wings of their respective churches.

[54]For India, see Herbert E. Hoefer, *Churchless Christianity* (Madras: Asian Program for Advancement of Training and Studies India, 1991); and Paul Hiebert, "The Christian Response
to Hinduism," in *Missiology for the 21st Century*, ed. Roger E. Hedlund and Paul Joshua
Bhakiaraj (Delhi: ISPCK, 2004), pp. 332-33. For Japan, see Mark R. Mullins, *Christianity
Made in Japan: A Study of Indigenous Movements* (Honolulu: University of Hawaii Press,
1998). For China, see Lian Xi, *Redeemed by Fire: The Rise of Popular Christianity in Modern
China* (New Haven, CT: Yale University Press, 2010).

[55]For the theologies of Nee and Wang, see Grace Y. May, "Watchman Nee and the Breaking
of Bread: The Missiological and Spiritual Forces That Contributed to an Indigenous Chinese Ecclesiology" (ThD diss., Boston University, 2000); and Thomas A. Harvey, *Acquainted with Grief: Wang Mingdao's Stand for the Persecuted Church in China* (Grand Rapids:
Brazos, 2002).

[56]A more recent essay by Sebastian Kim appears to take cognizance of grassroots movements
as part of the contextual landscape in Asia, but how these grassroots movements contribute

for example, Kosuke Koyama's *Waterbuffalo Theology*, which was reissued twenty-five years after it first appeared in 1974. One would expect to see some important updates after a quarter-century. But other than changes in style to more politically correct language, hardly anything was changed. Anyone who picked up the 1999 edition would have thought that Asian theology was frozen in time around the 1970s.

Many Asian theologians appear to be caught in a time warp because of the way they define the theological task. If the theologian's task is essentially a reflection on context—whether social, political or economic—such an approach can ostensibly produce interesting theologies if one believes that the various contexts are where God is at work. For instance, M. M. Thomas's reflection on the Asian Revolution in the 1960s and '70s was predicated on the belief that the Asian Revolution was where God was working to prepare Asians for the gospel.[57] Asian theologies of liberation are similarly predicated. But time and again these theologians have been proven wrong—sometimes terribly wrong (as we have seen in Song and Ting). It is becoming apparent that discovering the Spirit's work in the world is a lot more difficult in religiously plural cultures compared with the West, where a Christian universe of discourse is still assumed (even if it is not the case in fact).[58]

The situation calls for discernment. But here we encounter the problem of finding adequate criteria. This is highlighted in a recent work by Kirsteen Kim, who proposes four criteria for discernment: the ecclesial, ethical, charismatic and liberational. Kim suggests that these criteria need to be taken together, because separately "none constitutes conclusive proof of the Spirit's presence."[59] But as we have seen, it becomes virtually impossible to discern the Spirit's work in the world once we allow for the Spirit's working independently of the church, that is, when

---

to Asian theologies remains to be seen. "The Word and the Spirit: Overcoming Poverty, Injustice and Division in Korea," in *Christian Theology in Asia*, ed. Sebastian C. H. Kim (Cambridge, UK: Cambridge University Press, 2008).

[57]M. M. Thomas, *The Christian Response to the Asian Revolution* (London: SCM Press, 1966).

[58]For example, when "God" is mentioned in the West, it is almost always assumed that it refers to the Judeo-Christian God. The same assumption cannot be made in Asia.

[59]Kirsteen Kim, *The Holy Spirit in the World: A Global Conversation* (London: SPCK, 2007), p. 168.

the ecclesial criterion ("the confession of Jesus as Lord by the Christian community") is no longer regarded as essential and determinative. Kim's one Christian criterion is that the Spirit is the Spirit of Jesus Christ who points to Christ. But this is not helpful if "Christ" could mean anything to different Christians—the historic Jesus of Nazareth (Newbigin), the cosmic Christ (M. M. Thomas), the christic principle (Panikkar)—as she herself acknowledges.[60] We wonder: Where on earth is the Spirit of God, and what on earth is he doing?

With no certainty of where or how to locate the Spirit, there is little material left in the world to practice the theologian's craft. About the only situations where some confident pronouncements can still be made are those where the Spirit of God is *not* found—situations of oppression (especially of women and gays), the ecological crisis and unfair trading practices. This can be amply illustrated from the documents of the general assemblies of the Ecumenical Association of Third World Theologians over the years. The themes, especially for Asia and Latin America, are predominantly liberationist but are variously reconfigured to reflect changes in the socio-economic and political cultures of the Third World.[61] Such theologies can be considered no more than social critiques—which NGOs like Amnesty International and Greenpeace can do better. Is it any surprise that much of the so-called "ecumenical theology" in Asia today is a rehashing of old issues? Asian theologies will not advance much if we allow for only this kind of theology to count as theology.

Elitist tendencies. A fourth problem is that a culturally denominated theology tends to reflect an elitist perspective. While its subject matter may be the poor and marginalized—the Dalits and Minjung—seldom do we find views of the grassroots themselves being taken seriously; rather, what we see is how the theologian views the grassroots and how they might fit in to the theologian's grand scheme of things. As one astute critic has observed, "It would appear that *minjung* theology is not so much a theology *of the minjung* as it is a non *minjung* elite's theology *for*

---

[60]Ibid., p. 167.
[61]See "List of Asian Theological Conferences (ATC)," *Voices*, vol. 34, no. 3 (July–September 2011), p. 74, http://internationaltheologicalcommission.org/VOICES/VOICES-2011-3.pdf.

the minjung."[62] In other words, it promotes the views of the intelligentsia and largely ignores the views of the ordinary people themselves, especially the ordinary members of the church. It's the elite theologians who define the problem of the Minjung and decide what they really need: their problem is that they are victims of an oppressive social system, and what they need is a certain kind of political liberation. Similarly, for Asian women, the problem is patriarchy, and freedom for them is usually defined in terms of Western egalitarian ideals. But if the Minjung should desire a more spiritual kind of liberation, or if Asian women should desire to pursue the ideal of motherhood and family, they are accused of having "false consciousness" and therefore all the more in need of liberation.[63] Elite theologians may theologize about the poor and oppressed, but such a theology is not likely to find much traction among the poor themselves. The failure of such theologies is well summed up by one Latin American theologian who noted, "Liberation theology opted for the poor and the poor opted for Pentecostalism."[64]

ECCLESIAL EXPERIENCE AS ECUMENICAL THEOLOGY

If ecclesial experience must be distinguished from cultural experience, it must also be distinguished from individual experiences. It is hazardous to base theology on the private experiences of individuals no matter how important these experiences may be to the individuals themselves. Church history is peppered with examples of enthusiasts whose claims to special revelation, when taken too seriously, led to disastrous conse-

---

[62]Kim Seyoon, "Is Minjung Theology a Christian Theology?" *Calvin Theological Journal* 22, no. 2 (1987): 262.

[63]Such views have been roundly critiqued by some social anthropologists. See Elizabeth Brusco, *The Reformation of Machismo: Evangelical Conversion and Gender in Colombia* (Austin: University of Texas Press, 1995); Saba Mahmood, *The Politics of Piety: Islamic Revival and the Feminist Subject* (Princeton, NJ: Princeton University Press, 2005), pp. 5-39; R. Marie Griffith, *God's Daughters: Evangelical Women and the Power of Submission* (Berkeley: University of California Press, 1997).

[64]Cited by Donald Miller, "The New Face of Global Christianity: The Emergence of 'Progressive Pentecostalism,'" Pew Research Religion and Public Life Project, April 12, 2006, www .pewforum.org/Christian/The-New-Face-of-Global-Christianity-The-Emergence-of-Progressive-Pentecostalism.aspx. See also Donald E. Miller and Tetsunao Yamamori, *Global Pentecostalism: The New Face of Christian Social Engagement* (Berkeley: University of California Press, 2007), p. 215.

quences. Rather, ecclesial experience is the experience of the church, the whole people of God. This is what Prosper had in view when he formulated his rule. Ecclesial experience is that which is *ab apostolis tradita, in toto mundo atque in omni catholica Ecclesia* (handed down by the apostles to the whole world and the entire catholic church).[65]

In recent years, the importance of the lived theology of the ordinary people of God in shaping our theological endeavors is becoming more widely recognized. One could not agree more with this assessment from the World Council of Churches' ninth assembly in Porto Alegre, Brazil, concerning the need to develop ecumenism at the grassroots level:

> There is a growing awareness that if the ecumenical movement is not rooted in the life of people and is not looked at from the perspective of people, its authenticity and credibility will be considerably undermined. In fact, ecumenism is not something to be imported from the outside or developed on an institution-centred basis; rather, it must emanate from the very life of people and be owned by the people. It must touch the life of people in all its layers and dimensions.[66]

But for real ecumenical theology to develop, it should not be based merely on what elitist theologians are saying about the grassroots. This is the limitation of the "global perspective" of doing theology in the work of Stephen B. Bevans.[67] For all his attempts to take grassroots theology seriously, the "global" contexts are seen only through the lenses of elitist theologians who, as we have noted above, tend to impose their views on the grassroots and read their contexts selectively.[68] If real ecumenism is validated at the grassroots, then it is also at the grassroots level that our reflection on an ecumenical theology must begin. In other words, the experience of ecumenism among the people of God constitutes primary

---

[65]Prosper of Aquitaine, *Complete Works, Patrolgia Latina* vol. 51, ed. J.-P. Migne (Cambridge, MA: Harvard University Press, 1861), col. 209.

[66]"Report of the Moderator," World Council of Churches, Feb. 15, 2006, www.oikoumene.org/en/resources/documents/assembly/porto-alegre-2006/2-plenary-presentations/moderators-general-secretarys-reports/report-of-the-moderator.html.

[67]Stephen B. Bevans, *An Introduction to Theology in Global Perspective* (Maryknoll, NY: Orbis, 2009).

[68]Ibid., pp. 78-85. Note the usual sources cited for Asian theologies (pp. 311-13).

ecumenical theology and should become the starting point for further theological reflection.[69]

But the process of translating primary theology into secondary theology that commends wide acceptance is often long, tedious and fraught with difficulties. The problem is not so much a lack of understanding as a lack of will—more precisely, goodwill. This is due mostly to the presence of previous theologies deeply entrenched in different ecclesiastical institutions. The tendency of ecclesiastical authorities is to defend established doctrines that have served the church well. Their first response is usually to incorporate the new ecclesial experience into existing doctrines. If this can be successfully accomplished, the result is a deepening and expansion of the church's understanding of existing doctrines. But there are times when a new ecclesial experience challenges established beliefs at a more fundamental level. This requires much more careful consideration and explains why doctrinal development at this level is not as forthcoming.

Perhaps an example could be cited to illustrate this difficulty. A recent work by Connie H. Y. Au has shown that in the late 1960s to 1980s, charismatic renewal in the United Kingdom brought about a genuine spiritual unity at the grassroots level that cut across long-existing divisions, especially between Catholics and Protestants. Each side freely acknowledges that they experienced the genuine communion of the Holy Spirit. Yet when the question of eucharistic communion was raised, the Catholic side balked.[70] For the Catholic Church, to share in the Eucharist implies full communion in the one (Catholic) church, so intercommunion cannot be practiced until actual union has taken place—to do so would compromise a fundamental meaning of communion. But some Catholic priests in the renewal secretly celebrated the Eucharist with Protestants. For them the *theologia prima* of their shared experience was too real to be ignored. Sadly, intervention on the part of the Catholic hierarchy and impatience on the Protestant side prevented further development of what

---

[69]On the potential of shared experience for ecumenism, see Lindbeck, "The Unity We Seek," pp. 28-31.
[70]Connie Ho Yan Au, *Grassroots Unity in the Charismatic Renewal* (Eugene, OR: Wipf and Stock, 2011), chap. 4.

could potentially have become an ecumenical doctrine of communion. In hindsight, if Protestants had shown a little more patience and Catholics a little less rigidity, their shared *theologia prima* could eventually have formed a shared *theologia secunda*. But that process takes time. Protestants should realize that within the Catholic Church the outworking of Prosper's rule is measured not in terms of a few years but in terms of generations and perhaps centuries.

What we see in this study of charismatic renewal in Britain is an example of the vast potential for theological renewal if theologians begin to take ecclesial experience seriously. For if the living faith of the people of God (the living tradition) is the locus of primary theology, it is vital that the church's theology reflect that faith. The task of the professional theologian is not to tell the church what is good for it but to listen carefully what the Spirit of truth who indwells the church is saying through the people of God. Elitist theologians who fail to recognize what God is doing among his people by his Spirit are no better (and are perhaps worse) at recognizing what God is doing in the world.

FOLK CHRISTIANITY

But whether theologians do or do not acknowledge the significance of mass Christian movements like the Pentecostal-charismatic movement, historians and social scientists are showing keen interest as a result of these movements' unmistakable social impact. It is only in more recent times that their theological significance is also being taken seriously. For example, the type of theology represented by Cho Yonggi is increasingly recognized for the contribution it is making to Korean contextual theology.[71] What makes the Pentecostal-charismatic movement an important subject of theological investigation is that it is an example of

---

[71]See Wonsuk Ma, William W. Menzies and Hyeon-Sung Bae, eds., *David Yonggi Cho: A Close Look at His Theology and Ministry* (Baguio, Philippines: APTS, 2004); Yun Koo Dong, "Pentecostalism from Below: *Minjung* Liberation and Asian Pentecostal Theology," in *The Spirit in the World: Emerging Pentecostal Theologies in Global Contexts*, ed. Veli-Matti Kärkkäinen (Grand Rapids: Eerdmans, 2009), pp. 89-114; Yoo Boo-Woong, *Korean Pentecostalism and Its History and Theology* (Frankfurt, Germany: Verlag Peter Lang, 1987); Lee Young-hoon, *The Holy Spirit Movement in Korea: Its Historical and Theological Development* (Oxford, UK: Regnum, 2009).

perhaps the most successful contextualization of the gospel the world has ever seen. It effectively contextualizes the gospel in the primal religious contexts that pervade much of the non-Western world, making Pentecostalism one of the most visible forms of folk Christianity. It embodies an ecclesial experience that could be found in practically every ecclesiastical body. Even if one has good reason to find fault with it, one must still ask why it has gained such wide acceptance, from the highest level within the Catholic hierarchy to the simple adherents in popular indigenous Christian movements throughout the world.

Folk Christianity has much in common with folk religion in general. According to Hiebert, Shaw and Tiénou, folk religion deals with the "middle zone" between the questions of ultimate meaning handled by the "high religions" and the questions of the observable handled by science. The middle zone is the realm where the world of science and the world of high religions become mixed. It is the realm of spirits, demons and witch doctors.[72] Harold Turner, a pioneer in the study of new religious movements, has also noted the deep affinities between the biblical worldview and primal religions.[73] Turner overturns the commonly held view found in nineteenth-century comparative religious studies in which "primitive" religions and Christianity are located at opposite ends of the evolutionary scale (with the axial religions somewhere in the middle).[74] Their similarities mean that folk Christianity shares both the strengths and weaknesses of folk religiosity.

Among elitist theologians, however, folk Christianity is often prematurely judged as syncretistic and so much superstition. The Filipino

---

[72]Paul G. Hiebert, R. Daniel Shaw and Tite Tiénou, *Understanding Folk Religion* (Grand Rapids: Baker, 1999), pp. 47-72.

[73]Harold Turner, "The Primal Religions of the World and Their Study," in *Australian Essays in World Religions* (Bedford Park, Australia: Australian Association of World Religions, 1977), pp. 30-32.

[74]It is interesting to note that some strands of current New Testament scholarship have made a 180-degree turn to seeing the historical Jesus as a man who shared the primal religious worldview in which the unseen world of spirits is as much a fact as the visible world. See Marcus J. Borg, *Jesus: A New Vision* (New York: HarperCollins, 1991). But if the history of New Testament scholarship is anything to go by, that picture of the historical Jesus may yet change again. What is perhaps more certain is that the world of the Bible has much in common with the world other than the secularized West.

theologian Jaime Bulatao calls it "split-level Christianity," which he explains as "the co-existence within the same person of two or more thought-and-behavior systems which are inconsistent with each other."[75] Implied in this description is that the little traditions inevitably corrupt the big tradition that preserves a more pristine Christian belief system. But "split-level Christianity" represents only one side of the story. If the grassroots is where primary theology is lived out, the big tradition of institutional and elitist theology needs to take seriously the former if it hopes to continue to develop as a living tradition. Failure to take folk Christianity seriously, as we have seen in mainline Protestant Christianity, has resulted in either a fossilized tradition (mostly among the more conservative) or one that is subject to the whims of cultural changes (mostly among the more liberal). Christianity as a lived reality among ordinary folks has the unique characteristic of both preserving tradition and also changing it as it adapts to new challenges. The new expressions of Christianity seen especially in the Pentecostal-charismatic movement should not be prematurely judged as syncretism and "superstition." This is the problem with the theologically loaded phrase "split-level Christianity." It assumes that Christianity and primal religions are inherently incompatible, whereas, as we have noted in the studies of Harold Turner, they are in fact much closer to each other theologically. Their relationship could be better described with less-loaded terms supplied by the social sciences.

For instance, Singaporean sociologist Daniel Goh in his study of "Chinese religion" in Singapore and Malaysia suggests terms like "transfiguration" and "hybridization" to describe the phenomena arising from the interaction between charismatic Christianity and folk religions. Transfiguration refers to "the changing of forms of practices without the shift in essential meaning," while hybridization is "the change in meaning with little change to forms of religious practice."[76] Goh cites the Pente-

---

[75]Jaime Bulatao, *Split-Level Christianity* (Manila: Ateneo de Manila University, 1966), p. 2.
[76]Daniel P. S. Goh, "Chinese Religion and the Challenge of Modernity in Malaysia and Singapore: Syncretism, Hybridisation and Transfiguration," *Asian Journal of Social Science* 37 (2009): 113.

costal worship ritual of "the raising of hands with palms facing out and up" as an example of transfiguring the Chinese ritual of *baishen* (worship) in which the palms are always brought together.[77] The practice of the "prayer walk" understood as "spiritual warfare" is an example of hybridization. Here, the ritual is similar, but the tools of "enemies" (Chinese religion) are now turned against them.[78] To understand the changed practices and beliefs as transfiguration and hybridization is not to deny the need for discernment, but rather to recognize the need to fine-tune the discernment process.

In both phenomena a further question needs to be asked concerning theological significance. It seems that ritual change helps better to retain the distinctively Christian meaning of the transfigured rite. Christian hybridization, on the other hand, often indicates a prior shift in theology; the adoption of a ritual practice that closely resembles a non-Christian rite (prayer walks) follows from the theological shift rather than causes it. But even hybridization does not always mean that the gospel is hopelessly compromised. It depends on the proportion of the mix, the size of each component that goes into the hybrid. If the theological shift is sufficiently major, it is likely that the meaning of the non-Christian rite will predominate; if not, the respective ritual practices will be sufficiently distinguished to allow for a distinctive Christian meaning to emerge. Be that as it may, discernment is necessary. Many Pentecostal-charismatic practices are still in flux and therefore should not be too quickly dismissed or endorsed. The fact that the Pentecostal movement as a whole is generally recognized as part of orthodox Christianity suggests that perhaps the question with which we should begin is not "What is wrong with its beliefs and ritual practices?" but "What is right about them that makes this the most effective missionary movement since its beginning at the turn of the last century?" A more nuanced approach may result in a better understanding of the nature of contextualization and a genuine development of doctrine.

To cite a case in point, historian Mark Mullins in his study of Japanese

---

[77]Ibid., p. 130.
[78]Ibid., pp. 130-31.

indigenous Christian movements (JICMs) argues that JICMs challenge us to expand our understanding of Christian doctrines beyond our own culturally restricted interpretations.[79] For instance, Mullins notes that the JICM interpretation of salvation beyond the grave may provide fresh insights into the "descent into hell" of the Apostles' Creed and neglected passages of Scripture like 1 Peter 3:18-22; 4:6. While the practices following from their belief—namely, evangelism to and prayer for the dead—might unsettle our conventional notions, underlying this practice is a basically orthodox Christian belief that salvation for all can come only from a personal encounter with Jesus Christ who died and rose again.[80] In contrast, notes Mullins, a theology such as Song's, which considers any assertion of salvation through Christ alone as another case of missionary imperialism, betrays its Enlightenment prejudice. Song's is an elitist theology that may satisfy the Asian elite but completely ignores the real concerns of Asian folk Christianity.[81]

As Hiebert, Shaw and Tiénou have also shown, there is much that can be learned from primal religions. The primal religious view of life is both holistic and communal. Human life is intimately linked to the world of the unseen (spirits both good and evil) as well as the nonhuman world (animals, trees and rocks),[82] unlike the Christianity of the Enlightenment, which compartmentalizes the world into the "spiritual" and "physical," the unseen and seen, religion and science, subjective values and objective facts—and then having created its own kind of split-level Christianity, resolves the tension by reducing the spiritual realm into an aspect of one of the social sciences. Human life in primal societies is also communal, as seen in such rites of passage as birth, initiation, marriage and death. The names given to children at birth are not "arbitrary labels" but carry special significance for the community; initiation rites are events signifying incorporation into the community; marriage is not just between two persons but joins two families together; death is not the extinction

---

[79]Mark R. Mullins, "What About the Ancestors? Some Japanese Christian Responses to Protestant Individualism," *Studies in World Christianity* 4, no. 1 (1998): 41-64.
[80]Ibid., p. 60.
[81]Ibid., pp. 59-60.
[82]Hiebert, Shaw and Tiénou, *Understanding Folk Religions*, pp. 45-72.

of life but entrance into another mode of existence.[83] Primal religions' affinity with the Christian understanding of initiation, sacraments and the church will be explored more fully later. For now, let us acknowledge that this deep affinity gives us reason to believe that folk Christianity has more to teach us about Asian theology than what elitist Asian theologians are saying.

ECCLESIAL EXPERIENCE AND SOCIAL ENGAGEMENT

One reason folk Christianity (often derogatorily called "pietistic" Christianity) has not been taken seriously by elitist theologians in the past is that it does not appear to have a theology of social engagement. For example, M. M. Thomas believes that too much emphasis on "mission of preaching and Church Growth . . . contributed to the Christian indifference to secular politics which led to the rise of Hitler and Stalin in the West."[84] But Thomas's theory of social engagement causes him to miss what Barth clearly saw: that it was not pietistic indifference but direct endorsement on the part of those concerned about commending Christianity to its cultured despisers that led to the rise of a Hitler or Stalin. Thomas, however, acknowledges that in spite of a lack of a theology of engagement, the practice of conservative missionaries has had a positive impact on society.[85] Thomas seems to regard a theology of direct engagement in the sociopolitical process as the only theology possible. Anything else, even if it has had a positive impact on society, is not considered a theology of engagement at all. This assumption is so widespread in elitist circles that it is considered the received view.[86] To be sure, sometimes a spirituality of what Thomas calls "pietistic individualism" may have been used to support vested interests,[87] but the problem is not confined to this form of spirituality. To lump these people together with those who take preaching the gospel and church growth seriously reflects

---

[83]Ibid., pp. 95-122 *passim.*
[84]M. M. Thomas, *Salvation and Humanization* (Madras: Christian Literature Society, 1971), p. 7. Thomas's discussion is in reference to the mission theology of Peter Beyerhaus.
[85]Ibid., p. 12.
[86]For example, see Melanchthon, "Christologies: Asian," pp. 48-49.
[87]Thomas, *Salvation and Humanization*, pp. 12-13.

a failure to appreciate other theologies of social engagement.

The one-sided understanding of social engagement that dominates mainline Asian theology needs to be supplemented by a more comprehensive understanding recognizing other theologies of social engagement. There are, broadly speaking, two forms of theology of social engagement. For heuristic purposes, we shall briefly look at these forms in terms of two of the most influential theologians of the last century: Paul Tillich and Karl Barth. Tillich's basic method of relating Christianity to the world at large is the "method of correlation."[88] Philosophy poses the question of human existence, while Christianity formulates the answer. The primary task of theology is to translate particular Christian symbols into philosophical terms of the larger culture. Thus Christian "symbols" such as God and Trinity are translated into the "nonsymbolic" term "being itself." For Tillich, essence precedes existence. The particular is only an instantiation of the more general "abstract principle." Thus "Jesus of Nazareth [must be] sacrificed to Jesus as the Christ," the revelation of the "new being." Christianity, too, is itself not final but only a witness to the universal reality of being.[89] A recent example of the Tillichian methodology at work can be seen in Ian S. Markham's A Theology of Engagement.[90] Reinforcing this approach is Niebuhr's theology of culture. For Niebuhr, culture is the neutral, all-embracing reality ("reality sui generis") within which Christians discover their identities.[91] In this approach culture sets the agenda for the church; the church has to find its raison d'être in relation to the larger "culture."

There are a number of consequences when social engagement is seen in this way. First, it tends to create a low view of the church. If the church is simply a means to a higher end to be realized in the world and its raison d'être essentially instrumental, then its public and institutional character

---

[88]While the Tillichian approach to social engagement is found predominantly among "mainline" Asian theologians, it is not exclusively confined to them. Some evangelicals adopt a similar approach—for example, Paul Freston, Evangelicals and Politics in Asia, Africa and Latin America (Cambridge, UK: Cambridge University Press, 2001).

[89]Paul Tillich, Systematic Theology (Chicago: University of Chicago Press, 1951), 1:133-37 passim.

[90]Ian S. Markham, A Theology of Engagement (Oxford, UK: Blackwell, 2003).

[91]H. Richard Niebuhr, Christ and Culture (New York: Harper Brothers, 1951), pp. 30-32.

becomes irrelevant. On this view, church becomes, as David S. Yeago has noted, "only . . . a vehicle for something essentially disembodied and non-public: a set of beliefs and values, an abstract 'message,' an inward religious experience."[92] Thus M. M. Thomas would rather not see any clear demarcation between the church and the world, since the church's goal is only to realize God's larger purpose in the world, namely, the humanization of society. The church must lose itself as a "religious community" and find its fulfillment in the "Christ-centred fellowship of faith and ethics" that embraces people of all faiths sharing the same Christian-human principles.[93] Second, if the church loses its distinctive character as a "religious community," its gospel too is also reconceived as a set of principles. Thus Song considers any attempt to proclaim the gospel of salvation to non-Christians as "Christian ecumenical imperialism."[94] The rhetoric is always repetitively similar: since Christianity is only a minority religion in most Asian countries, it must assume a humbler position and proclaim with all the great Asian religions a shared message of God's universal purpose for humanity and creation centering on such themes as justice and peace. Song sees the particularization of the gospel as Western but fails to see that his own brand of the gospel is an uncritical application of the Tillichian correlationist theology in which the concrete particularity of the gospel is reduced to an abstraction. Third, its assumption that the world is the primary locus of the Spirit's operation has often led to a dismal failure in discernment, as we have already noted. Finally, it is no coincidence that when the church's responsibility is seen almost exclusively in terms of direct social engagement, spirituality is reduced to sociopolitical liberation and sin essentially a social condition of injustice, oppression and so on. Little consideration is given to the personal cultivation of the spiritual life or to the sinfulness of human nature. Doing so is regarded derogatorily as "pietism." As one critic has observed, there is no place for a spirituality of everyday life if the more

---

[92]David S. Yeago, "Messiah's People: The Culture of the Church in the Midst of the Nations," *Pro Ecclesia* 6, no. 1 (Spring 1997): 149.

[93]M. M. Thomas, *Salvation and Humanization*, pp. 40-41.

[94]C. S. Song, *Jesus in the Power of the Spirit* (Minneapolis: Fortress, 1994), pp. 176-79.

important work of the church is to be found in political struggles.[95]

Barth's theology could be said to entail a different form of social engagement—or, to be more precise, his theology could be said to lay the
foundation for a different theology of social engagement. Central to
Barth is his insistence that the very possibility of theology—the knowledge
of God—is God's self-revelation since "God is who He is in the act of His
revelation."[96] And God's self-revelation is not about some generic being
but specifically the triune God: Father, Son and Holy Spirit. In one bold
stroke Barth undercut the European theology dominant in the nineteenth and early twentieth century, which sought to locate God in some
aspect of human experience, either in ethical experience (neo-Kantians)
or in religious consciousness (Schleiermacher).

Barth's theology is perhaps best summed up in George Hunsinger's
description of its "shape" in terms of four main motifs: actualism, particularism, objectivism and personalism. These four motifs are inter-
related and may be expressed as follows: God is not a static being but
"lives in a set of active relations" (actualism). God in his act (as Father
loving the Son and Son loving the Father in the unity of the Spirit) reveals
himself in the concrete "particularities of the biblical witness, especially
its narrative portions" (particularism). This particular story of God's revelation in Jesus Christ is objectively real (objectivism) and concretely
personal (personalism).[97] The personal, objective and particular that
mark Barth's theology (contra Tillich) is affirmed in an oft-repeated
dictum: "The general exists for the sake of the particular."[98]

> The Bible is not interested in God's power over everything—the power that
> creates, upholds and moves the world—as a reality to be considered for

---

[95]Arne Rasmussen, *The Church as Polis: From Political Theology to Theological Politics as Exemplified by Jürgen Moltmann and Stanley Hauerwas* (Notre Dame, IN: University of Notre
Dame Press, 1995), p. 372.

[96]Karl Barth, *Church Dogmatics* 2.1 (Edinburgh: T & T Clark, 1957), p. 257.

[97]See George Hunsinger, *How to Read Karl Barth: The Shape of His Theology* (New York: Oxford
University Press, 1991), pp. 27-42. Hunsinger includes two other motifs, "realism" and "rationalism" (pp. 43-49). These can be understood as further elaborations of Barth's objectivism. Realism stands between literalism and expressivism, while rationalism refers to reason
operating between the limits of revelation.

[98]Barth, *Church Dogmatics* 2.2, 8, 53 and so on.

itself. On the contrary, it is interested in God's power because it forms the ground and place, the space and framework, in which he is active as the Lord of this history. It is not the general that comes first but the particular. The general does not exist without this particular and cannot therefore be prior to the particular. It cannot, then, be recognized and understood as the general prior to it, as if it were itself a particular. Thus we cannot move from the general to this particular, but only in the opposite direction— from this particular to the general.[99]

This personal particularism of Barth's thought is one his most important contributions to an alternative theology of engagement. Perhaps the best known contemporary example of this approach is that of Stanley Hauerwas.[100] It is a theology with three distinct emphases. First, the distinctive truth of God's revelation in Christ makes a difference in the world. This means that the gospel of Jesus Christ in all its particularity is the means for the total transformation of the world. Contrary to Song, preaching the gospel of salvation through Jesus Christ is not imperialism but simply a way of recognizing that this is God's way of transforming the world. Second, Christians influence the world by their distinctive character as Christians rather than by promoting social programs for the common good, although the latter is not to be ignored since Christians inevitably share some common space with non-Christians.[101] Third, the primary community that gives Christians their most basic identity is the church. The gospel, so central to the church's proclamation, is also that which gives the church its own distinctive identity. To be the church of Jesus Christ is to be shaped by the gospel story.

---

[99]Barth, *Church Dogmatics* 2.1, p. 602.

[100]Two of Hauerwas's earlier works that best sum his view are *A Community of Character: Toward a Constructive Christian Social Ethic* (Notre Dame, IN: University of Notre Dame Press, 1981) and *The Peaceable Kingdom: A Primer in Christian Ethics* (Notre Dame, IN: University of Notre Dame Press, 1983).

[101]Within the Hauerwasian framework differences exist concerning the desirability of developing a theology of public life based on different perceptions of whether common ground exists between the church and the larger public. Charles Mathewes, unlike Hauerwas, thinks that there is such common ground. See his *A Theology of Public Life* (Cambridge, UK: Cambridge University Press, 2007). Asian Christians are likely to find their world less secular than the West and more in common with people of other faiths and therefore closer to the world envisaged by Mathewes than Hauerwas (see Mathewes, *A Theology*, p. 2).

In many respects the global Pentecostal phenomenon and Asian Christianity in particular exemplify a more Barthian-Hauerwasian than Tillichian-Moltmannian approach to social engagement.[102] Miller and Yamamori in their study of "progressive Pentecostalism" note that the Pentecostals' distinctive approach is not so much to directly challenge the existing sociopolitical order but to create "an alternative social reality" within the existing system that could become quite subversive in the long term.[103] This approach seeks to create a community of transformed persons (see also Hauerwas's "community of character") who will in turn leaven the surrounding culture. Miller and Yamamori also note the "organic" metaphors that describe this social reality: the "growing" and "nurturing" needed to realize the "body of Christ," which suggests that Pentecostalism takes a long-term view of social transformation. In contrast, the kind of engagement represented by, say, liberation theology calls for direct confrontation to bring about immediate changes to sociopolitical structures.[104] Besides Pentecostalism, a similar pattern of engagement has also been observed in Asia among grassroots Christian movements. Gao Shining of the Chinese Academy of Social Sciences in her research among urban Christians in China concludes that "although criticism of Chinese society by individual Christians is limited, as a community Chinese Christianity has already become an important power in the reconstruction of Chinese ethical morality."[105] This point is not lost on another observer:

> It is interesting that young educated people who are the most successful section of the population are embracing Christianity. Christianity can serve as an ethic for the new urban middle class: it gives a sense of respectability,

---

[102]The different theologies of engagement exemplified in Tillich and Barth continue today in the respective theologies of Jürgen Moltmann and Stanley Hauerwas. For an excellent study of their contrasting approaches see Rasmusson, *Church as Polis*. Here Rasmusson (pp. 370-72) shows that the later Moltmann shares some of Hauerwas's concerns, such as the need to build a contrast community, but Moltmann's understanding of the "public" is still fundamentally Tillichian.

[103]Miller and Yamamori, *Global Pentecostalism*, pp. 4-5.

[104]Ibid., pp. 214-15.

[105]Gao Shining, "The Faith of Chinese Urban Christians: A Case Study of Beijing," in *Christianity and Chinese Culture*, ed. Miikka Ruokanen and Paulos Huang (Grand Rapids: Eerdmans, 2010), p. 272.

plus it has an empowering capacity in that a person who is able to change his or her private life feels able to cope with the challenges of a changing society. Christianity also promotes the ethic of moderation; money is not wasted on gambling or drinking. Furthermore, a strict Christian lifestyle brings good health and appearance, and promotes hard work and good manners, all of which are an advantage in professional life.[106]

Another remarkable feature of this form of social engagement is that it develops quite spontaneously with minimal influences from foreign missionaries. This has been observed from Latin America to China.[107] It is a theology arising from the grassroots—that is, from ecclesial experience.

Thus the way grassroots Christianity, especially Pentecostalism, has impacted the larger society as noted by Miller and Yamamori[108] and its creative adaptation in primal religious contexts as noted by Turner, Mullins and others makes it a significant point of reference for developing an Asian theology that takes seriously both sociopolitical and ethnographic contexts, integrates these two poles, and offers an alternative approach to social engagement. This is the approach that we will take. We believe that such an approach will allow theology to go beyond the impasse currently seen in mainline Protestant and liberal Catholic theologies in Asia.[109]

ORGANIZING PRINCIPLES OF THEOLOGY IN ASIA

If what we have said thus far constitutes the formal method of doing theology in Asia, what might constitute its content if this method is pursued? Saphir Athyal, in an important essay on theological methodology, proposes that Asian theology must be systematized around con-

---

[106]Zhang Minghui, "A Response to Professor Gao Shining," in *Christianity and Chinese Culture,* p. 275.

[107]For Latin America, see Elizabeth E. Brusco, *The Reformation of Machismo: Evangelical Conversion and Gender in Colombia* (Austin: University of Texas Press, 1995). For China, see Zhang, "A Response," p. 275.

[108]See, for example, Harvey Cox, *Fire from Heaven: The Rise of Pentecostal Spirituality and the Reshaping of Religion in the Twenty-first Century* (Cambridge, MA: Da Capco Press, 2001).

[109]In many respects, the liberal wing of the Catholic Church in Asia, as reflected in some of the Federation of Asian Bishops' Conferences (FABC) Papers, is very similar to mainline Protestantism.

textual issues in Asia. Just as the organizing principle of Calvin's theology
is the sovereignty of God, Luther's justification by faith, and Barth the
theology of the Word, Athyal suggests that the organizing principle of an
Asian theology might be the God who acts redemptively and controls
history, in light of the penchant for myths and stories in many Asian
societies.[110] This would also suggest that a narrative approach might be
an appropriate way of presenting such a theology.[111] There is much to be
said for this approach. It connects well with a characteristic found in
many traditional societies in Asia and Africa—what one philosopher
calls "body thinking."[112] Understanding is achieved not by breaking up
reality into its constituent parts and analyzing each part separately, but
by grasping it in its concreteness. It is not so much an analytical as an
imaginative process. Not only stories but painting and poetry are basic
modes of thought for coming to terms with reality.[113] This penchant for
the concrete and the imaginative may explain why some of the most influential preachers in Asia were also great storytellers, such as Sadhu
Sundar Singh, Wang Ming Dao and John Sung.[114]

    Athyal's proposal is typically evangelical—and perhaps too restrictive
if the central focus is the God who acts redemptively in human history.
A more adequate way of organizing an Asian theology is to center it in
the doctrine of the triune God as the divine family. This is not an arbitrary choice but faithfully reflects the fundamental way in which the first
two persons of the triune God are revealed, namely, as Father and Son.
In much of Asia a person's foremost identity is defined in relation to his

---

[110]Saphir Athyal, "Toward an Asian Christian Theology," in *What Asian Christians Are Thinking,* pp. 68-84.

[111]As seen, for example, in Gabriel Fackre, *The Christian Story,* 2 vols. (Grand Rapids: Eerdmans, 1984, 1987).

[112]Wu Kuang-Ming, *On Chinese Body Thinking: A Cultural Hermeneutic* (Leiden, NY: Brill,
1997).

[113]Ibid., pp. 7-8.

[114]Sundar Singh, *At the Master's Feet,* trans. Arthur Parker (London: Revell, 1922); Wang Ming
Dao, *A Call to the Church: Twenty Pre-Prison Messages of Conviction and Courage* (Washington, PA: Christian Literature Crusade, 2002); John Sung, *Forty John Sung Revival Sermons,*
2 vols. (Singapore: Christian Life Book Centre, n.d.). C. S. Song, too, is well known for his
story approach to theology. For example, see *Tell Us Our Names: Story Theology from an
Asian Perspective* (Maryknoll, NY: Orbis, 1984).

or her family, and not just the immediate family but also the extended family, which may include an entire clan, and the linear family, which includes deceased ancestors. Given its importance, the concept of God as the trinitarian family could serve as theology's organizing principle.

This way of organizing theology highlights a neglected feature. Take, for example, Christology. In terms of Christ's triple office, the contextual theologies of Asia are dominated by the prophetic and kingly office. Thus the mission of the church is a matter of "kingdom concerns" backed up by prophetic boldness.[115] The priestly ministry, however, is largely neglected. Yet both in Africa and Asia, the priestly office might be a far more significant way of conceptualizing the essential character of theology and ministry. As John Parratt has observed, "The Christian ministry in Africa should be a genuinely sacerdotal one, making full use of African ideas of priestcraft."[116] Asia is not very different in this regard. The focus on the family and the rites associated with ancestral veneration and filial piety are best understood within the context of priestly ministry, where sacrifices are a significant part of religious expression—for example, the offering of food to deceased ancestors and the offering of gifts such as the *hong bao* (money wrapped in red packets) to living ancestors on auspicious occasions such as the Lunar New Year and birthdays. Biblically, too, there is much to be said for this approach. Paul describes his ministry in terms of his priestly work of offering up the gentiles as an acceptable sacrifice to God (Rom 15:16).

If our theology is oriented towards the family, then the following loci of theology will have a different emphasis:

The Trinity. Modern conceptions of the Trinity have tended to stress the triune relationship as a society of equals (for example, see Moltmann). Yet if the proper name of God is Father, Son and Holy Spirit, as Jenson argues,[117] then the family may offer a better analogy. God as the divine family is essentially the Father, who eternally generates his only begotten

---

[115]For example, Ken R. Gnanakan, *Kingdom Concerns: A Biblical Exploration Towards a Theology of Mission* (Bangalore: Theological Book Trust, 1989).

[116]*Reinventing Christianity: African Theology Today* (Grand Rapids: Eerdmans, 1995), p. 43.

[117]Robert W. Jenson, "The Triune Name of God," in *Christian Dogmatics*, ed. Carl E. Braaten and Robert W. Jenson (Philadelphia: Fortress, 1984), 1:87-96.

Son and, by virtue of his creating the world, is Father to the whole human race (Eph 3:14-15; 4:6). The Father-Son relationship cannot be conceived in purely egalitarian terms but implies a certain order (*taxis*). Karl Barth, for example, has maintained that an essential aspect of the relationship between the Father and the Son is that the Father commands and the Son obeys. The command-obedience dynamic belongs to their very nature as the first and second "modes of being."[118]

Humanity and sin. Humans are not discrete individuals but relational beings. In Asia the most primary expression of human relationship is the ordered family, such as between husband and wife and parents and children (see Eph 5:22-33; 6:1-5). While the instructions to husband and wife are preceded by the command to submit to one another (Eph 5:21), the command does not detract from the fact that their relationship requires them to fulfill different roles. Their reciprocity includes a certain order in which their respective roles are played out. Their relationship is analogous to that of Christ and his church, in which Christ initiates love and the church responds in submission.[119] Within the family context, sin is not just the wrong an individual does against some objective law. It is an affront to God's honor (Anselm) and an act that dishonors the family name. Modern discussions of the atonement have tended to be restricted to the question of guilt, whereas in the Scripture it clearly involves the question of shame. The idea of sin as shame implies that sin is not against an impersonal law but against a community of which the sinner is a member. It breaks the harmony of the community.

Christ and salvation. If the central focus is on Christ as priest instead of prophet and king, then the first thing to remember is his identification with those he called his "brothers" (Heb 2:11-12, 17). The book of Hebrews shows that priesthood and family are closely related. Jesus is apostle and high priest in God's household on behalf of his "brothers," and as high priest he sanctifies them by his blood and he consecrates them to God (Heb 9:26) so that they become "holy brothers" (Heb 3:1-2 ESV).

---

[118]Barth, *Church Dogmatics* 4.1, pp. 203-10. See next chapter.
[119]See the fine discussion on this subject by P. T. Forsyth, *Marriage: Its Ethic and Religion* (Blackwood, South Australia: New Creation, 1999), pp. 69-79.

Salvation is the restoration of one's standing in the family (see the parable of the Prodigal Son). Christ's saving work means that people who were once unholy are now made holy, sharing the same family values, so that Christ is "not ashamed to call them brothers" (Heb 2:11). Another biblical image is that of adoption (Rom 8:15). When salvation is seen in this way, the focus is on communion with God and one another within the one household of faith. In this family Christ serves essentially as the high priest, the "firstborn among many brothers" (Rom 8:29) whose chief role is as a mediator between the Father and those Christ addresses as his brothers. Mission too is a priestly work of offering people up as acceptable sacrifices to God (Rom 15:15-16).

The Holy Spirit. The Spirit is the bond of love between the Father and the Son and the bond between the church and Christ. Thus, the Spirit could be considered the one who actualizes the essential trinitarian bond and the bond of the extended family of God. The Spirit effects communion between the church on earth and the church in heaven. As the bond of love he "hypostatizes" the rest of creation through the church.

The Church as the communion of saints. The priestly work of offering up the Gentiles is to create the church. The church, as the creed confesses, is the communion of saints. Thus communion could be said to be the ultimate end of the *missio Dei*: "Man's chief end is to glorify God and enjoy him forever." This communion is anticipated in the church's liturgical celebration of word and sacrament made possible by the ordered relationship of leader and people. The word is the prophetic proclamation that finds its fulfilment in the Eucharist. Thus the Eucharist plays a key role in defining the nature of the church; it is that which makes the church the church. In eating and drinking the church proleptically participates in the marriage supper of the Lamb. This understanding of the church again presupposes the Christian life as a family in which the people of God are joined in the communion with the Father, Son and Holy Spirit.

Our approach to Asian theology will attempt to take full cognizance of the spiritual resources of the church, that is, Scripture and tradition as ecclesial experience or the living tradition, which is the ongoing experience of the Holy Spirit expressed primarily in the liturgy and other core practices of the church. Contextually, it will seek to relate especially to the grassroots, taking seriously the beliefs and practices of folk Christianity and folk religions by understanding them on their own terms rather than by demythologizing them. This is not to say that nothing could be learned from an elitist interpretation but that, as far as Asia is concerned, it has its limitation in constructing a local theology.

2

GOD IN ASIAN CONTEXTS

IN MUCH OF THE HISTORY of theology in the West, the doctrine of
God has revolved around the question of divine immanence and transcendence. Grenz and Olson in their study of twentieth-century theology
regard "the interplay of transcendence and immanence as the central
theological concern" that "has contributed greatly to determining the
specific path that theology has taken over the last hundred years."[1] But
the terms are not always understood in the same way. Western theology
took a major turn in the seventeenth century when the doctrine of divine
transcendence-immanence was redefined in terms of God's "distance" in
relation to the world rather than, as was the case prior to that time, a way
of pointing to the mystery of God who transcends metaphysical categories. By understanding God's relation to the world as a matter of distance, the rational mind could then "domesticate" God.[2]

The question of God, then, becomes a matter of playing out the contrast between transcendence and immanence: how far or near is God in
relation to the world? This "contrastive" view of God has since dominated
Western theological discussion.[3] Context plays a critical role in deciding
which side of the contrast is to be preferred. In a culture of optimism in
the nineteenth century, fostered by material prosperity and military

[1]Stanley J. Grenz and Roger E. Olson, *20th Century Theology: God and the World in a Transi-
tional Age* (Downers Grove, IL: InterVarsity Press, 1992), p. 10.
[2]William C. Placher, *The Domestication of Transcendence: How Modern Thinking About God
Went Wrong* (Louisville: Westminster John Knox, 1996).
[3]Ibid., p. 7.

power and supported by the theory of evolutionary progress, the accent fell heavily on God's immanence: God must be present in our world, perhaps even on our side! This was how European colonial expansion was justified. But by the mid-twentieth century after the shattering experience of two world wars, optimism turned to despair. Immanence was now replaced by an absent "God," who for many meant no God at all.

Unlike the Western church in the last two hundred years, the issue for Asian Christians has not been God's presence or absence, or whether God exists or not. In most religious traditions and especially in the world of primal religions, God's existence is never in doubt but always presupposed. The question is not God's existence or non-existence but God's identity and nature. The most urgent question for Christians is not theism vs. atheism or agnosticism but how to make sense of the Christian understanding of God in contexts filled with a plethora of vastly different conceptions of deity. In this chapter, the part surveying elitist responses will be brief and may not do full justice to the subject matter; its aim is to alert us to the complexity of the task of commending the Christian view of God. The daunting task is further complicated when we consider that within any religious tradition the question of God could be understood from the perspective of the religious elite as well as from its folk expressions.

GOD IN ISLAMIC CONTEXT

In the Muslim context the question of identity and difference is one of the most pressing issues because of a partially shared history. Is Allah identical with the Father of Jesus Christ? First, there are sufficient similarities between the Christian and Muslim conceptions of God to affirm an ontological identity. Together with the Jews, Muslims share with Christians the fundamental belief in the oneness of God. Considerable similarities can also be seen in the Muslim view of the divine attributes. One cannot read the ninety-nine beautiful names of God in the Koran and not notice a remarkable resemblance to the God revealed by Jesus Christ.[4] Even the Koran affirms this identity (Koran 29:46). Furthermore,

---

[4]Timothy George, *Is the Father of Jesus the God of Mohammad?* (Grand Rapids: Zondervan, 2002), p. 72.

there are points of convergence in their respective understandings of salvation history. Both agree that their God is the God of Abraham, although they disagree over what Abraham's God did after Abraham: whether he chose Isaac or Ishmael to continue his covenantal relationship. All these suggest that they are talking about the same God. There is enough convergence to suggest identity. But there are also fundamental differences. Muslims deny the doctrine of the Trinity. Christians are often accused of worshiping three gods. The concept of God as Father, so foundational to the Christian conception of God, is anathema to the Muslim. Their respective theologies affect religious expressions such as worship and perhaps even ethical behavior, even though both have sufficiently specific and similar predications of God as not to render identification improbable.

The situation is not helped by certain modern trinitarian conceptions, such as Moltmann's, which tends almost toward tritheism.[5] One wonders if a better case could be presented to the Muslim via a Thomistic conception of the Trinity. Scholasticism may have fallen out of favor with modern theologians, but it has the conceptual tools to make important distinctions that are often obscured in modern theological discussions. For example, Thomas's concepts of God as "pure act" (simple, perfect, without potentiality and change) and of divine "operations" (such as "generation" and "procession") might serve as a better point of contact between the Muslim and the Christian. It makes distinction in God conceivable without compromising the divine perfection and oneness. Perhaps in an age when Muslim and Christian theologians shared the same Aristotelian framework, it was possible for fruitful dialogues to be pursued.[6] But given the postmodern climate, it is more difficult to discover a common language. However, as we shall see later, it does not render dialogue impossible; rather, starting with the recognition of difference in the faith traditions may open up more fruitful paths to genuine

---

[5]Jürgen Moltmann, *The Trinity and the Kingdom of God* (San Francisco: Harper & Row, 1981).
[6]See David Burrell, *Knowing the Unknowable God* (Notre Dame, IN: University of Notre Dame Press, 1986).

dialogue than beginning by subsuming the differences under an assumed universal reason.

Perhaps the most compelling accounts that seem to confirm the idea that the Christian and Muslim conceptions of God share a common identity have come from Muslims themselves who became Christians. These converts do not feel that they have switched their allegiance to another God but that they have come to relate to him in a new and more meaningful way. They are worshiping the same God differently. The story of Bilquis Sheikh is typical and shows that the doctrine that most fundamentally divides Christianity and Islam, namely, the person of Jesus Christ, is at the same time the most existentially significant. The deepest human need is not answered in the God who is only "the Everlasting, the All-High, the All-Glorious" (Koran 2:256), but the God who is also eternally loving because he is eternally the triune personal God, the one whom Bilquis Sheikh and all Christians dare to call "Father."[7] In Islam power is the primary attribute of God rather than love. In the strict monotheism of Islam, love could be actualized only after God created. In Christianity, God's eternal love for his Son is revealed supremely in the sending of his Son to die for the sins of the world. The Christian experience of the God-who-sent-his-Son highlights another important feature in the Muslim convert's experience of God: the decisive turning point is almost always a personal encounter with Jesus as Son of God. The testimonies of converts from far-flung and unrelated contexts are quite consistent; they almost always involve Jesus' coming to them either in a dream or vision, or in some deeply existential moment.[8] One is reminded of St. Paul's experience on the Damascus road, which radically transformed his Jewish monotheism.

TRINITY AS A DOCTRINE OF CHRISTIAN EXPERIENCE

The Muslim converts' experience of God reconfirms Prosper's rule. The Christian awareness of the Trinity arises from the encounter with God's revelation of himself in Jesus Christ and in the Holy Spirit. This idea is

---

[7]See the story of Bilquis Sheikh, *I Dared to Call Him Father* (Grand Rapids: Baker, 1992).
[8]See Gulshan Esther, *The Torn Veil* (Fort Washington, PA: CLC, 2010), pp. 74-76, 128.

not new but was developed quite early by the church fathers. Only God can save humanity, and if Jesus is indeed the Savior then he has to be God.[9] The doctrine of the Trinity is the result of Christians reflecting upon and seeking to make sense of their experience of God's mission to humanity. The Word spoken by God is incarnated in Jesus Christ, the Son of the Father. The Spirit is sent from the Father through the Son and thus continues the trinitarian mission in the Church. In their encounter with divine revelation, Christians discover that the primary character of God is love, that God's love for humanity is grounded in his very nature from eternity. God is the eternally loving God since even before creation there is differentiation in the one God that makes the relationship of love possible. Thus it was from the uniquely Christian experience of God that Christians eventually came to identify God as Father, Son and Holy Spirit. It took the church many years to articulate the doctrine, but its experience of the God revealed in Jesus Christ and the Holy Spirit is what sets its monotheism apart from Jewish and Islamic monotheism.

The way in which Christians' trinitarian awareness developed from its roots in Jewish monotheism may help shed light on the recent "Allah controversy" in Malaysia. When some Malaysian Muslims insist that "Allah" is the Muslim God and cannot be used by any other religion, they are in effect arguing that Islam has a tradition of interpretation that links the term uniquely to Islam, a link that is not shared with any other religions. It carries a certain theological freight unique to Islam. In short, "Allah" carries different connotations for Muslims than it does for Jews and Christians. For Christians and Jews, "Allah" in Abrabic is simply a generic name for God, whereas for Muslims, "Allah" functions as a proper name.[10] For Jews and Christians the term "God" does not sufficiently carry the full freight of their respective experiences of God, whereas in the history of Islam "Allah" carries the full weight of their experience.

This development from a common name to a proper divine name is not unique to Islam but can be found in both Judaism and Christianity.

---

[9]Athanasius, *On the Incarnation* 3.13, 4.20.
[10]Timothy C. Tennent, *Theology in the Context of World Christianity* (Grand Rapids: Zondervan, 2007), pp. 45-46.

For the Jews the tetragrammaton (YHWH) was probably a generic term originally ("I will be") but came to be identified with the one who established his covenant with Israel and therefore the proper name of the God of Israel.[11] Similarly, the "Christ" (anointed one) was a generic name before it became the proper name of Jesus; that is to say, for Christians, there are no other "Christs" except the one who is called Jesus of Nazareth. Along a similar line, Robert Jenson has argued that "Father, Son and Holy Spirit" are the proper names of the triune God.[12] For Jews, then, it is "Yahweh" rather than *elohim* that carries the full weight of their experience of God, while for Christians it is "Father, Son and Holy Spirit" (for which the term "Trinity" is the shorthand) that functions in the same way as "Yahweh" for the Jews and "Allah" for Muslims. If Father, Son and Holy Spirit are the proper names of God carrying a uniquely Christian experience, substituting these names with functional equivalents such as Creator, Redeemer and Sanctifier would undermine their uniquely Christian significance. We could therefore understand the apprehension of some Muslims that the use of "Allah" by non-Muslims might confuse the simple-minded Muslim, since it carries different connotations for Muslims and non-Muslims. It is quite another matter, however, to insist that on that account only Muslims hold exclusive right to the use of the name.

GOD IN INDIAN CONTEXT

The situation, however, is quite different when we move from the Muslim to the Hindu context. Between the Christian and Muslim monotheistic conceptions of God the main question concerns identity and difference, but in the Hindu context the issue concerns the personhood of God vis-à-vis the impersonal conception of the ultimate.

Much of traditional Indian Christian theology is an attempt to relate basic Christian beliefs to philosophic Hinduism, especially how Brahman, as the impersonal, attributeless mystery could be related to the supremely

---

[11]Robert Jenson, *Christian Dogmatics*, ed. Carl E. Braaten and Robert W. Jenson (Philadelphia: Fortress, 1984), 1:89-90.
[12]Ibid., pp. 92-95.

personal conception of God as Trinity. One of the earliest attempts at correlation between Brahman and the Trinity was made by the "Hindu-Christian" Keshab Chandra Sen (1838–1884), the successor of Ram Mohan Roy (1772–1833), founder of *Brāhma Samāj*, a movement seeking to reform Hinduism through the ethics of Jesus but without becoming Christian. Sen saw in the doctrine of Brahman as *Saccidānanda* (*Sat, Cit, Ānandà*: being, intelligence, bliss) a link to the Trinity.[13] His work represents one of the most significant contributions to the development of an Indian Christian theology. Robin Boyd has this to say about Sen's theological achievement:

> Sen is perhaps here feeling his way towards a completely new and fully Indian formulation of the mystery, in terms of *Sat, Cit, Ānandà*. And it may be that the road here marked out by him and later followed by others will prove more effective for the Christian mission in India than concepts derived from Greek philosophy, and the Roman Theatre or even from modern western personalism.[14]

The question of contextualizing the Christian doctrine of God is usually framed in terms of whether the Trinity should be understood in terms of the *advaita* (nondualistic) doctrine of Brahman as interpreted by Sankara or in terms of the "qualified nondualism" of Ramanuja. An early attempt to relate the Trinity to the non-dualistic doctrine can be seen in Brahman-brandhab Upādhayāya (Bhavāni Charan Bānerji, 1861–1907). The way Upādhayāya went about it was to argue that God as Brahman is necessary being (*sat*) while creation (*asat*: nonbeing) is not nothingness but contingent being. Using Thomistic categories, he reinterpreted *Maya* (illusion) as *creation passiva*. According to Robin Boyd, what Upādhayāya did with Sankara's doctrine of Brahman parallels what Aquinas did with Aristotle.[15] Along similar lines of argument, Raimundo Panikkar attempts to show that the tensions found in the various philosophical schools of Hinduism—between Brahman as absolutely unrelated to the world and

---

[13]Robin Boyd, *An Introduction to Indian Christian Theology* (Bangalore: Christian Literature Society, 1969), pp. 28, 34-35.
[14]Ibid., pp. 34-35.
[15]Ibid., pp. 75-77 *passim*.

yet in some sense the cause of the world—can be understood in trinitarian terms: the Son of God who links God in his absolute mystery to the world.[16] Christ most closely parallels Isvara of Hinduism. Isvara is the relational side of Brahman, just as Jesus Christ reveals the Father. Panikkar argues that at the "intentional level" and "analogical level" there must be some common ground between the Christian and the Hindu when each respectively calls Jesus Christ and Isvara "Lord."[17]

If Upādhayāya and Panikkar represent interpretations of the Trinity in terms of nondualistic Hinduism, A. J. Appasamy seeks to understand the Trinity in relation to the "qualified nondualism" of Ramanuja (eleventh century). Ramanuja rejected the strict monist interpretation of Sankara and stressed the personal dimension exemplified in the personal devotion to Krishna, the incarnation of Vishnu, as seen in the Bhagavadgita. It is from this devotional tradition known as *bhakti* that Appasamy develops his theology. Central to his theology is the Logos (*antaryamin*), the God who is immanent in the world before his incarnation. But the coming of Christ is where the Logos fully dwells. God is related to the world as the Logos, who is also the agent of creation. He is related to the world as the soul is related to the body (an analogy derived from Ramanuja).[18] Unlike Hindu nondualism, which sees the nameless absolute (*nirguna Brahman*) as higher than Isvara, the personal God, Appasamy proposes two ways of conceiving God: God understood in terms of personal attributes and God who transcends these attributes.[19] This is not very different from the traditional *via positiva* and *via negativa*. The *bhakti* tradition, as we shall see, plays an important role in popular forms of Christianity in India.

While traditional Christian theology seeks to relate to the religious context of India, more recent forms of Indian Christian theology has sought to relate to the sociopolitical context. An example is M. M. Thomas. For Thomas, God is the God of history, one who effects his-

---

[16]Raimundo Panikkar, *The Unknown Christ of Hinduism: Towards an Ecumenical Christophany* (London: Darton, Longman and Todd, 1981), pp. 155-60.
[17]Ibid., p. 101.
[18]Boyd, *An Introduction*, pp. 124-27.
[19]Ibid., pp. 129-30.

torical fulfilment. Thomas wrote at a time when India was going through radical sociopolitical changes, which he designated "the Asian Revolution." Specifically, the Asian Revolution was an instrument of Western democratic humanism and technological development, both of which would result in the creation of an Asian self-identity. Thomas sees these changes as generally positive because they not only posed a fundamental challenge to the rigid caste system that has kept India in a hopelessly cyclical pattern of karmic existence but also promises to bring social and political liberation. Democratic humanism enables each person to discover his or her personal identity as a self-determining agent, while technological development offers hope of escape from abject poverty. These forces create conditions for greater selfhood and national identity—in Thomas's term, "humanization." Thomas believes that through the Asian Revolution God is preparing Asia to face the challenge of the gospel, whose central focus is on historical hope and persons as free agents.[20]

There are others, however, who seek to transcend the foregoing forms of theologizing, whether from the religious or sociopolitical contexts. This is because, according to Avind P. Nirmal, considered the father of Dalit theology, much of "Indian Christian theology" is obsessed with "the Brahminic tradition" while ignoring the concerns of the outcastes.[21] Dalit theology is strongly opposed to the system that has left Dalits completely subjugated for centuries. It would therefore have nothing to do with attempts at accommodation with the Brahminic tradition. Instead, from the early 1980s Dalit Christians have been calling for a theology from a "subaltern" perspective in opposition to the "homogenizing propensities of elite theology." Dalit theologians stress not only the God of history (à la M. M. Thomas) but the God who brings historical liberation to the Dalits. They recognize that a general liberation theology from the perspective of the privileged caste will not do.[22] Theirs is the "servant-God"

---

[20]M. M. Thomas, *The Christian Response to the Asian Revolution* (London: SCM Press, 1966).
[21]Arvind P. Nirmal, "Towards a Christian Dalit Theology," in *A Reader in Dalit Theology*, ed. Arvind P. Nirmal (Madras: Gurukul Lutheran Theological College and Research Institute, n.d.), p. 55.
[22]Dhyanchand Carr, "Dalit Theology Is Biblical and It Makes the Gospel Relevant," in *A Reader in Dalit Theology*, pp. 71-73.

revealed in Jesus Christ, the servant of Yahweh.[23] If Thomas's view of history can be described as eschatological, which places confidence in the sociopolitical processes to bring about gradual improvement ("humanization"), the view of Dalit Christians is apocalyptic, rejecting and overturning the "master narrative" of the theological elite.[24] Dalit theologians, however, are careful not to define Dalit theology only in opposition to the dominant theology; to do so would mean letting the dominant theology serve as their point of reference. Rather, they seek a theology in which Dalits themselves are the subjects of their own history.[25]

GOD IN CHINESE CONTEXTS

In ancient China, the concept of the supreme deity is designated by two terms: *Shang-di* and *Tian*. While the meanings and connotations of *Shang-di* and *Tian* underwent significant changes through the long history of China, they could be thought of as corresponding roughly to the two primary names of God in the Old Testament respectively: Yahweh and Elohim. Yahweh is the covenantal name of God, God in relation to his people, while Elohim is God in relation to the universe. *Tian*, however, does not seem to have the personal connotations of the Old Testament names.[26]

In Confucianism the concept of *Tian* evolved over many centuries from that of the supreme deity (probably in Confucius himself)[27] to that of an impersonal ethical ultimate (among the neo-Confucianists), so that Confucianism as we know it today is largely perceived as an ethical rather than a religious system. Some modern Confucian scholars are aware that there is no reason that Confucianism—simply as an ethical system sup-

[23]Nirmal, "Towards a Christian Dalit Theology," pp. 63-65.
[24]Sathianathan Clarke, "Dalit Theology: An Introductory and Interpretiave Theological Exposition," in *Dalit Theology in the Twenty-First Century: Discordant Voices, Discerning Pathways*, ed. Sathianathan Clarke, Deenabandhu Manchala and Philip Vinod Peacock (New Delhi: Oxford University Press, 2010), pp. 19-20.
[25]Ibid., pp. 27-29.
[26]Chuang Tsu-Kung, "*Shang-di*: God from Chinese Perspective," in *The Global God: Listening to God and Learning from Culture*, ed. Aída Besançon Spencer and William David Spencer (Grand Rapids: Baker, 1998), pp. 189-92.
[27]Hans Küng and Julia Ching, *Christianity and Chinese Religions* (London: SCM Press, 1989), p. 67.

ported by ritual practices—should be observed at all. Thus the Confucian scholar Tu Wei-Ming has sought to reroot Confucianism in a transcendent point of reference. That is to say, if Confucian ethics is to be taken seriously, it has to have some "religious" basis. For Tu, then, "the Confucian way of being religious [is] ultimate self-transformation as a communal act and as a faithful dialogical response to the transcendent."[28] Seen in this way, the Confucian sense of the ethical ultimate has the character of a religious conviction. Its religious character is further confirmed by its interface with the cult of ancestors going back to very ancient times.[29]

Besides Confucianism, there are other philosophical traditions in China that Christian theology must address, namely, Taoism and Buddhism. One attempt at relating Christian theology to philosophical Taoism can be seen in the work of Lee Young Jung. When the Trinity is adapted to the Taoist universe, the Trinity can be seen as a "becoming" or the principle of change itself. According to Lee, the Tao is the "supreme ultimate." It is characterized by the harmony of opposite, the *yin* and *yang*. This harmony of opposite is not a synthesis in the Hegelian sense, but relationality: "What is intrinsic to the *yin-yang* relationship is not its entity or being but its change."[30] God is "change itself," which remains changeless. Here, Lee's view seems remarkably close to what the process philosopher Alfred North Whitehead calls the "primordial nature" of God, while his explication of the trinitarian relationship corresponds to Whitehead's "consequent nature."[31] In terms of the principle of change, Father is change itself, Spirit is power of change, and Son is manifestation of change.[32]

---

[28]Tu Wei-Ming, *Centrality and Commonality: An Essay on Confucian Religiousness* (New York: State University of New York Press, 1989), p. 94. A similar conclusion has been drawn by Zhang Qingxiong, "Sin and Evil in Christian and Confucian Perspectives," in *Christianity and Chinese Culture*, ed. Miikka Ruokanen and Paulos Huang (Grand Rapids: Eerdmans, 2010), pp. 35-36.

[29]Küng and Ching, *Christianity and Chinese Religions*, p. 76.

[30]Lee Young Jung, *The Trinity in Asian Perspective* (Nashville: Abingdon, 1996), p. 27.

[31]Alfred North Whitehead, *Process and Reality: An Essay in Cosmology* (Cambridge, UK: Cambridge University Press, 1929), pp. 484-97.

[32]Lee, *The Trinity*, p. 66.

But Lee also seeks to understand the trinitarian relationship in more concrete ways. For example, *Yang* is the Father; *Yin* is the Spirit (Mother); Son in his two natures is the unity of Father and Mother, the work of both the Most High (Father) and the Spirit (see Luke 1:47-48).[33] The Son as the archetype of humans is also the unity of male and female.[34] Elsewhere the Spirit is the *qi*, the activity of *yin* and *yang*. *Qi* is the wind or breath that flows through the universe and the microcosm of the human body bringing healing. This concept underlies the healing techniques of acupuncture, Tai Ji and so on, which seek to let the *qi* flow harmoniously through the body.[35] One interesting feature of Lee's understanding of the Trinity in terms of the *yin-yang* relationship is the concept of complementarity or the irreducible distinction of the male and female. Part of the problem of modern society, claims Lee, is that masculine characteristics such as "positiveness, firmness, creativity, and strength" have become the norm to be desired by all, including women. The result is gender competition in a world defined by a male value system:

> When the female becomes like the male, the distinction disappears. When the distinction disappears, men and women do not reflect the Trinitarian principle, which is the core of community life. . . . The denial of gender distinction is also an ontological sin, for God made man and woman to complement each other.[36]

Complementarity and distinction extend also to the ordering of society. Hierarchical orders or classes need not be oppressive; the alternative to order is not a classless society but disorder. Lee himself had seen the dismal failure of communism to create a classless society. In North Korea he discovered that the elimination of the upper class merely resulted in its replacement by an elite proletariat. We might add that the egalitarian ideals of modernity underlying its discourse on rights, justice and

---

[33]Ibid., pp. 74-75.
[34]Ibid., p 80. Here Lee refers to Carl Jung's observation that every male has female components and vice versa.
[35]Ibid., pp. 95, 97.
[36]Ibid., pp. 203-4.

freedom are similarly destined to fail.[37] Lee therefore calls us to "consider the possibility that the structure of the social classes reflects the functional hierarchy in the Trinity."[38]

Taoism as a philosophy has always held a certain attraction to Chinese Christians. A case in point is Lin Yutang, the Chinese humanist who rejected the Christianity of his childhood to become a Taoist for the next forty years, only to return to the faith of his parents in his old age. But Lin never gave up on Taoist philosophy. The spirit of Taoism that unconsciously shaped his experience of God in his earlier days continued to shape him more consciously upon his return to Christianity: The beauty of mountain and water (*shan shui*) reminded him of God's omnipresence; he appreciated the Taoist ethics of simplicity, humility and nonresistance, which reminded him of Jesus' Sermon on the Mount. Even the simplicity of Taoist folk religion was something he appreciated, although after his return to Christianity he criticized its superstitions.[39]

GOD IN PRIMAL RELIGIOUS CONTEXT

The idea of the supreme being that we have seen in Confucianism and Taoism shows significant nuances in the religions of China. But it must be remembered that what we are looking at is the "great tradition" of these religious systems. They represent the views of the intelligentsia. Things are quite different at the level of folk religiosity (the "little tradition"). Here we find Confucianism, Taoism and Buddhism so syncretized as to become almost indistinguishable from each other so that when the phrase "Chinese religion" is used, it usually refers to the syncretism of popular forms of these religions.[40] "Chinese religion" is often characterized as pragmatic. The gods or spirits are worshiped and sought after for general protection and prosperity. But in more serious problems such

---

[37]See, for example, the critiques of Stanley Hauerwas on the Enlightenment projects on justice and freedom in *After Christendom?* (Nashville: Abingdon, 1999), pp. 45-92.

[38]Lee, *The Trinity*, pp. 204-5.

[39]He Jianming, "Dialogue Between Christianity and Taoism: The Case of Lin Yutang," in *Christianity and Chinese Culture*, pp. 129-42 *passim*.

[40]See John Clammer, ed., *Studies in Chinese Folk Religion in Singapore and Malaysia* (Singapore: Institute for the Study of Religions and Society, 1983).

as prolonged illness or the collapse of a business venture, professional help is sought from mediums and geomancers.[41] The same pragmatism is seen among the Koreans. As one American educator who came to Korea in the early twentieth century, Homer B. Hulbert, observed, "The all round Korean is a Confucianist when in society, a Buddhist when he philosophizes, and a spirit-worshipper when in trouble."[42]

Folk Christianity too shares similar pragmatic impulses. One Chinese researcher has noted how pragmatism is largely responsible for the popularity of certain forms of Christianity in rural China: Christianity does not require the use of expensive joss sticks whereas Buddhism and Taoism do! The practical benefits of embracing the Christian faith are aptly captured in this Christian folk song:

> It is really worthwhile to believe in Jesus, one neither drinks [alcohol] nor smokes, one does not have to burn joss sticks and paper money, and one will not gamble either; in such a way one can save much money every year. When money is saved, one may have better food and clothes; it will not be difficult anymore to have a better life, and after death one can even go into heaven. Please tell me, whether this is worthwhile or not?[43]

It would be a mistake, however, to see the influence of folk religions on Christianity as only one-way, resulting in what Bulatao calls "split-level Christianity."[44] We could look at the situation exemplified by the above folk song as another instance of the impact of the pragmatic mindset of folk religiosity on Christianity, or we could also see it as a case of effective contextualization of Christianity. Christianity in such a context poses as much a challenge to folk religions as an adaptation to them. It offers an alternative lifestyle (no drinking, smoking or gambling) and encourages thrift and, consequently, upward social mobility. Its engagement with popular culture should

---

[41]Ju Shi Huey, "Chinese Spirit-Mediums in Singapore: An Ethnographic Study," in *Studies in Chinese Folk Religion*, pp. 21-24.

[42]Cited by Bong Rin Ro, "Communicating the Biblical Concept of God to Koreans," in *The Global God*, p. 315.

[43]Gao Shining, "The Impact of Contemporary Chinese Folk Religions on Christianity," in *Christianity and Chinese Culture*, pp. 176-77.

[44]Jaime Bulatao, *Split-Level Christianity* (Manila: Ateneo de Manila University, 1966).

not be understood purely in terms of pragmatic accommodation but also creative adaptation.

This is perhaps best exemplified in the Pentecostal-charismatic forms of Christianity, which are perhaps the most dominant forms of Christianity in Asia today. Here we find the "big tradition" and the "little tradition" confusedly juxtaposed. The received orthodoxy expressed in theological concepts sits side by side with what appear to be contradictory practices. But to call this "split-level Christianity" does not do it full justice. Its adaptation to folk religiosity not only produces positive practical outcomes but also theological achievements. If the Asian context is marked by the poles of poverty and religiosity (Pieris),[45] Pentecostalism has the greatest potential to bring these two poles together. In fact, it integrates these poles in a manner that Pieris did not quite foresee. It is both the religion of the poor and the religion that directly addresses the primal religious instinct that pervades Asia. The God of the Pentecostals is active in the world and also possesses absolute sovereignty over the entire universe.

What is unique to Pentecostals is that they have an unwavering confidence in such a God in everyday life. Their belief in divine immanence and transcendence finds practical expression in praying for the sick, exorcising demons and so on. God encounters us in concrete realities, in worship and in dreams and visions. God is concerned for the whole person and so Pentecostals do not treat poverty as a social issue in isolation from the broader religious context. Its message is "God can change you spiritually, free you from spiritual bondage, and also heal your body and supply all your needs." This message is succinctly captured in Cho Yonggi's "threefold blessings." The main weakness of Pentecostal Christianity is that it does not adequately address the "big tradition." An educated Buddhist would probably not find Pentecostalism very attractive (or, for that matter, folk Buddhism), but even so, he cannot completely avoid the primal religious context, and that is where Pentecostalism establishes an attractive point of contact.

---

[45]See below p. 98.

THE *VESTIGIA DEI*

As we have observed in chapter 1, Christianity is closer in many respects
to primal religions than to the axial religions. This is why it tends to be
more readily accepted in primal religious societies than in societies dominated by the axial religions. One of the reasons for the welcome Christianity receives is that the message concerning God seems to find deep
resonance within the collective memory in these societies.[46] Traditionally, this contiguity between Christianity and primal religions is designated the *vestigia dei* (the footprints of God) or *prisca theologia* (ancient
theology). The idea has a long history in the church and can be found in
many church fathers, including Justin Martyr, Irenaeus, Clement of Al-
exandria and Origen.[47] The eighteenth-century American theologian
Jonathan Edwards argues that the presence of *prisca theologia* shows that
there are elements of true religion in non-Christian religions and
thinkers.[48] Edwards saw these religions as "once visited by and still re-
taining traces of the light of revelation."[49] But under the impact of
modern historiography the *vestigia dei* concept is cast into considerable
doubt. It is consigned to the realm of "primeval history," a subject for
anthropologists rather than historians. But that does not render the
concept itself theologically irrelevant. Whether the knowledge of a supreme being in many ancient cultures owes its origin to some primeval
revelation or traces of ancient people's memory of a prelapsarian state,
the fact of the matter is that it is often a concrete point of contact between
primal religious societies and the gospel. It constitutes a de facto *praeparatio evangelica*. It prepares the way for the gospel and accounts for its
ready reception in these societies.

One variation and application of this teaching is seen in a recent work
of evangelical Calvinist Terrance Tiessen, who believes that those who

---

[46]See Don Wilkinson, *Eternity in Their Hearts* (Ventura, CA: Regal, 1981); Chan Kei Thong,
Finding God in Ancient China (Grand Rapids: Zondervan, 2009).

[47]Gerald McDermott, *God's Rivals: Why Has God Allowed Different Religions? Insights From the
Bible and the Early Church* (Downers Grove, IL: InterVarsity Press, 2007).

[48]Gerald R. McDermott, *Jonathan Edwards Confronts the Gods: Christian Theology, Enlightenment Religion, and Non-Christian Faiths* (New York: Oxford University Press, 2000), p. 8.

[49]Ibid., p. 12.

die without an explicit knowledge of the gospel proclaimed by the church are still included in God's various covenants with humanity, which go back to his creation covenants with Adam and Noah (provided that they are faithful to the conditions of those covenants). According to Tiessen, we can therefore conclude that these people are saved.[50] But would such a view of salvation not make knowledge of Christ extraneous? Tiessen believes that the encounter with Christ can come at death rather than after death. This is in line with his belief that the opportunities to be saved are given only in this life (citing Heb 9:27-28; Lk 13:23-30).[51]

Whatever explanations that might be given regarding primal religions' contiguity with Christianity, the fact that it is recognized as such in the religious consciousness of the folk religionist belies the oft-repeated claim that Christianity is a foreign religion in Asia. Christianity may seem foreign in the world of the axial religions and the religious intelligentsia at the conceptual level. But in the primal religious context the perception is often quite different. Plus, the perception of foreignness is not uniformly true even among the intelligentsia. As noted earlier, a supernatural encounter with Jesus Christ is often the turning point for Hindu or Muslim converts, even among the elite. Primal religiosity runs deep in Asia; it is no respecter of one's educational or religious background. A similar phenomenon is observed among the "cultural Christians" of China.

"Cultural Christians" (CC) are Chinese intellectuals who are sympathetic to but not openly identified with the Christian church.[52] According to Chen Cun-fu, the director of the Christian Research Center at Zhejiang University, CCs are already playing a vital role because of their intimate knowledge of Chinese culture, their translation of Western works on theology and philosophy into Chinese, and their interpretation of

---

[50]See Terrance L. Tiessen, "The Salvation of the Unevangelized in the Light of God's Covenant," *Evangelical Review of Theology* 36 (July 2012): 231-49.
[51]Terrance L. Tiessen, *Who Can Be Saved? Reassessing Salvation in Christ and World Religions* (Downers Grove, IL: InterVarsity Press, 2004), pp. 221-22.
[52]David Aikman, *Jesus in Beijing: How Christianity Is Transforming China and Changing the Global Balance of Power* (Washington, D.C.: Regnery, 2003), pp. 245-62.

Christianity, which has helped overturn erroneous concepts (such as "religion is the opium of the people").[53] Yuan Zhiming is one such Chinese intellectual best known for his highly-acclaimed TV documentary "River Elegy," which reinterprets the cherished symbols of Chinese civilization, such as the Great Wall and Yellow River, as symbols of isolation and oppression. Yuan was one of the leaders of the democracy movement that ended in the 1989 Tiananmen Square massacre. After his escape to the West, Yuan saw that the Western democracy he idealized was not the answer to China's problem. His conversion to Christianity in the West gave Yuan a new perspective. He now sees that conversion to Christ is the true hope of society.[54] Perhaps after the failed Tiananmen experiment in democracy, he realized that something more than ideas and ideals was needed to change the world. What is needed is the power of faith that goes beyond knowledge, that is, a relationship with God that gives to the soul an "explosive power" to transcend the most extenuating circumstances. As Yuan puts it, "When faith sinks its roots deep within the soul, the strength of heaven descends upon it."[55]

At times Yuan sounds like Solzhenitzyn, warning against the destructive individualistic freedom in the West[56] and arguing, à la Niebuhr, for the necessity and possibility of democracy based on the doctrine of human sin and the *imago Dei*.[57] Yuan is concerned not only with the Christian basis of a free society but also grapples with the relationship between Christianity and Chinese culture and philosophy by appealing to a form of "primitive monotheism." Yuan represents a growing number of Chinese intellectuals who see Christianity as providing the spiritual resource that can address the various ills of their nation. Their understanding of Christianity is still evolving and at times seems naïve and

---

[53]Cun-Fu Chen, "The 'Cultural Christian' Phenomenon: An Overview and Evaluation," in *Chinese Intellectuals and the Gospel*, ed. Samuel and Stacey Bieler (Vancouver, BC: China Horizon, 1999), pp. 99-101.

[54]Yuan Zhiming, "The Dream of Those Years: Beginning from a Reassessment of 'River Elegy,'" in *Soul Searching: Chinese Intellectuals on Faith and Society*, ed. Carol Lee Hamrin, Samuel Ling and Daniel Baida Su (Pasadena, CA: China Horizons, 1997), pp. 9-16.

[55]Yuan Zhiming, "The Authority of the Soul," in *Soul Searching*, pp. 70-71.

[56]Ibid., pp. 80-81.

[57]Yuan Zhiming, "God and Democracy," in *Soul Searching*, pp. 55-65.

even unstable,[58] but they possess a youthful and vibrant faith that augurs well for Christianity in China.

THE CHALLENGE OF THE TRINITY

The brief foregoing consideration of Asia's multireligious contexts shows that there is no one theology of God that suits every situation. Each religious context has its own set of issues that Christians must address. This does not, however, mean that the Christian view of God should change to suit each religious context. Central to the Christian faith is the doctrine of the Trinity, but in each context there are different ramifications. Muslims have difficulty with the Trinity, whereas in India the Trinity is almost a necessity in relating to the Hindu philosophical system. We see this, for example, in the Hindu-Christian Keshab Chandra Sen's attempt to relate the Trinity to the concept of Brahman as *Saccidānanda* (being, intelligence, bliss).

Again, the challenge in the Muslim context is not about God's personhood as such but how that personhood is defined: whether God's person is a pure monad or a triunity.[59] While the Trinity may be a stumbling block to the Muslim, it also presents a formidable challenge. Against Islam's strict monotheism, the Fatherhood of God in Christianity implies that personal relationship is marked chiefly by love rather than submission to an absolute power. In the Hindu context, on the other hand, where personhood is largely seen as inferior to an impersonal ultimate, the challenge is to make sense of the trinitarian personhood as the ultimate reality. In the Confucian context, the main challenge is to show that the ethical ultimate must ultimately be grounded in divine personality. The Trinity as relational being also poses a serious challenge to the Confucian understanding of a distant and impersonal supreme being.[60] In Confucian and Taoist societies, the doctrine of the Fatherhood of God as found in the Orthodox concept of the monarchy of the Father also

---

[58]Chen, "The 'Cultural Christian' Phenomenon," p. 99.
[59]A. Christian van Gorder has suggested that perhaps "triunity" is to be preferred over "Trinity" in the Islamic context as the former term highlights the unity of God. *No God but God: A Path to Muslim-Christian Dialogue on God's Nature* (Maryknoll, NY: Orbis, 2003), p. 116.
[60]Ro, "Communicating," p. 208.

makes a lot of sense against the backdrop of an ordered society marked by differentiation of roles and reciprocal relationships.

With respect to folk religiosity, a general feature of the Asian religious scene is the deep divide between the high religions and their folk expressions. Folk religionists operate in the world of many gods and spirits, but the supreme being who rules over these lesser gods is not one with whom ordinary people can relate.[61] The doctrine of the Trinity addresses the problem of both the high religions as well as the folk religions of Asia. The "one God and Father of all, who is over all" is also "through all and in all" (Eph 4:6 ESV). He is both supremely transcendent and immanent because he is Trinity, the God in relation.

In the doctrine of the Trinity the Son gives God a name and a face. Often this is the way many Asians first come to know the God of Christianity. The personal God revealed in Jesus is their first point of contact and the main reason for Christianity's attraction. It is not coincidental that Muslim converts often testify to their personal encounter with Jesus Christ in vision or dream as the decisive turning point in their lives. The God they used to know as the transcendent and mysterious one is now experienced as the loving Father of Jesus Christ and their Father. This truth is relevant not only to the Muslim but among adherents of other Asian religions as well. There is something to be said about the evangelical message of introducing Jesus as personal Lord and Savior: it appeals to the instinctual longings for personal relationship present in the Asian soul as much as in any other. It fills a religious void in the merely ritualistic religions (such as popular Taoism). For all the speculation that the doctrine of the Trinity has undergone in the West, it is a profoundly practical doctrine in Asia.

With great importance placed on the family in Asia, the Trinity as the divine family takes on a special significance. The ideal Asian family is an ordered relationship with differentiated roles and reciprocal responsibilities that reflect the order of the Trinity. The trinitarian order is not a projection of a cultural ideal; rather, it is the archetype that sets the order

---

[61]Norman Anderson, *Christianity and World Religions: The Challenge of Pluralism* (Downers Grove, IL: InterVarsity Press, 1984), pp. 115-16.

of the traditional family. Modern theology in the West generally stresses the equality of the three persons of the Godhead, reflecting the egalitarian ideal that has become increasingly influential even among western evangelicals.[62] The one notable exception is perhaps Karl Barth. According to Barth, the glory of the Trinity is seen in the Father's sending his Son who, in his obedience to the Father, reveals what the inner Trinitarian relationship is like.[63] Both "divine superiority" and "divine subordination" reveal their respective "modes of being." That is to say, the subordination is based on the hypostatic distinction of Father and Son, not an essential distinction; therefore, it does not imply subordinationism. This ordered relationship is also a fellowship of love, brought about by the third mode of being, the Spirit.[64] Barth thus affirms both mutuality and hierarchy in the Trinity and extends this ordering to the relationship between male and female.[65]

Modern egalitarians, while affirming mutuality, have serious difficulty with hierarchy, especially in human relationships.[66] But as we have seen in the Korean theologian Lee Young Jung, the human hierarchy is patterned after the "functional hierarchy in the Trinity." This view comes much closer to the traditional Catholic and Orthodox doctrine of the monarchy of the Father, which understands the Father as the one "without origin" and the "sole principle" (*monē archē*) by whom the Son is generated and from whom the Spirit proceeds.[67] The Father's generation of the Son and spiration of the Spirit imply personal distinction and order,

---

[62]For example, see Elaine Storkey, "Evangelical Theology and Gender," in *The Cambridge Companion to Evangelical Theology*, ed. Timothy Larsen and Daniel J. Treier (Cambridge: Cambridge University Press, 2007), pp. 161-76.

[63]Karl Barth, *Church Dogmatics* 4.1 (Edinburgh: T & T Clark, 1957), pp. 203-4.

[64]Ibid., pp. 209-10.

[65]*Church Dogmatics* 3.4, pp. 168-77.

[66]See for example Jone Salomonsen, "'Love of Same, Love of Other': Reading Feminist Anthropologies with Luce Irigaray and Karl Barth," *Studia Theologica* 57 (2003), pp. 103-23. Salomonsen's argument that Barth's human hierarchy is based on the vertical relationship to God as *creator singularis* fails to take account of Barth's idea (in *Church Dogmatics* 4.1) that a hierarchical relationship exists between the Father and the Son in their respective modes of being (p. 114). It would be more true to say that the order of the male-female relationship is analogous to the Father-Son order.

[67]Vladimir Lossky, *Orthodox Theology: An Introduction*, trans. Ian and Ihita Kesarcodi-Watson (Crestwood, NY: St. Vladimir's Seminary Press, 1989), pp. 47-48.

yet the relationship can also be described as mutually dependent. Just as the Son and the Spirit depend on the Father for their origin, the Father is dependent on the Son to reveal his Fatherhood and lordship and on the Spirit's glorifying the Father and the Son to reveal his deity.[68] In the Orthodox tradition, this relationship of order and reciprocity is reflected in the liturgical *taxis*.[69] All this is to say that the hierarchical view of the Trinity has greater claim to universality than the egalitarian model. In the chapters that follow, the ramifications of this particular trinitarian doctrine will be further developed.

---

[68]Wolfhart Pannenberg, *Systematic Theology* (Grand Rapids: Eerdmans, 1991), 1:316, 322, 330.
[69]For example, Nicholas Afanasiev, *The Church of the Holy Spirit*, trans. Vitaly Permiakov, ed. Michael Plekon (Notre Dame, IN: University of Notre Dame Press, 2007). Barth's argument for the family *taxis* is remarkably similar to the Orthodox trinitarian *taxis* (*Church Dogmatics* 3.4, pp. 172-76.)

3

HUMANITY AND SIN

IT IS CUSTOMARY IN THEOLOGICAL anthropology to give pride
of place to the doctrine of the creation of humans in the image of God
beginning with the Genesis account. The doctrine carries vast sociopolitical implications as it touches on the question of the nature of human
dignity, rights, freedom and so forth. It has a special bearing on situations
of mass poverty and human rights abuse, which pervade many Asian
societies. But important as it is, we will not address it directly; rather, I
take human uniqueness as a theological given, not because humans
possess certain inherent qualities like freedom and rationality, but because as *imago Dei*, they stand in a special relationship to God. More
specifically, human dignity is predicated on the incarnation, which reveals God's ultimate goal for humanity in Christ. The *imago Dei* can only
be properly understood proleptically in the light of the coming of the
Logos (Jn 1), that is, in light of humanity's final destiny.[1]

Humans have an inherent worth because they are created for communion with the triune God. If personhood were based strictly on certain
distinctively human qualities such as freedom, rationality, creativity, self-
consciousness and so on, then those who lacked these capacities either
because of birth defects or through disease or injury would be less than
persons. The dignity of human beings can be properly maintained only
in the Christian view that sees human personality as grounded ultimately
in communion with the divine persons. A victim of Down syndrome is

---

[1]Wolfhart Pannenberg, *Systematic Theology* (Grand Rapids: Eerdmans, 1991), 2:190.

no less a person because he or she is loved and known by God. Without such an understanding we run the risk of reducing a human being to an object to be discarded once it has outlived its usefulness. These givens are shared in common with the best in the Christian tradition.[2]

The relational nature of the *imago Dei* in Genesis has special reference to the relationship between male and female, not just any interpersonal relationship.[3] It is this understanding that has led to the view of marriage and family as foundational to the created order and the most fundamental way of ordering human society, a view that is also widely held in traditional societies. Underlying this understanding of the human family is the archetypal Trinity as the communion of Father and Son in the unity of the Spirit, as noted in the previous chapter. But how is the family relation ordered? This question will be taken up below.

But before that, there is a question in older dogmatics concerning the person's "constituent elements" that merits some consideration: Is the human being made up of one (monism), two (body and soul) or three (body, soul and spirit) basic elements? The belief that human nature consists of more than one element may have its roots in Platonic dualism, which has generally fallen out of favor, and explains why contemporary theological anthropology has tended to dismiss it in favor of Hebraic holism (see below). But the question is not without significance if it is rerooted in other aspects of biblical anthropology to yield a better account of human nature. This is especially the case when we look at the Asian primal religious context, where questions regarding the place of the dead among the living are, quite literally, life and death issues. We need to move beyond the impasse in the traditional debates between the monist, dichotomist and trichotomist. Perhaps with some help from Wittgensteinian ordinary language analysis we might yet discover that these traditional debates provide different insights into the complexity of human nature. Wittgenstein has taught us to be aware that similar terms may actually hide different logical functions, each being governed by its own set of rules or "language game." Dichotomy and trichotomy may

---

[2]Ibid., pp. 175 and following.
[3]Karl Barth, *Church Dogmatics* 3.1 (Edinburgh: T & T Clark, 1957), pp. 185-91.

appear to be talking about the same thing: the single metaphysical problem of human nature's "constituent elements." This is the way the issue is usually framed in older dogmatics,[4] but further probing reveals different logics or language games.[5]

The logic of dichotomy is located in individual eschatology.[6] It seeks to make sense of the biblical data that for human beings death is not the final reality. But in the Old Testament this conviction does not stem from a doctrine of the immortality of the soul in contrast to a perishable body, but from the belief that not even death can break human beings' fellowship with the eternal, covenant-keeping God.[7] In other words, dichotomy seeks to preserve the Christian doctrine of hope of a future life. In this respect it does not differ functionally from a nonreductive monism, that is, the view that "the phenomenological experiences that we label 'soul' are neither reducible to brain activity nor evidence of a substantial, ontological entity such as a 'soul,' but rather represent essential aspects or capacities of the self."[8] The difference between traditional dichotomy and nonreductive monism or holism lies in their respective understandings of the makeup of the self: is the person made up of composite elements (dichotomy) or is it ontologically one (monism)? But they share a common understanding that biblical anthropology requires a view of the self that is capable of transcending temporal existence. However, dichotomy does more than that: it serves also as a pointer to a reality traditionally designated the intermediate state and also as a rationale for the traditional doctrine of eternal damnation.[9] The monistic view rejects

---

[4]For example, see Louis Berkhof, *Systematic Theology* (London: Banner of Truth Trust, 1984), pp. 191-95.

[5]It is quite clear that Erickson's endorsement of dichotomy is predicated on the Christian understanding of the "intermediate state," as seen in his rejection of the monistic view of man (*Christian Theology*, pp. 530-36), while in his discussion of trichotomy he recognizes its functional validity (p. 521).

[6]John W. Cooper, *Body, Soul, and Life Everlasting: Biblical Anthropology and the Monism-Dualism Debate* (Grand Rapids: Eerdmans, 1989).

[7]Pannenberg, *Systematic Theology*, 3:567.

[8]Joel B. Green, *Body, Soul, and Human Life: The Nature of Humanity in the Bible* (Grand Rapids: Baker, 2008), p. 31.

[9]Jerry L. Walls, *Hell: The Logic of Damnation* (Notre Dame, IN: University of Notre Dame Press, 1992).

the concept of an intermediate state in favor of immediate resurrection at death, but in so doing it fails to deal adequately with the biblical idea of a final resurrection.[10] On the whole dichotomy serves as a better pointer to the doctrine of the future life. If understood as "holistic dualism," as John Cooper has argued,[11] it has, in my view, a slight edge over the monistic view when it comes to the question of the intermediate state. Monism tends to be hedgy over what happens to the person between death and final resurrection.

Further, modern monistic views, perhaps as an overreaction against Platonic dualism, fail to clarify the distinction between Platonic dualism's concept of a wholly incorporeal soul and the concept of "ethereal bodily beings" commonly found in primal religious societies.[12] The distinction is important. In the primal religious conception, "the dead are never dead" but continue to exist in solidarity with the living.[13] The person after death is still truly a person in a different mode of existence, not a partial human being as implied in Platonic dualism where death is the separation of the "soul" from the body. This belief in the continuing existence of the person after death is widely acknowledged.[14] Africans have their concept of the "living dead" while in many Asian societies it is presupposed in the practice of ancestral veneration. It forms one of the most important backdrops for the contextualization of the gospel. Failure to address the issue of ancestral veneration in a satisfactory manner has been a major hindrance to the acceptance of Christianity in Asia. Elitist attempts to bracket its ontological status and treat it merely as a question for the social sciences (for example, as a means of social cohesion) have failed to assuage the deep concerns of its grassroots practitioners; a theology that ignores the grassroots is not likely to go very far. In short, holistic dualism offers a better fit in primal religious contexts than holism.

The logic of trichotomy, on the other hand, is best understood within the context of human psychology. For example, the functional trichotomy

---

[10]As pointed out by Pannenberg (*Systematic Theology*, 3:573-89) and others.
[11]Cooper, *Body*, pp. 73-80.
[12]Ibid., p. 74.
[13]Uchenna A. Ezeh, *Jesus Christ the Ancestor* (Berne, Germany: Peter Lang, 2003), pp. 89-90.
[14]See John Hick, *Death and Eternal Life* (San Francisco: Harper & Row, 1976), pp. 55-73.

of Victor Frankl has opened up a fuller understanding of human nature by recognizing the human capacity for transcendence and their quest for ultimate meaning—a point that finds concrete expression in Christian eschatology and in the logic of dichotomy. Trichotomy also alerts us to the ever-present danger of various forms of psychological reductionisms.[15] The logics or "language games" of dichotomy and trichotomy are important for defining two aspects of the Christian view of the self, vis-à-vis certain Eastern understandings where the self is metaphysically indistinguishable from the world (Hinduism) or the view that it has no substantial existence (Buddhism). Against these stands the Christian affirmation of the irreducibility of the person whose participation in God as the ultimate tripersonal being is the basis for the doctrine of eternal life.[16] Any contextual account of Christian theological anthropology must start from this basic given.

The discussions of monism, dichotomy and trichotomy that are usually set in the context of Platonic philosophy in the West take on a different character and direction when placed within a primal religious context in Asia and Africa.

Order in Human Relations

Modern discussions of humanity have generally shifted the focus from the question of the essence of the self to its sociopsychological functions, especially its relational nature, as the basic definition of human identity. The relational understanding is often set in opposition to the Cartesian construal of the person as a self-referencing agent idealized in the concept of the robust, independent and self-made individual. In this respect it has much in common with Asian and other traditional societies where the person is part of a network of interpersonal relationships.

But within the relational definition, the focus in the West, especially in mainline Protestantism and evangelicalism, has increasingly shifted toward an egalitarian conception, as distinguished from a differentiated and hier-

---

[15]Victor E. Frankl, *Man's Search for Meaning: An Introduction to Logotherapy* (New York: Washington Square Press, 1968).

[16]Pannenberg distinguishes between "fellowship" with God, which does not necessarily guarantee the continuation of life beyond death, and "participation," which does (*Systematic Theology*, 2:272).

archical conception. Historically, egalitarian aspirations may have been the outcome of the rapid socioeconomic changes that characterize modern societies,[17] but when an ideal that functions well in industrial relations is projected to the family and various structures of human relations, it runs into difficulties. The household codes of Ephesians and Colossians have proved to be some of the most intractable problems for advocates of egalitarianism. Even they have to admit that these codes "do not fully articulate new roles for women, reaching only a modified or benevolent patriarchy."[18] The problem for egalitarians is that they begin by assuming the truth of egalitarianism and then proceed to read the Bible in the light of this overarching idea.[19] And if a picture emerges in the Bible that does not fit their ideal, it is interpreted as indicative of the failure to follow the (supposedly) scriptural "trajectory" toward egalitarianism. This is how some feminists interpret the Ephesian household codes. For example, its juxtaposition of mutual submission with the submission of wife to husband is interpreted as a failure "to complete its trajectory" toward egalitarianism.[20] Along the same line of argument, the later New Testament writings, such as 1 Peter and 1 and 2 Timothy, in which male headship is clearly taught are interpreted as a "retreat" of the post-Pauline church:

> Increasingly the structure of the early church began to reflect the hierarchical patterns of the middle-class patrons in whose homes the *ecclesia* met. The process began to reverse the pre-Pauline pattern: there *ecclesia* shaped family, but in the latter church traditional family patterns began once again to influence *eccelsia*.[21]

---

[17]For example, see Merry E. Wiesner, "Family, Household, and Community," in *Handbook of European History 1400-1600*, ed. Thomas Brady, Heiko A. Oberman and James D. Tracy (Leiden: Brill, 1994), 1:51-70.

[18]Bonnie Miller-McLemore, "A Feminist Christian Theologian Looks (Askance) at Headship," in *Does Christianity Teach Male Headship?* ed. David Blankenhorn, Don Browning and Mary Stewart Van Leeuwen (Grand Rapids: Eerdmans, 2004), p. 61.

[19]For a critique of this feminist assumption, see Esther Yue L. Ng, *Reconstructing Christian Origins? The Feminist Theology of Elisabeth Schüssler Fiorenza: An Evaluation* (Carlisle, UK: Paternoster, 2002).

[20]Don S. Browning, Bonnie J. Miller-McLemore, Pamela D. Couture, K. Brynolf Lyon and Robert M. Franklin, *From Culture Wars to Common Ground: Religion and the American Family Debate* (Louisville: Westminster John Knox, 1997), p. 147.

[21]Ibid., p. 148.

This is the hermeneutics of setting up a canon within a canon based on what egalitarians think is the ideal pattern of the pre-Pauline church. Feminists would be more honest by abandoning their project of reconstructing from Scripture and accepting Rosemary Radford Reuther's assessment of the Bible for feminist theology: "Feminist theology cannot be done from the existing base of the Christian Bible. The Old and New Testaments have been shaped in their formation, their transmission, and finally, their canonization to sacralize patriarchy."[22]

Against the theological capitulation to modernity, both the official teaching of the Catholic Church and that of Eastern Orthodoxy have consistently maintained the tradition of an ordered relationship based on the order (*taxis*) of the Trinity. Even though these traditions differ in their understandings of the relationship of the Son and the Spirit to the Father (the *Filioque* clause is still a sticking point), the document of the joint commission of the Catholic and Orthodox churches titled "The Mystery of the Church and of the Eucharist in the Light of the Mystery of the Holy Trinity" clearly affirms their common doctrine of the monarchy of the Father. The monarchy of the Father means the Father is "the sole source of the Trinity"; the Father is responsible for the eternal generation of the Son and the procession of the Spirit.[23] Without the doctrine of the monarchy of the Father there is no meaningful concept of the unity of the Trinity. It is a doctrine supported by the liturgical prayer of the church:

> That is why the eucharistic mystery is accomplished in the prayer which joins together the words by which the word made flesh instituted the sacrament and the *epiclesis* in which the church, moved by faith, *entreats the Father*, through the Son, to send the Spirit so that in the unique offering of the incarnate Son, everything may be consummated in unity.[24]

This joint teaching reflects faithfully the overall thrust of the New Tes-

[22]Rosemary Radford Reuther, *Womanguides: Readings Towards a Feminist Theology* (Boston: Beacon, 1985), p. ix.
[23]"The Mystery of the Church and of the Eucharist in the Light of the Mystery of the Holy Trinity," Joint Commission for Theological Dialogue Between the Roman Catholic Church and the Orthodox Church, Vatican, 1982, www.vatican.va/roman_curia/pontifical_councils/chrstuni/ch_orthodox_docs/rc_pc_chrstuni_doc_19820706_munich_en.html.
[24]Ibid. Emphasis mine.

tament where the Father is explicitly identified as God (consider the oft-repeated Pauline greeting "from God our Father and the Lord Jesus Christ") and as the sender of the Son and the Spirit.[25] At this point, the Catholic and Orthodox churches have shown a far more serious commitment to the Bible than some modern Western evangelicals.

Among modern Protestant theologians Karl Barth stands out as a rare exception in his defense of this traditional understanding. Barth has cogently argued that although man and woman are equal, "there is no simple equality." They are also as different as A and B. "They stand in a sequence" that cannot be "reversed." They stand in an order that implies super- and subordination.[26] The exploitation that comes from this divine order represents an abuse of the order; it is not due to the nature of the order itself. The abuse can come from both man and woman when each exploits his or her respective "rights" and fails to accept personal obligations.[27] Barth examines the biblical evidence and shows that the man-woman sequence is analogous to the order in the Trinity between the Father and the Son. It is precisely in her subordinate position that woman stands as a perfect type of the church.[28] One has good reason, therefore, to question whether egalitarianism is the scriptural trajectory in light of the overwhelming testimony of the Christian tradition, both Catholic and Orthodox, of the hierarchical nature of trinitarian and human relations.

THE FAMILY ORDER

The Asian church too, except where mainline Protestant influence has been particularly strong, has generally maintained this traditional understanding. In Asia the relational nature of humanity finds its most basic expression in the family. It explains why the primary locus of religion in Asia is found in the home. This is true of most Asian religions.[29] Concern

---

[25]For a fuller account, see my discussion in *Pentecostal Ecclesiology: An Essay on the Development of Doctrine* (Blandford Forum, Dorset, UK: Deo, 2011), pp. 106-15.
[26]*Church Dogmatics* 3.4, p. 169.
[27]Ibid., pp. 170-71.
[28]Ibid., pp. 174-76.
[29]See chapter six.

for the solidarity and perpetuation of the family is the main reason why ancient societies made various arrangements, such as polygamy-polygyny and the levirate law (Deut 25:5-10), to ensure the continuation of the family line. Polygyny exemplifies the traditional concern of putting the larger social concern before personal gain. Far from representing the ultimate in personal self-fulfillment for the man, it is in some instances— such as levirate marriage—an act of self-sacrifice. The refusal to consummate such a relationship resulted in severe divine judgment (Gen 38:6-10). The story of Ruth highlights the exemplary character of Boaz in redeeming the ancestral land and marrying Ruth. His action was portrayed as a noble and selfless act, compared with that of a nearer kinsman who refused to marry her for fear of jeopardizing his own inheritance.[30] Given the rationale and altruistic motivation behind the ancient practice of polygyny, it is understandable that from time to time the idea of its reintroduction has been mooted as an answer to the alarming decline in birth rate in modern society.[31]

Polygamy is only one of many ways of ensuring the perpetuation of the family; what is far more important is how family solidarity is maintained. Here, the major East Asian religious traditions have been quite consistent. They generally see relationship in reciprocal and hierarchical terms—much the way the larger Christian tradition perceives it. For instance, the Confucian concept of the "five relationships" are remarkably similar to the New Testament household codes with regard to their respective mutual obligations and orders.

1. Kindess of the father is reciprocated with filial piety of the son.

2. Favors of the ruler are reciprocated with loyalty of the subjects.

3. Dutiful behavior of the husband is reciprocated with obedience of the wife.

---

[30]The marriage between Boaz and Ruth was strictly speaking not a levirate marriage since Boaz was not the brother-in-law.

[31]For example, see Philip L. Kilbride, *Plural Marriage for Our Times: A Reinvented Option?* (Westport, CN: Bergin and Garvey, 1994); Lee Kuan Yew, "Keeping Our Bearings in Midst of Rapid Changes," *The Straits Times*, December 15, 1986, p. 18. Lee, the former prime minister of Singapore, even questioned the wisdom of monogamy!

4. Graciousness of the oldest son is reciprocated with respect of the younger siblings.

5. Between friends, a gift from one is reciprocated with a gift from the other.[32]

The basic difference between the Confucian and Pauline concepts of relationship is that the latter is governed by their basic unity in Christ. But equality in Christ does not abrogate the distinction in roles and functions whether in the church or in the family.

The Taoist *yin-yang* or female-male understanding of human relationship is another variation on the same theme. The relationship could be described as different yet complementary, ordered but mutually dependent and mutually enriching. Again, its similarity to the household codes has not been lost on Asian Christians and various attempts have been made to develop a more nuanced Christian view of the male-female relationship based on this Taoist understanding. We have seen previously how the Korean theologian Lee Young Jung has adapted the doctrine of the Tao, "the great ultimate," to the male-female relationship and warned against committing the "ontological sin" of abrogating their distinction (chapter 2).

A slightly different approach has been advocated by the Asian-American feminist Young Lee Hertig. Like Lee, Hertig also rejects certain forms of Western feminism substituting male domination for female domination as reductionistic. She proposes the Taoist way of *yin-yang* harmony, which recognizes the need for complementarity. But Hertig qualifies the complementarity in two ways. First, she tries to minimize the male-female difference by introducing the Jungian idea that there is a female element in the male and vice versa. One wonders, however, if Hertig has not abrogated the very *yin-yang* distinction that is necessary to her project, even though she tries to maintain a qualified distinction by saying that "*yin* in male and *yin* in female are not the same."[33] Second, by offering a "*Yinist* paradigm" in which *yin* comes to the foreground and *yang* recedes to the

---

[32] "*Wu lun* (Five Human Relations)," *RoutledgeCurzon Encyclopedia of Confucianism*, ed. Yao Xinhong (London: RoutledgeCurzon, 2003), 2:664.

[33] Young Lee Hertig, "The Asian-American Alternative to Feminism: A Yinist Paradigm," *Missiology* 26, no. 1 (1998): 19.

background,[34] one wonders if she is still being faithful to the Taoist principle of harmony. For example, when Hertig says, "The Asian American often portrays a *Yinist* Jesus—vulnerable, humble, merciful, loving, sacrificial and steadfast, in contrast to a *Yangist* God, ruler, king, mighty and omnipotent,"[35] isn't this precisely setting forth a one-sided portrait of Jesus? A more faithful Taoist approach would be to recognize both the *yinist* and *yangist* sides of Jesus: He is *yinist* toward the Samaritan woman and *yangist* toward the Pharisees. But by preferring one to the other, Hertig is simply offsetting one form of alleged imbalance with another.

This off-balance is apparent when Hertig, in defence of her preference for a *yinist* God, starts to pit Pelagius against Augustine in favour of Pelagius: "My preference for Pelagius over Augustine is obvious because I am *Yinist*."[36] Hertig fails to realize that the whole controversy between Augustine and Pelagius was part of the Latin tradition where divine sovereignty versus freewill became a zero-sum game. That the issue is still being discussed in this manner shows that the Western church has not quite transcended the old problematic.[37] There is no real harmony here because the two positions mutually exclude and threaten each other. One cannot be both Augustinian and Pelagian at the same time; the conflictual relation has to be resolved by prioritizing one or the other: it's either *yang* or *yin* that must have the upper hand.

Closer to the spirit of Taoist harmony and against this rationalistic and conflictual Latin paradigm stands the Eastern Orthodox concept of synergy.[38] The doctrine of synergy, according to Vladimir Lossky, is "faithful to the apophatic spirit of the Eastern tradition" and "expresses the mystery of the coincidence of grace and human freedom in good works, without recourse to positive and rational terms."[39] It is not a *via media* between

---

[34]Young Lee Hertig, "Why Asian American Evangelical Theologies?" *Journal Of Asian And Asian American Theology* 7 (2006): 12.

[35]Ibid., p. 13.

[36]Ibid., p. 11.

[37]See David Basinger and Randall Basinger, eds., *Predestination and Freewill: Four Views of Divine Sovereignty and Human Freedom* (Downers Grove, IL: InterVarsity Press, 1986).

[38]For an account of the nature of Orthodox synergy, see Vladimir Lossky, *The Mystical Theology of the Eastern Church* (London: James Clarke, 1957), pp. 196-99.

[39]Ibid., p. 198.

the Augustinian and Pelagian polarities but a different paradigm that transcends both. Lossky cites the example of John Cassian, whose position on the debate between Augustine and Pelagius was interpreted in the West as semi-Pelagianism. It shows the failure in the West to take the Eastern doctrine on its own terms.[40] Eastern synergy affirms simultaneously God's sovereign action and human action. It accepts fully the reality of divine and human freedoms but refuses to rationalize about their relationship. Coupled with the monarchy of the Father as seen in the larger Christian tradition and Barth, we could, with Barth, speak of "superordination" and "subordination" as well as complementarity of *yang* and *yin* without implying domination of one by the other. Contra Hertig, we do not have to choose between a *yangist* or a *yinist* God.

The Western debate between Augustine and Pelagius, however, is not without its significance in another Chinese context. They have their counterparts in the history of Confucianism. Julia Ching notes that between the great Confucian thinkers Mencius (c. 372–289 B.C.) and Xunzi (c. 312–238 B.C.) the former sees human nature as essentially good but corrupted by its environment while the latter sees human nature as inherently wicked. By the time of the neo-Confucianists (from the eleventh century A.D.) Mencius's view seemed to have prevailed. Ching compares the two Confucian thinkers to Gregory of Nyssa and Augustine respectively.[41] But there is a limit to the comparison, as Ching herself admits. Christianity, whether in its Augustinian or Orthodox form, is ultimately a religion of grace, whereas Confucianism, as a humanistic philosophy, albeit open to transcendence, tends to emphasize human striving.[42] In this respect the Confucian emphasis on human perfectibility might be closer to Pelagianism. This seems to be the case, at least at the popular level. Sin (*jui*) is seen more as an act than a state. It connotes serious crimes rather than petty wrongdoings.[43] Thus, when a Christian evangelist tells devotees of "Chinese religion" that they need a Savior because

---

[40]Ibid.

[41]Julia Ching, *Chinese Religions* (Maryknoll, NY: Orbis, 1993), pp. 75-77.

[42]Ibid., p. 8.

[43]See also Julia Ching and Hans Küng, *Christianity and Chinese Religions* (London: SCM Press, 1989), p. 73.

they are "sinners," the hearers are likely to feel deeply offended. Their usual response is likely to be, "I haven't killed or burned down anyone's home; how dare you call me a sinner?" But there is another aspect of Confucianism that comes closer to the biblical conception of sin: sin is also failure to uphold proprieties (*li*) in personal relations, not just transgression of an objective law. In this respect it has much in common with cultures marked by concepts of honor and shame (see below).

SIN

The nature of humanity and sin needs to be defined against two forms of reductionism: the sociopolitical reductionism found predominantly in Asian and Latin American liberationist theologies and the individualistic reductionism of modernity found predominantly in the West.

In much of so-called ecumenical discussion on humanity and sin, human life tends to be defined largely by the sociopolitical context of conflict between the poor and rich, oppressor and oppressed, and so on. The goal of life is freedom and justice, which is again sociologically defined. Sin is equated with oppression, unjust distribution of wealth and so on. This way of understanding has hardly changed over the years, as can be seen in the Ecumenical Association of Third World Theologians,[44] although the hermeneutical basis may have shifted from Marxist analysis to postcolonial interpretation, from the class struggle between capitalists and the proletariat to the unequal relationship between colonizer and colonized.[45] The focus has tended to shift from sin to the "sinned-against."[46] This is understandable when sin is understood as the unequal relationship between oppressor and oppressed or conqueror and vanquished. The sinner is always the oppressor; the oppressed is the "sinned-against." But victims are sinners too in their own ways, even if we think

---

[44]See chapter five for further discussion of this point.

[45]Rasiah S. Sugirtharajah, *Postcolonial Reconfigurations: An Alternative Way of Reading the Bible and Doing Theology* (St. Louis: Chalice, 2003); *Postcolonial Criticism And Biblical Interpretation* (Oxford, UK: Oxford University Press, 2002).

[46]Raymond Fung, "Compassion for the Sinned Against," *Theology Today* 37, no. 2 (July 1, 1980): 162-69; Andrew Sung Park and Susan L. Nelson, eds., *The Other Side of Sin: Woundedness from the Perspective of the Sinned-Against* (Albany: State University of New York Press, 2001).

that the greater sinners are still the oppressors. And while the ecumenical viewpoint may represent an important perspective, it is by no
means the only one. Here again we see how grassroots Christianity transcends these polarities. For example, the way Pentecostals empower
people to take charge of their own lives shows that the poor are not
always passive victims of an oppressive system. Even though many have
come from the lower strata of society, they refuse to see themselves
simply as victims, the sinned-against, but as active agents renewed by
the Spirit. This gives them a sense of being in charge and of the hope of
change. When drunkards and womanizers are converted, the result is a
more stable family and consequently upward social mobility.[47] When
Dalits experience conversion in India they begin to realize that change
is possible, and with this realization, they experience freedom from the
inevitable law of karma.[48]

The example of the Pentecostals shows that important though sociopolitical analysis may be, it becomes reductionistic when not comple-
mented by the cultural-religious. The latter is probably even more important for understanding the problem of sin since it runs more deeply
in the Asian consciousness. In fact, it is in addressing the problems at the
cultural-religious level that the sociopolitical is also addressed. This is
apparent in cultures shaped by concepts of shame and honor.

HUMANITY AND SIN IN AN HONOR-AND-SHAME CULTURE

In many Asian societies to be called "shameless" is the worst possible
insult. A shameless person is one without any sense of honor, whereas to
be able to feel shame implies that one is acutely aware of the loss or di-
minishment of honor. Bruce Malina defines honor as "basically a claim
to worth that is socially acknowledged." In the modern world honor is
defined economically. A person's status is often measured by possessions,
success and so on whereas in the ancient world it was defined by kinship.
It is "the value of a person in his or her own eyes . . . plus that person's

---

[47]Elizabeth E. Brusco, *The Reformation of Machismo: Evangelical Conversion and Gender in Colombia* (Austin: University of Texas Press, 1995).
[48]Vishal Mangalwadi, *Truth and Social Reform* (London: Spire, 1989).

value in the eyes of his or her social group. Honor is a claim to worth along with the social acknowledgement of worth."[49]

In an honor-and-shame culture sin takes on two major characteristics. First, sin is a personal-relational problem. Sin is offending the honor of another person or the community. A person who sins brings shame to those with whom he or she is closely identified, especially his or her family and the community to which the family belongs. This concept of sin reminds us of Anselm's satisfaction theory of the atonement. Sin, according to Anselm, is the failure of humans to render to God the honor that is due him. Further, according to Anselm, it is not sufficient that the offence be removed; some form of "compensation for the anguish incurred" is necessary. "So then, everyone who sins ought to pay back the honor of which he has robbed God; and this is the satisfaction which every sinner owes to God."[50] Second, sin is pollution that can be removed only through purification. Thus purification rituals are important. They are not so much for achieving personal purity as for maintaining public or social order: They show the person's conformity to what is culturally appropriate, which leads to restoration of honor.[51]

Recent biblical studies drawing from cultural-anthropological studies of the ancient world have underscored the importance of the shame-honor motif in the New Testament. In fact there is more said in the Bible about shame and honor than about guilt and innocence. Guilt is mentioned 145 times in the Old Testament and ten times in the New, while shame occurs three hundred times in the Old Testament and forty-five times in the New Testament.[52] Biblical scholars have shown that by applying the honor-shame motif as an interpretive template, much of the New Testament makes better sense.

It is always tempting for modern readers to psychologize biblical char-

---

[49]Bruce Malina, *The New Testament World: Insights form Cultural Anthropology,* 3rd rev. ed. (Louisville: Westminster John Knox, 2001), pp. 29-30.

[50]Anselm, *Cur deus homo?* 1.11.

[51]Jayson Georges, "From Shame to Honor: A Theological Reading of Romans for Honor-Shame Contexts," *Missiology* 38, no. 3 (July 1, 2010): 295-307.

[52]Timothy C. Tennent, *Theology in the Context of World Christianity* (Grand Rapids: Zondervan, 2007), p. 92.

acters, often imposing on them modern notions of the self or motivations and strategies typical of the modern world. Appreciation of the ancient psychology of honor and shame offers more authentic cultural and historical reading of those social dynamics.[53]

The results of some of these studies are worth reflecting on in some detail as they have deep implications for understanding the doctrine of humanity and sin in Asian contexts. Western missionaries often complain that in an honor-and-shame-based culture there is no sense of absolute right or wrong, that sin is relative to communal norms, and so on. But this is using one culture-specific theory of ethics to judge another. If in fact much of the New Testament can be better explained against the backdrop of an honor-shame culture of the first-century Mediterranean world, a society with a similar backdrop may be better placed to understand the New Testament and to live out its Christian values in terms of the thought patterns of the New Testament world. The issue is not the honor-shame culture itself but what constitutes honor and shame in the New Testament. It is clear that while the New Testament presupposes such a background it also redefines the nature of honor and shame in terms of one's relation to God and his community, the church.

Robert Jewett's use of the honor-shame template in Romans has yielded some interesting results. He shows, for example, that the term "righteousness," which is often understood forensically in Romans, is "virtually synonymous" with honor and glory. Thus "being justified" is better understood as "to be set right." It is less about a forensic act of acquittal as a divine act in which the sinner's shame is removed and a new status of honor is bestowed in Christ. Salvation, then, has to do with being given a new status of honor in Christ.[54] Christianity redefines the nature of honor by locating it in the God who dispenses it. Commenting on Paul's affirmation "I am not ashamed of the gospel of Christ," he says,

---

[53]Jerome H. Neyrey, "Despising the Shame of the Cross: Honor and Shame in the Johannine Passion Narrative," *Semeia* 68 (January 1, 1994): 113-37, esp. p. 133.
[54]Robert Jewett, "Honor and Shame in the Argument of Romans," in *Putting Body and Soul Together: Essays in Honor of Robin Scroggs*, ed. A. Brown, G. F. Snyder and V. Wiles (Valley Forge, PA: Trinity Press International, 1997), pp. 270-72 *passim*.

If what the world considers dishonorable has power, it will prevail and achieve a new form of honor for those who have not earned it, an honor consistent with divine righteousness. All who place their faith in this gospel will be set right, that is be placed in the right relation to the most significant arena in which honor is dispensed: divine judgment. Thus the triumph of divine righteousness through the gospel of Christ crucified and resurrected is achieved by transforming the system in which shame and honor are dispensed.[55]

If righteousness is the restoration of honor, sin is the loss of honor. Sinners have fallen short of the glory of God (Rom 3:23). To fall short of the glory of God is to fall short of "the ultimate standard of honor they are intended to bear." Without honor, sinners can only hang their heads in shame. The picture of Adam in the Garden may have been in Paul's thought. Adam, who was clothed with the divine glory before he sinned, lost the glory when he disobeyed and became ashamed and sought to cover himself. In an honor-shame society, such a concept makes a lot of sense and actually comes closer to the way much of the New Testament is to be understood. In such a culture it makes more sense to see sin as bringing shame to God's name and to his family, the church, than as breaking a set of impersonal rules, even if they are utterly compelling rules. Needless to say, the ramifications of such a view are far-reaching. It redefines the nature of Christian life as essentially communal: sinning against God and against community are virtually indistinguishable.

In the New Testament honor and shame have an absolute character because they are defined in relation to God, the supremely honorable one who bestows his honor on those who give up their shameful ways. Further, although honor and shame are socially acknowledged values, that does not make them merely relative, because they ultimately refer back to God. In an honor-shame culture the values are communal, but they are relative only if they are defined solely by the community itself. For Christians, the communally defined values are also values bestowed by God on the community, namely, God's righteousness or "glory" bestowed on the community in Christ. This is how we are to understand the various exhorta-

---

[55]Ibid., p. 265.

tions or rules in the Pauline letters, including the household codes. Peter Gosnell in his study of Ephesians shows that the honor-shame motif runs through every section of Ephesians and serves as a point of unity between the first and second half of the letter. In the first half Paul shows that the God who is supremely honorable confers a reputation on Christians at conversion that raises their status and honor. The exhortations in the second half, then, are challenges to maintain their honor as Christians: "Honor from God as benefactor is established as the foundation for the obligation of performing the prescribed deeds"; "the sense of honor developed in the first half of the letter establishes the basis for the honor lifestyle challenges that appear in the second."[56]

How might our understanding of the Scripture in light of the social environment of honor and shame impact the theology we are trying to develop in Asia? First, Asian Christians would discover that their world is not too far removed from the world of the Bible; on the contrary, it has deep affinities with the biblical world. At the same time they would also discover that the biblical concepts challenge their own cultural concepts. The Bible challenges by relocating honor and shame in a new network of relationships. God is now our heavenly Father who possesses supreme honor; the ecclesial community into which Christians are incorporated is the new family. Every Christian is now a brother or sister. Social communities like the family, clan or tribe are not abrogated but relativized. The previous definitions of honor and shame are still important, but they are not everything. In fact, only as they are seen in relation to the eschatological community that Jesus himself established can these social institutions be truly redeemed.

Second, Asian Christians are better positioned to appreciate the corporate and relational nature of life, both as sinners and as Christians. Much of Christianity today has been shaped by one dominant culture that celebrates "the rugged individual." From this perspective, a sinner is one who is guilty because he or she has broken the law of God, while a Christian is one who possesses certain desirable moral virtues like

---

[56]Peter Gosnell, "Honor and Shame Rhetoric as a Unifying Motif in Ephesians," *Bulletin for Biblical Research* 16, no. 1 (2006): 113-14.

honesty and courage to stand, if need be, against what "the rest of them" might think. It follows that spirituality is largely a matter of individual formation. The conscience of the individual becomes the primary arbiter of right and wrong. Such rugged individualism has its downside: It is in danger of falling into legalism, which is often the source of church splits to which Protestants are particularly prone. But a theology deriving from a culture that understands the logic of honor and shame provides a necessary corrective, as Tennent has noted:

> The great contribution from shame-based cultures seems to be the reminder that the legacy of sin is far more than the objective guilt we incur because of the transgression of specific commands. We have dishonored the Triune God, brought shame on ourselves, and caused a breach in the divine-human relationship. As we become aware of God's righteousness and our sinfulness, it should be experienced not only as an internal realization of guilt, but also as an increased awareness that we collectively stand ashamed before God. In other words, God's righteousness not only declares us forensically guilty, it also places us as relationally distant and shamed before the presence of the Triune God. It is not just his Word that condemns us; it is his Triune person who shames us.[57]

Both sin and righteousness have an irreducibly corporate dimension. Just as "being a sinner means that we are collectively embedded as members of a race who together stand ashamed before God because we have corporately robbed God of his honor,"[58] similarly, salvation is more than just my personal acquittal before the righteous God. We are justified "in Christ" corporately: Just as "in Adam" all die, "in Christ" all shall be made alive (1 Cor 15:22).

Closely related to this is that since honor and shame are "socially acknowledged" values, an individual cannot escape shared responsibility. The sin of one person shames the entire community, but the honor one receives uplifts the whole community. Failure to appreciate this strong sense of corporate responsibility has led to ineffective evangelical preaching on individual salvation. This is because an individual who breaks with one's culture

---

[57]Tennent, *Theology*, p. 97.
[58]Ibid., p. 96.

by becoming a Christian brings shame and dishonor to the entire community. Christian mission experiences this most acutely in Muslim societies,[59] but it occurs in varying intensities where relationships are ordered around a communally defined shame and honor.[60]

Third, Christians in an honor-shame culture may be better placed to appreciate the biblical meaning of worship. Biblically, to worship is to give God the glory and honor due him, to acknowledge God for who he is (Ps 96:8). This is how worship is understood in the doxology in Ephesians 1. As Gosnell has observed,

> The letter begins by honoring God. The opening *berakah* establishes God as praiseworthy and extols his activities of blessing "in Christ" the "saints . . . and faithful in Christ Jesus" "with every spiritual blessing in the heavenly places" (1:3). The readers and writer together are direct beneficiaries of God's generosity. They are to join in their recognition of God as one most worthy of praise, celebrating his high reputation.[61]

Much has been said in recent years about the "dumbing down" of worship and the conspicuous absence of a sense of reverence and awe in so-called contemporary worship.[62] But the underlying problem is a culture of consumerism and self-fulfillment. The church is expected to be a service provider to meet the needs of its consumer members. In this consumerist context, people are not likely to encounter anything like the *fascinans et tremendum* that humans experience in the presence of the holy God.[63] Traditional words such as "holy," "praise," "honor" and "majesty" are still freely bandied about, but for the modern Christian, worship is largely a personal experience in a celebratory and friendly atmosphere. There will be a lot of acclamations about God's goodness, love and intimacy but little that suggests the awesome presence that elicits reverence and awe, fear and trembling (Heb 12:28-29; Ps 96:8-9)

---

[59]Bahar Cavary, "Miss Elsa and the Veil: Shame, Honor, and Identity Negotiations," *Journal of Feminist Studies in Religion* 25, no. 2 (2009): 47-66.
[60]Tennent, *Theology*, p. 98.
[61]Gosnell, "Honor and Shame Rhetoric," p. 115.
[62]For example, see Marva J. Dawn, *Reaching Out Without Dumbing Down: A Theology of Worship for the Turn-of-the-Century Culture* (Grand Rapids: Eerdmans, 1995).
[63]See Rudolf Otto, *The Idea of the Holy* (Middlesex, UK: Penguin, 1959).

leading to bowing or prostration (Ezek 1:28; Rev 1:17). The inability to understand these qualities has resulted in considerable shrinking of modern worship.[64] The rich meaning of honoring someone of a higher status than ourselves that is available to an honor-based society is no longer available to a culture where individual egalitarianism is the norm, so that even God is dragged down to the human level!

Fourth, in an honor-shame culture, the loss and restoration of honor are not private matters but public events. A person is truly shamed when the fault is made public. Honor is not honor unless it is publicly bestowed. Thus Christ by his death and resurrection made "a public spectacle" of the devil's defeat (Col 2:15 NIV). His resurrection is a public declaration by God before the world of the restoration of his honor (see also Rom 1:4).[65] Perhaps this is why in such societies the public nature of theology is better appreciated. The Kantian dichotomy of fact and value—one having to do with truth, the other with opinion or preference—would be quite incomprehensible to people in an honor-shame culture. Religious truth is not what each individual understands it to be, nor is it a matter of private "opinion"; all truth, including religious truth, is public truth.

CONCLUSION

We have seen that certain traditional doctrines concerning humanity and sin need to be recast within the Asian context. Particularly, the question of man's constituent nature, which used to be discussed within the context of Platonic dualism, needs to be reexamined against the pervasive belief in the existence of the spirit world, which finds expression in such practices as veneration of the dead, divination, necromancy and so on. Perhaps the "holistic dualism" of John Cooper comes closest to meeting the concerns of people in primal religious societies that "Hebraic holism" cannot adequately address. On the question of human relations, the modern tendency to read democratic egalitarianism into all aspects of human relations needs to be seriously questioned in the light of the larger

---

[64]See Ronald P. Byars, *The Future of Protestant Worship: Beyond the Worship Wars* (Louisville: Westminster John Knox, 2002).
[65]Jewett, "Honor and Shame," p. 271; Tennent, *Theology*, pp. 94-95.

Catholic and Orthodox traditions based on an ordered Trinity and the Asian concept of an ordered universe. The conception of sin as shame and dishonor develops from a context that has deep affinities with the New Testament, where sin is more an infinite affront against God's honor than a breach of a legal code, more relational and communal than private and juridical. As Tennent observes, "Shame and honor are public values and are external, whereas guilt and innocence are more naturally thought of in private terms and tend to be interiorized."[66] The biblical concept of shame and honor shows that the Christian life is really about community and relationships and how they must be ordered, and as such it addresses wider concerns beyond the Asian context.

---

[66]Tennent, *Theology*, p. 94.

4

CHRIST AND SALVATION

THE ONTOLOGICAL QUESTION concerning Christ's divine and human natures and their relationship in one person that has occupied christological discussions in the past is probably not the first question the Asian church asks. Rather, the question of who Christ is usually surfaces in relation to what he does. The ontological status of Christ is presupposed, but the question in the foreground is his work as Savior. For most people, the humanity of Christ is not an issue. Hindus revere him as a great moral teacher, Muslims as a great prophet. The issue of his divinity is a little more complex. Hindus are quite prepared to accept him as a god among many other gods, while Muslims, like Jews, reject the Christian's claim as it would undermine their strict monotheism.

The issue of the divinity of Christ is resolved in different ways. Sometimes the truth of who Jesus is comes from answered prayer, such as during a personal crisis. Many Christians in Asia testify that what convinced them of the truth of the gospel was an experience of divine healing or seeing a relative healed.[1] At other times the issue is resolved in a personal encounter with Christ resulting in a radical change of worldview. Sadhu Sundar Singh's encounter with the risen Christ, he tells us, brought about a new awareness that completely overturned his Hindu pantheistic worldview. The meeting with Jesus Christ convinces him of the ontological distinction between God and humanity. God is not within us but

---

[1]For example, see Tony Lambert, *China's Christian Millions: The Costly Revival* (London: Monarch, 1999), pp. 109-20.

comes from "outside" to confront us. In his own words: "If we want to rejoice in God we must be different from Him; the tongue could taste no sweetness if there were no difference between it and that which it tastes."[2] Similarly, in story after story of Muslim conversion, we notice a common pattern: a visionary encounter with Christ decisively resolves the question of his divinity.[3] One is reminded of St. Paul's Damascus Road encounter, which decisively reshapes his understanding of the nature of God and of Christianity.

Thus it is more appropriate to discuss Christology not as an abstract question of ontology but within the rubric of salvation and mission. This is not to suggest that Christology in Asia is merely functional; rather, it is out of the experience of the risen Christ that the ontological question is settled. This is clearly a Christology "from below."[4]

CHRISTOLOGICAL QUESTIONS: TWO STARTING POINTS

Contemporary discussions of Christology "from above" and "from below" are essentially methodological questions stemming from the Chalce-donian doctrine of the two natures of Christ. A Christology from below starts with the humanity of Christ and proceeds to ask how this man Jesus is also understood as divine; the Christology from above starts from the presupposition of Christ's divinity, which entails a doctrine of his preexistence, and proceeds to understand how the second person of the Trinity becomes man. In contrast, the fundamental question in Asia is how Christ is related to a religiously plural context. Basically, there are two approaches to Christology in Asia. One is to begin with the givens in the Christian tradition and then proceed to answer the questions the

---

[2]Cited by Robin Boyd, *An Introduction to Indian Christian Theology* (Bangalore: Christian Literature Society, 1969), p. 95.

[3]For example, see Gulsham Esther, *The Torn Veil* (Fort Washington, PA: CLC, 2010), pp. 74-76; Jean-Marie Gaudeul, *Called from Islam to Christ: Why Muslims Become Christians* (London: Monarch, 1999), pp. 287-88; R. W. F. Wootton, ed., *Jesus More Than a Prophet: Fifteen Muslims Tell How They Found Forgiveness, Release and New Life* (Leicester, UK: Inter-Varsity Press, 1982), pp. 24-25. Anecdotal evidence from those working in closed Muslim contexts show many more cases of visionary encounters with Christ than the selective anthologies such as those of Gaudeul and Wootton might suggest.

[4]See also Timothy C. Tennent, *Theology in the Context of World Christianity* (Grand Rapids: Zondervan, 2007), p. 113.

Asian context poses. The big question from this approach would be: How is Jesus as the final revelation of God for the salvation of the world to be understood in the midst of the great Asian religions with their various ways of salvation? This is the approach adopted by traditional Christianity, including the Catholic Church. Traditional Christianity has always insisted that if Jesus is the only Savior of the world, then the essential mission of the church is to make that truth known. The proclamation of the gospel and, through it, the personal encounter with Jesus Christ is of utmost importance and constitutes the bare minimum of the gospel. But how is this to be done in a context where concepts of God, the world, salvation and so on are significantly different?

The other approach is to begin with the questions posed by the Asian context and then proceed to ask how the Christian faith can adapt to the distinctive questions it poses. For many, the big question in the Asian context is the great Asian religions: In a world dominated by these great religions, how is Christianity as a minority faith to express itself authentically? The other issue is poverty, which is something Asians share with much of the underdeveloped world, although in recent years great strides have been made in terms of economic development in some Asian nations, including the two largest, China and India.

At first glance, the two approaches appear to be only a matter of difference in starting point. The first begins with text-tradition while the other begins with context-culture. But in point of fact, these approaches entail divergent tendencies that become apparent only as their ramifications are further developed. When the starting point is the givenness of the "text" or the Christian tradition, the tendency is to use text-tradition as the interpretive lens with which to view context-culture. This will result in giving Scripture and tradition a more critical role in evaluating culture. It does not exclude dialogue with culture, but dialogue is a means of fulfilling "the church's mission of bringing salvation to all peoples in Asia."[5] But when the starting point is context, the tendency is to give culture a more determinative role in reshaping tradition. Dialogue be-

---

[5]Peter C. Phan, ed. *The Asian Synod: Texts and Commentaries* (Maryknoll, NY: Orbis, 2002), chap. 3.

comes the main mode of the church's relation to culture. There is reti-
cence in the second approach to engage in direct proclamation of the
gospel for fear that it will be perceived as proselytization and that it will
treat the "other" as an object of conversion.[6]

These divergent tendencies can be seen in post-Vatican II theology in
Asia. In 1998 John Paul II called a synod of bishops in Asia as part of the
preparation for the "Great Jubilee" of 2000. The Asian Synod was one of
five Special Synods of Bishops: Africa (1994), America (1997), Asia (1998),
Oceania (1998) and Europe (1999). The Lineamenta (Outline) for discussion proposed by the Roman Curia focused on what might be considered a traditional understanding of Christ, salvation and the church.
It presupposed the uniqueness of Christ as Savior of the world, the need
for the proclamation of the gospel and the centrality of the church in
God's mission. But some of the Asian bishops reacted with deep unease.[7]
They would have preferred to start with dialogue rather than proclamation.[8] They perceived the Lineamenta as overtly "Western" and "overly
self-complacent and introverted."[9] No doubt cultural differences may
have been a factor in some of the Asian bishops' reaction, but looking at
the issue as a non-Catholic, the problem between the Asian bishops and
Rome shows as much a cultural as a theological divide. While Rome is
concerned to stress the uniqueness of Christ as Savior, some of the Asian
bishops would prefer Christ as "symbol" of salvation. Rome's theology
was more Barthian, stressing the particularity of Christ, while some of
the Asian bishops' more Tillichian, stressing the christic principle.[10]

ELITIST CHRISTOLOGIES

The tension seen in the relation between the Asian bishops and Rome

---

[6]See Jonathan Y. Tan's evaluation of the Indonesian and Japanese bishops' responses to the
Lineamenta: "The Responses of the Indonesian and Japanese Bishops to the Lineamenta," in
Asian Synod, pp. 59-72.
[7]Not all are as radical as the bishops from India and Japan. The response from the bishops of
Malaysia, Singapore and Brunei was very much a straightforward response to the Lineamenta
questions and probably more in line with Rome's expectation.
[8]Especially the Indian bishops. See Phan, Asian Synod, p. 22.
[9]The Japanese bishops were particularly critical. Ibid., pp. 27, 31.
[10]See above pages 36-40.

shows what can happen when the question of contextualization or inculturation is approached from an elitist perspective. This is evident not only in the Catholic Church but in mainline Protestantism as well. An elitist approach tends to frame the questions of contextualization in terms of institutional relations and the "big questions" posed by the intelligentsia. Take, for example, the matter of relation with the West (or in the Catholic case, with Rome). The current fashion is to explain the relationship in terms of postcolonial hermeneutics, a relation of unequal power arrangement in which the more powerful West, if given the chance, will impose its will and ways upon a weaker East, politically, culturally and religiously: a new colonialism.[11]

In point of fact, the situation is much more complex. With the shift in the "center of gravity" of Christianity to the non-Western world, the influence is hardly one-way. In a globalized world where ideas and modes of operation are often selectively taken from one culture and adapted in another, it is not surprising to find religions displaying the same phenomenon. The process is dialectical and multilateral, producing new configurations or complex "hybridity." This is especially the case with Pentecostalism, a global phenomenon that does not respect social and cultural boundaries.[12] As the historian Mark Noll has argued, features of American Christianity found in other parts of the world are not so much due to the direct influence of popular American culture but the result of critical assimilation of aspects of American culture (such as its voluntarism) that are found to be workable in other parts of the world.[13]

Again, we see this in global Pentecostalism, particularly in the form of mass movements and megachurches. They may resemble phenomena in America and may have had their original inspiration from the West, but in Asia they are also highly indigenized, using local resources such as indigenous styles of music and appealing to the deep primal religious

---

[11]For example, see Rasiah Sugirtharajah, ed., *Voices from the Margins: Interpreting the Bible in the Third World,* 3rd ed. (Maryknoll, NY: Orbis, 2006).
[12]Michael Wilkinson, "Religion and Global Flows," in *Globalization, Religion and Culture,* ed. Peter Beyer and Lori Beaman (Leiden: Brill Academic, 2007), pp. 385-88.
[13]Mark Noll, *The New Shape of World Christianity: How American Experience Reflects Global Faith* (Downers Grove, IL: InterVarsity Press, 2009).

consciousness of local people.[14] Even in a highly globalized city like Singapore where we see many popular Western forms of Christianity replicated, we also see examples of hybridization and transfiguration as Christianity interacts with the local cultures.[15] Creative indigenization of Christianity has been going on in much of Asia at the popular level with or without the input of Western or Asian theologians and missionaries. This is the case with many indigenous churches in China, such as the True Jesus Church.[16] In the missionary expansion of the church into new locales, there is both continuity with older traditions and discontinuity as it faces a set of new questions and challenges. In short, the grassroots approach to the question of relationship between Asian and Western churches shows that their relationships are more multilateral than unilateral.

What is perhaps still apparent in this multiplex situation is the same deep theological divide that we noted in chapter 1. The issues in Christology are no exception. For example, is Christ's uniqueness as Savior to be understood in terms of the particular history of the person of Jesus Christ or in terms of certain salvific principles found in all religions that Jesus exemplifies? If the former, then the primary responsibility and mode of the church's communication is the proclamation of the gospel in all its particularity: the events of the life, death and resurrection of Jesus Christ. But if the latter, then the church's basic responsibility must be expressed through dialogue, inculturation and the common pursuit of sociopolitical liberation.[17] In the West this issue used to be discussed in terms of three main theories of religion: exclusivism, inclusivism and

---

[14]For example, see Charles E. Farhadian, "A Missiological Reflection on Present-Day Christian Movements in Southeast Asia," in *Christian Movements in Southeast Asia: A Theological Exploration*, ed. Michael N. C. Poon (Singapore: Genesis Books, Trinity Theological College, 2010), pp. 101-20.

[15]See above p. 32-33.

[16]Daniel H. Bays, "Independent Protestant Churches in China, 1900-1937: A Pentecostal Case Study," in *Indigenous Responses to Western Christianity*, ed. Steven Kaplan (New York: New York University Press, 1995), pp. 124-39. For more examples, see Daniel H. Bays, *A New History of Christianity in China* (Oxford, UK: Wiley-Blackwell, 2012), pp. 128-40; Lian Xi, *Redeemed by Fire: The Rise of Popular Christianity in Modern China* (New Haven, CT: Yale University Press, 2010).

[17]See chapter six.

pluralism,[18] but more recently, it has been framed in terms of the principles of particularity or generality.[19]

THE COSMIC CHRIST

If dialogue is the primary way of engaging the world, its theological basis is usually the cosmic Christ. As the Christian Conference of Asia in its statement on dialogue (1970) puts it,

> Jesus Christ, Lord and Man of history as of the cosmos, can never be brought in or added to man's cultural and spiritual life. It need, therefore, cause no surprise that we may discern his Presence everywhere, prior to that moment toward which we look forward eagerly when men will recognize his Presence.[20]

This may explain why as far as Christology is concerned the cosmic Christ is probably the most dominant motif in so-called ecumenical theology in Asia. It is the belief that the Christ whom the Christian church explicitly acknowledges is also present anonymously in the world carrying out his salvific work in different ways in various religions. The concept is succinctly captured in the words of Raimundo Panikkar:

> The mediatorship of Christ is total and unique, and this by definition, so that if something or somebody could be the link between God and the world, this would be Christ. Christian faith enters in not indirectly denying anything of the religions of the world, but in affirming that the Christ, which all religions in one way or another acknowledge . . . finds his full or at least his central epiphany in Jesus, the son of Mary. We mean to say that this ontic mediatorship of Christ is independent of the religion an individual may profess, and from the place and time of this existence on earth, whether inside or outside Christianity, or within or without the historical existence of the visible church. What Christ claims to be and to perform is valid for the Animist, Hindu, Muslim, etc. as well as for the Aztec, the Mongol, Greek, European, etc., as also for the Cro-Magnon man,

---

[18]Gavin D'Costa, *Theology and Religious Pluralism* (Oxford, UK: Basil Blackwell, 1986).

[19]For example, see George R. Sumner, *The First and the Last: The Claims of Jesus Christ and the Claims of Other Religious Traditions* (Grand Rapids: Eerdmans, 2004).

[20]"The Concern for Dialogue in Asia: CCA Statement," in *What Asian Christians Are Thinking*, ed. Douglas Elwood (Manila: New Day, 1976), p. 336.

for those who lived 15,000 years ago or for the man of our time. If we lose sight of this catholic christic perspective, we may easily falsify all relationship among Christians and the so-called non-Christians.[21]

The kerygma is about "something which is already there, which is at work before the messengers come." It is not bringing Christ to them, but "bringing him forth" from them. "The Church brings every true and authentic religion to its fulfillment through a process of death and resurrection."[22] It is also the basis, as we have seen earlier, for C. S. Song's collapsing of salvation history and general history. Christ is equally present in all human histories as their fulfillment.[23]

The cosmic Christ not only addresses Christ's presence in other religions but also his presence among the poor in Asia. But the two motifs are not readily reconciled. As Levison and Levison have noted, Asian Christologies have tended to focus either on the religiocultural or socioeconomic aspect. The exceptions, in their view, are M. M. Thomas and Aloysius Pieris, who integrated these two dimensions by introducing the cosmic Christ as "the meeting point of religions as they struggle for justice."[24] But they have successfully integrated the two poles of religiosity and poverty only by reducing the role of religion to that of primarily promoting the cause of social justice. Both Pieris and Thomas have little or nothing to say about the role that religions play, for example, in the form of popular piety. Thomas, as we have seen, simply dismisses such forms of "devotionism" as having no role in shaping the larger society.

The cosmic Christ is also the basis for understanding other Christological themes, namely, the suffering Christ, the liberating Christ and the enlightened Christ.

The suffering Christ. It is not coincidental that the theology of the suffering Christ that developed out of the ravages of the Second World War finds its most poignant expression among Japanese theologians. The

---

[21]Raimundo Panikkar, "Christians and So-Called 'Non-Christians,'" in *What Asian Christians Are Thinking*, p. 358.

[22]Ibid., pp. 361-62.

[23]C. S. Song, "The Decisiveness of Christ," in *What Asian Christians Are Thinking*, p. 17.

[24]Priscilla Pope-Levison and John R. Levison, *Jesus in Global Context* (Louisville, KY: Westminster John Knox, 1992), p. 73.

war brought untold sufferings to the Japanese, culminating in the dropping of atomic bombs on Hiroshima and Nagasaki. For the Japanese nation, however, it was not a simple case of victimization. Japan also suffered as an aggressor. Out of this context comes Kazoh Kitamori's theology of the pain of God: the God who suffers pain by giving up his own Son for the sake of a rebellious world. Basic to Kitamori's theology is that God's love is rooted in pain. Unlike the sympathy of the Buddha, it is not a pain that arises in response to human pain; rather, the pain is found in his very essence as God. It arises from his essence as both love and wrath. "The pain of God is his love—this love is based on the premise of his wrath, which is absolute, inflexible reality."[25] It is a pain seen in Luther's theology of the cross. The cross manifests the inner struggle of God between divine judgment on sin and a yearning love for the sinner: "God fighting with God" and in pain for humanity. It is important to remember that the theology of the pain of God addresses humans as the offender who despite the offence are embraced by God. The God who "resolves our pain and heals our wounds" is himself the wounded God whose love is "rooted in his pain."[26] The pain of God awakens the pain of our own sin against God and others and so the sinner who is so embraced must live a life of cross-bearing and self-denial. In this respect, it is quite different from the God of liberation theology who stands on the side of the victim as the one who is sinned against rather than as the active sinner.

Perhaps the greatest contribution of the theology of the pain of God is the spirituality it fosters. First, the theology of the pain of God is a theology of wonder. It is a shocking truth that God would love the sinner who deserves nothing but wrath. "The most urgent business before the church and theology today is the recovery of wonder, the pronouncement of the gospel afresh in order to make this wonder vivid again."[27] The good news is shocking news, and if it has lost its capacity to shock, perhaps we have failed to appropriate the news that God died as good

---

[25]Kazoh Kitamori, *Theology of the Pain of God* (London: SCM Press, 1966), p. 27; see also p. 45.
[26]Ibid., p. 21.
[27]Ibid., p. 44.

news.[28] It is a theology of wonder precisely when it is a *theologia crucis*, not a *theologia gloriae*.[29] This wonder at the pain of God, secondly, calls Christians to the cruciform life. We "serve the pain of God by our own pain" and in so serving, our pain is healed.[30] Such service challenges all that the modern world stands for: power, control, and efficiency.

> Jesus Christ came. He walked towards the "full stop." He lost his mobility. He was nailed down! . . . At this point of "full stop," the apostolic church proclaims that the love of God to man is ultimately and fully revealed. God walks "slowly" because he is love. If he is not love he would have gone much faster.[31]

The theology of the pain of God is particularly relevant in some Asian contexts where Christians who have achieved a measure of economic success and power are often tempted to become triumphalistic. It challenges the megachurch mentality and the self-assured attitude that equates prosperity and health with divine approbation and regards poverty and sickness as signs of a lack of faith.

The liberating Christ. Given the rampant poverty of the masses, the wide gulf between the rich and poor, and the ensuing exploitation of the poor by the rich, it is hardly surprising that the emphasis on Christ as liberator of the poor from oppression and injustice constitutes a primary motif in much so-called ecumenical theology. It is the recurring theme in many conferences organized by the Ecumenical Association of Third World Theologians. But while these theologians share a common language of liberation, the way in which liberation is pursued differs widely. A more explicitly sociopolitical liberation is evident in countries such as the Philippines, where Christianity is the faith of the majority (very similar to Latin America). Here people share a common discourse that enables liberation theologians to seek to disseminate their views and implement their program for the larger society. Similar approaches are

---

[28]Kitamori is clear that he is not advocating patripassianism here. It is not the Father who died, but God. Ibid., pp. 15-16.

[29]Ibid., p. 47.

[30]Ibid., pp. 51-53.

[31]Kosuke Koyama, *Three Mile an Hour God* (London: SCM Press, 1979), p. 7.

possible where Christianity is a significant minority but holds common sociopolitical aspirations with people of other faiths, such as in Korea. The situation in India is a little more complex. Christians from diverse backgrounds may speak of liberation since the struggle for their rights is aided by a shared democratic tradition that provides a common framework and language for political liberation to be pursued in cooperation with like-minded people. But for the Dalits, the motif of the liberating Christ is given a different twist. Arvind P. Nirmal, the father of Dalit theology, regards Jesus as a Dalit, whose dalitness was seen in his identification with the poor and outcast and in his suffering in the hands of the religious elite, including Christian elite![32] This is why Nirmal and other Dalit theologians are highly critical of liberation theologies expounded by the elite who are often not the victims of oppression.[33]

For example, M. M. Thomas's grand concept of the "humanization" of society based on "democratic humanism" and the awakening of "personhood" that brings hope and freedom may sound hopeful, but in a context where laws are flouted or ignored, such a humanization benefits only the higher-caste Christians with access to power but not the "subaltern." In Muslim countries such as Indonesia, liberation takes yet another turn. For Indonesian Christians, liberation may consist of joining with other liberative movements (such as NGOs) to advance the common ends of society.[34] But to press for religious freedom, especially the freedom of propagation, would be perceived by some as a threat even if such freedom is constitutionally guaranteed. Such is the case in Malaysia. For example, the constitutionally guaranteed religious freedom is severely undermined by attempts to stop Christians from using the word "Allah" as the translation for God in the Malay Bible, as noted above. In short, the vastly divergent contexts of Asia make the sociopolitical type

---

[32]Arvind P. Nirmal, "Towards a Christian Dalit Theology," in *A Reader in Dalit Theology*, ed. Arvind P. Nirmal (Madras: Gurukul Theological College and Research Institute, n.d.), pp. 65-69.

[33]Cf. Dhyanchand Carr, "Dalit Theology Is Biblical and It Makes the Gospel Relevant," in *A Reader in Dalit Theology*, pp. 71-73.

[34]Josef P. Widyatmadja, "A Spirituality of Liberation: An Indonesian Contribution," in *Asian Christian Spirituality*, pp. 49-63.

of liberation theology as the only type highly doubtful. One might even ask if a totally different approach is called for as the means to achieving certain desirable goals as citizens. For example, what sort of options are open to Christians living under the constant threat of Muslim extremism? In such a context, one wonders if the language of liberation itself is helpful. This explains why the kind of liberation rhetoric seen in the Philippines is almost totally absent in Indonesia and Malaysia.

The enlightened Christ. In the Buddhist context, some Christians call for a view of Jesus as "the enlightened one" or a "Buddha," not just as enlightener. This point is also noted by John Paul II in his Apostolic Exhortation *Ecclesia in Asia.*[35] But how is Jesus as the enlightened one to be conceived? One way, suggested by Peter Phan, is to see Jesus as man who was subject to all human limitations, including that of self-knowledge, but who gradually became "enlightened" to who he was as God.[36] It is not clear, however, how such an image of Jesus Christ as enlightened one could help advance dialogue with Buddhists. In the first place, how faithful is this image to the Christian tradition given that it is largely a result of "historical reconstruction" from rather slender evidence? That being the case, how would it serve the course of dialogue? Dialogue is better served when both parties bring out their respective core teachings and practices and compare their commonalities as well as differences in their core teachings and practices. A better point of contact is not to compare Jesus and Buddha as the enlightened one, but to compare the Buddha with Christians as enlightened ones. The Christian doctrine of salvation includes the illumination of the Holy Spirit as a prerequisite. To be a Christian is to be enlightened by the Spirit to know Christ, who is the truth (Eph 1:17-19).

The various images of Christ that we have briefly reviewed address the three recurrent concerns in much mainline understanding of the mission of the church, namely, dialogue, inculturation and liberation. The cosmic and the enlightened Christ motifs address the concern of inculturation

---

[35]*Ecclesia in Asia* §20.
[36]Peter Phan, *Being Religious Interreligiously: Asian Perspectives on Interfaith Dialogue* (Maryknoll, NY: Orbis Books, 2004), pp. 133-36. Such a view is not very different from the one proposed by Edward Schillebeeckx, *Christ, the Sacrament of the Encounter with God* (London: Sheed and Ward, 1963).

and dialogue with other religions; the suffering Christ and liberating Christ address the concern of the poor and oppressed. All these images of Christ are subsumed under the all-embracing christic principle: the presence of Christ in all religions, cultures and liberating movements providing the basis for dialogue, inculturation and works of liberation. For many Asian mainline theologians, the particularity of the gospel continues to be a scandal. They fear that too much stress on Jesus Christ as "the one and only Savior" would undermine dialogue with Asian religions, cultures and the poor.[37]

GRASSROOTS CHRISTOLOGIES

Elitist Christologies begin with how the doctrine of Christ might serve the "big" questions regarding the church's relation with the sociopolitical and cultural-religious contexts, and the answer is through the cosmic Christ who liberates the poor and oppressed and is inculturated in Asian religions and cultures. They seek to show how the church's involvement in these contexts can be achieved primarily through dialogue. They often do not ask the more fundamental questions: How do ordinary Christians experience Christ? Why are poverty-stricken Asians, notwithstanding what liberation theologians have to say, attracted to Pentecostal churches instead? Elitist theologians often do not take seriously grassroots experiences. For the liberationists, the poor need sociopolitical liberation and justice, and if they are not aware of their need, it is the task of the theologians to create the awareness through "conscientization."

It does not occur to these theologians that the poor may be looking for another kind of liberation: spiritual liberation from fear and fatalism created by centuries of internalizing the law of karma; freedom from the fear of spirits; deliverance from demonic oppression, real or perceived; healing for their sicknesses, and so on. This serious disconnect between the elite and the grassroots explains why the poor are not too attracted to the "preferential option for the poor" but instead opt for Pentecostalism.[38] Without first addressing the kind of liberation the grassroots

---

[37]Phan, *The Asian Synod*, p. 62.
[38]Donald E. Miller and Tetsunao Yamamori, *Global Pentecostalism: The New Face of Christian Social Engagement* (Berkeley: University of California Press, 2007), p. 251.

seek, there cannot ultimately be any sociopolitical liberation. People need first to experience change within themselves before they can even envisage the possibility of change in the sociopolitical realm.[39] Our Christology will not have much traction with the poor if it does not answer this primal cry for a different kind of freedom.

For the grassroots, this freedom cry is answered in their personal encounter with Jesus Christ. We cannot underestimate the radical paradigm shift that takes place when a person experiences conversion. In countless instances, the personal encounter is in the form of a Christophany remarkably similar to the experience of the apostle Paul. According to New Testament scholar Kim Seyoon, "The Christophany on the Damascus road was an objective vision of the risen Lord. This affected Paul to the innermost part of his life, creating the conviction in the seat of his understanding, thought, feeling and will that what appeared to him was Christ, revealed by God in glory."[40]

Kim believes that Paul's gospel—the new understanding of Jesus and his relation to Israel—is best understood in terms of his conversion experience on the Damascus road.[41] Remarkably, the pattern of Paul's conversion finds its parallel in many conversion accounts in Asia. The conversion of Sadhu Sundar Singh involving a vision of Jesus is well known.[42] But there are many more similar encounters with Jesus among Muslim converts. These encounters seem to follow a common pattern. There is first a Christophany where Jesus Christ clearly identifies himself, and out of this encounter, the recipient's perception of Jesus is radically altered. The account of Gulshan Esther, a Muslim convert, is typical.[43] She found her room filled with light; Jesus identified himself and showed her the holes in his hands; he taught her the Lord's Prayer, which addresses God as Father. For a Muslim, the concept of God as Father is nothing short of

[39]Vishal Mangalwadi, *Truth and Social Reform* (London: Spire, 1989).

[40]Kim Seyoon, *The Origin of Paul's Gospel* (Grand Rapids: Eerdmans, 1981), p. 7.

[41]Ibid., p. 31.

[42]A. J. Appasamy, *Sundar Singh: A Biography* (Madras: Christian Literature Society, 1966), esp. chap. 5.

[43]Anecdotal evidences are quite plentiful. In the northeastern Indian state of Assam, Naga missionaries have told me of Muslim migrants who became Christians after having a vision or dream of Jesus Christ.

revolutionary. It "was a name that clutched at my heart, that filled its emptiness."[44] But it is important to note that the encounter with Jesus reconfigures Muslim monotheism. Jesus is not just a prophet but the Son of God who is worshiped.[45] Somehow the christophanic encounter also brings God closer: The transcendent God of Islam is also the loving Father.

Christophanic experiences are the beginning of a trinitarian faith for many Muslim converts. These converts' religious experience is remarkably similar to the early Christians' experience of the risen Christ. New Testament scholars believe that the trinitarian faith began with the early Christians' encounters with the risen Christ, whom they proclaimed as "Lord." Their experience of the risen Lord was paradigmatic, and Paul's would prove particularly significant for the development of a new kind of monotheism: a "binitarianism" that in subsequent centuries developed further into a full-fledged trinitarian faith.[46] Just as the doctrine of the Trinity arose from the early Christians' christophanic encounters, it is the same for many Muslim converts today. Many Asian Christians know from experience that in Christ dwells the fullness of the Godhead. Through Christ God's true nature is revealed. Perhaps one reason the trinitarian experience occurs so frequently among converts from Islam is that this is their main obstacle to faith in Christ. Their situation is not unlike that of the Jews with their strong monotheistic faith. Both Jews and Muslims could not have made the quantum leap into Christianity without a real encounter with the risen Christ.

Although the divinity of Jesus Christ is less of an issue outside the Jewish and Muslim contexts, the experience of the person of Christ is no less critical, albeit in somewhat different ways. Here, the Christology that resonates most deeply is a Spirit-Christology.[47] In a tradition such

---

[44]Gulshan Esther, *The Torn Veil* (Fort Washington, PA: CLC, 2010), pp. 74-76. See also Bilquis Sheikh, *I Dared to Call Him Father* (Grand Rapids: Chosen, 1978).

[45]Gulshan's brother had a similar encounter in a death experience. *Torn Veil*, p. 198.

[46]See for example Larry W. Hurtado, *How on Earth Did Jesus Become a God?: Historical Questions About Earliest Devotion to Jesus* (Grand Rapids: Eerdmans, 2005), pp. 48-53, and *Lord Jesus Christ: Devotion to Jesus in Earliest Christianity* (Grand Rapids: Eerdmans, 2003), pp. 64-78.

[47]For a traditional study of Spirit-Christology see Ralph Del Colle, *Christ and the Spirit: Spirit-Christology in Trinitarian Perspective* (New York: Oxford University Press, 1994).

as Buddhism, which stresses salvation as enlightenment, the most natural point of contact with Christianity is the Spirit of illumination (Eph 1:17-19) and the Spirit who gives the gifts of knowledge and wisdom (1 Cor 12:8). In both references the objects of the Spirit's enlightenment are the Christians. The Spirit rests on Jesus, the anointed one who went about doing good and healing all who were oppressed by the devil (Acts 10:38). In this sense Jesus could be called the enlightened one—but only in a limited sense since the primary focus of Spirit-Christology is the fulfillment of Christ's messianic mission rather than his evolving God-consciousness (contra Peter Phan).[48] But Jesus who receives the anointing of the Spirit is himself the baptizer of the Spirit. The ministry of the church is an extension of the ministry of Jesus in the power of the Spirit. The focus is not on spiritual gifts as such but on Jesus Christ, who gives the gift of the Spirit, and by the Spirit the church is gifted with all spiritual gifts.

Spirit-Christology is the Christology of the classical Pentecostals who believe that the "baptism in the Spirit" enables them to experience the "full gospel" of Jesus Christ. Pentecostal spirituality is driven by the desire for a deeply personal relationship with God, by the need for intimacy signaled by glossolalic prayer.[49] It is not coincidental that glossolalia features prominently in the Pentecostal revivals in the early twentieth century as well as in the charismatic revivals among mainline Protestants and Catholics in the 1960s.[50] Pentecostals are not satisfied with a superficial relationship or an occasional personal encounter but desire a relationship with God as familiar friend and intimate lover. Their relationship may not always be very mature, but there is no question they have discovered a God they can approach in childlike simplicity and with total abandon. The sense of God's nearness and familiarity gives to Pentecostals a holy, if sometimes reckless, boldness to "attempt great things for

---

[48]See above p. 102.
[49]Simon Chan, *Pentecostal Ecclesiology: An Essay on the Development of Doctrine* (Blandford Forum, Dorset, UK: Deo, 2011), chap. 5.
[50]One could not have missed the strong affirmation made of the connection between glossolalia and baptism in the Holy Spirit by the early Protestant charismatics. See Dennis J. Bennett, *Nine O'Clock in the Morning* (London: Coverdale House, 1974).

God." Prayers, for them, are not about generalities commonly found in the "general intercessions" of mainline churches; they expect God to answer very specific prayers: healing for the sick, deliverance from demons, rain in drought-stricken lands, babies for barren women. They travel to the far-flung mission fields "by faith" believing that God will meet all their needs—miraculously if need be. What makes such a relationship possible is their "baptism in the Holy Spirit," which results in a major paradigm shift in their religious consciousness. This is not to say that everything in Pentecostal spirituality is desirable; but it embodies a way of life that ordinary people everywhere, poor in body and spirit, starved of meaningful relationship, can readily identify with.

Pentecostals are seldom precise when speaking of their intimate relationship with God. More commonly, when they narrate their spiritual experience—contrary to popular perception—it is the person of Jesus who features prominently rather than the Spirit. As Steven Land has accurately observed of Pentecostal spirituality, "Jesus is the center and the Holy Spirit is the circumference."[51] Jesus becomes the center through Spirit baptism; more precisely, Spirit baptism mediates the person of Jesus as Savior, sanctifier, baptizer, healer and coming king.[52] Through Spirit baptism, Jesus is experienced as more than "the Savior of my soul" (à la evangelicalism), but as the powerful Christ anointed by the Spirit as well as the giver of the Spirit. This fivefold gospel[53] gives to Pentecostals their distinctive identity and also explains their tendency toward devotion to the name of Jesus, a devotion which, for some, unfortunately, ended with the reduction of the Trinity to the person of Jesus.[54]

This broadly demarcated Pentecostal Spirit-Christology is not very dif-

---

[51]Steven Land, *Pentecostal Spirituality: A Passion for the Kingdom*, supplement 1, *Journal of Pentecostal Theology* (September 1993): 23.

[52]See Christopher Thomas, ed. *Toward a Pentecostal Ecclesiology: The Church and the Fivefold Gospel* (Cleveland, TN: CPT, 2010).

[53]The fivefold gospel was developed by the Wesleyan-Holiness Pentecostals who inherited from John Wesley the doctrine of entire sanctification as distinct from salvation while the Reformed Pentecostals collapsed salvation and sanctification into a single work, resulting in the fourfold gospel (Jesus as Savior, baptizer, healer and coming king).

[54]David Reed, *"In Jesus' Name": The History and Beliefs of Oneness Pentecostals* (Blandford Forum, Dorset, UK: Deo, 2008).

ferent from the Christology that emerges from the African context. Tennent highlights six characteristics of African Christology: Jesus as healer and life-giver, liberator, chief, mediator, master of initiation, and ancestor/elder brother,[55] all of which except perhaps master of initiation are highly relevant to Asia. This is not surprising given their shared primal religious background.

Jesus as healer. Within the ecumenical world, healing is increasingly recognized as an important part of the churches' ministry. This is no doubt due to the impact that the many Pentecostal-like churches are creating around the world. Globalization has brought many immigrant churches to the West, and they are demonstrating to older churches long used to stagnation and steady decline that this is not the way the church is supposed to be. One World Council of Churches observer describes what happened at a consultation jointly organized by the Latin American Council of Churches and the World Council in 2005:

> For the first time, Pentecostal Christians were by far in the majority, so that they could make their mark on the gathering. Times have changed. The powerful trumpet of liberation theology is no longer being heard. The Gospel is now above all understood as a force for healing and reconciliation. Testimonies showed how many find the way of discipleship through healing, to themselves or to friends or neighbours. "Lord, I have no money for a doctor, but I know you as a God who is alive and who saves."[56]

Healing can be seen as an inclusive paradigm for a more holistic mission. Healing is not just physical and spiritual healing (soteriology); there is also the healing of community and relationships (ecclesiology) and cosmic healing, which incorporates the *Christus Victor* theme (eschatology).[57]

There might be sociological and cultural reasons for the Pentecostal emphasis on physical healing. The obsession with good health and good looks characteristic of our modern consumerist culture may be a motivating factor, and charismatic preachers such as Benny Hinn and Morris

---

[55]Tennent, *Theology,* pp. 125-27.
[56]Wout van Laar, "Churches as Healing Communities: Impulses from the South for an Integral Understanding of Healing," *Exchange* 35, no. 2 (Jan. 1, 2006): 226-41.
[57]Tennent, *Theology,* p. 119.

Cerullo know how to capitalize on this modern obsession by making healing the linchpin of their evangelistic campaigns. But there is a good theological reason why Pentecostals have put strong emphasis on physical healing. It is in the very nature of the Spirit to relate to the material world, as one contemporary writer has noted.[58] The Spirit was responsible for the Son to be incarnated in the womb of Mary (Lk 1:35). He came upon the Son at his baptism, making him the Christ and thrusting him into the wilderness where for forty days he faced the devil's temptation and encountered wild animals (Mk 1:10-13). At Pentecost, the Spirit came in his own person to indwell the church, the body of Christ, turning a group of motley believers into the temple of the Spirit. The Spirit continues his work in the church, especially in the Eucharist where created things—bread and wine—are "transfigured" into the body and blood of Christ. Finally, the Spirit who is the "firstfruits" of the new creation will free the whole creation from its bondage to decay and redeem mortal bodies (Rom 8:19-23). The Spirit is not just concerned with things spiritual; he seems to have a special relation to the material world. As Eugene Rogers puts it, the Spirit "befriends matter."[59] While there is increasing recognition that the Spirit's healing work is more than physical, Pentecostals instinctively understand the Spirit's special relation to the physical dimension of existence.

Besides the theological reason, there are other practical reasons that the healing motif has become so central to mission especially within the Majority World. First, there are still many places in Asia where medical facilities are extremely basic or nonexistent, and even where they are available, they are often beyond the reach of the poor. In such a situation, the ministry of healing takes on a special significance. It is often in the midst of ministering in such abject conditions that the church is forced to consider the place of divine healing. The Indian theologian Vishal Mangalwadi recounts his experience of serving in a poor Indian village, which forced him to engage in prayer for the sick and demon-possessed

---

[58]Eugene Rogers, *After the Spirit: A Constructive Pneumatology from Resources Outside the Modern West* (Grand Rapids: Eerdmans, 2005), chap. 3.
[59]Ibid., p. 55.

for which his own evangelical training had not quite prepared him.[60] This type of healing ministry is quite different from the health-and-wealth gospel. It addresses genuine needs rather than panders to the obsession of the affluent. Second, in situations where the demonic is more than just a metaphor for abnormal psychology or oppressive socio-political structures, the gospel that proclaims Christ's victory over Satan becomes more than just one of the theories of the atonement or a slogan to support a political agenda but a practical necessity.

Recognizing the importance of the healing ministry of the church, however, does not lessen the need for a holistic theology of healing. If there is one danger that Pentecostal-charismatics tend to fall into, it is the temptation of an overrealized eschatology that expects all the blessings of God to be realized in the here and now, in material form. The gift of the Holy Spirit after all is only the "firstfruits" of the new creation; his works give us a foretaste of heavenly reality and not its fullness. The effects of sin in our world will not be fully overcome until the parousia. In the meantime, the church must learn to exist in the tension of the "already-not yet." Finding the balance is always a challenge in pastoral ministry. When do we pray and "claim" the healing grace of the Spirit, and when do we learn to let go? How do we distinguish between faith and presumption, surrender to God's will and fatalism? In a context where the law of karma runs deep in human consciousness, one can understand why the tendency of many charismatics is to err on the side of presumption.

But fatalism cannot be overcome by presumption. A theology of healing must also include an understanding of faith that accepts sickness as a present reality and that complete healing must await the resurrection of the body. There is a faith that sees beyond the present; it is a faith that merges into hope, which enables the Christian to face various exigencies of this present life (Heb 11). All these challenges require the cultivation of spiritual discernment, which includes the charism of the Spirit to speak words of practical wisdom to specific situations, the kind we see in the desert fathers.[61] It is wisdom that discerns the specific will of God in

---

[60]Mangalwadi, *Truth and Social Reform*, pp. 34-37.
[61]Kallistos Ware, "The Spiritual Father in Orthodox Christianity," in *Spiritual Direction: Con-*

a given situation. Such wisdom does not come from the application of general rules, although learning the rules of discernment might come in useful at times; rather, it is wisdom that comes from deep personal acquaintance with the all-wise God through prayer. There is no separation between theology and spirituality.

Jesus as liberator and victor. Christ decisively defeated the devil at the cross, and after his resurrection and ascension, he continues to exercise his authority in heaven and on earth as high priest seated at God's right hand (Mt 28:18; Heb 8:1; 10:12; 12:2). According to Hebrews 2:14-15, the purpose of Jesus Christ's death was that "through death He might destroy him who had the power of death, that is, the devil, and release those who through fear of death were all their lifetime subject to bondage" (NKJV). Similarly, Colossians 2:14-15 reads, "having wiped out the handwriting of requirements that was against us, which was contrary to us. And He has taken it out of the way, having nailed it to the cross. Having disarmed principalities and powers, He made a public spectacle of them, triumphing over them in it" (NKJV). The handwriting probably refers to a certificate of indebtedness or IOU, while the "debt" the sinner owes is the obedience required by the law (*tois dogmasin*: "decrees"; see also Eph 2:15). As C. F. D. Moule puts it, "I owe God obedience to his will. Signed, Mankind."[62] But the debt was canceled by Christ at the cross. A further outcome of his death is the triumph over "principalities and powers." Their defeat is made apparent by their being "disarmed" or stripped bare. The powers are pictured as vanquished and publicly disgraced, like prisoners who are led in a triumphal procession behind the victorious general.

In both passages the defeat of Satan is due to Christ's death on the cross. But how does Christ's work on the cross overpower Satan? Images from patristic literature that pictured the cross as a kind of mousetrap baited with the divinity of Christ hidden under his humanity, which Satan unwittingly swallowed, are not helpful,[63] but

---

temporary Readings, ed. Kevin G. Culligan (Locus Valley, NY: Living Flame, 1983), pp. 21-23.

[62]Cited by Douglas J. Moo, *The Letters to the Colossians and to Philemon*, Pillar New Testament Commentary (Grand Rapids: Eerdmans, 2008), p. 210.

[63]See Gustav Aulén, *Christus Victor*, trans. A. G. Hebert (New York: Macmillan, 1958), pp. 51-53.

neither is the excessively juridical emphasis seen in atonement theories since the Reformation.

The Colossians passage explicitly juxtaposes the legal and the triumphal while the Hebrews passage does so implicitly. In Colossians the
connection between verse 14 and verse 15 is that by removing the indebtedness to God—in other words, by freeing humankind from sin—they
were no longer under the power of the devil who had a claim on them
because of sin. While sin is primarily against God, it puts one under
bondage to the devil. As 1 John 3:8 puts it, "He who sins is of the devil, for
the devil has sinned from the beginning." The sinner aligns himself with
the devil, doing what the devil is best at. By doing what the devil would
have done, the sinner comes under the devil's bondage. But John also says,
"For this purpose the Son of God was manifested, that He might destroy
the works of the devil." In Hebrews, Christ's death overcame death and
consequently the fear of death, because sin, the cause of death, was
overcome at the cross. Freedom from the fear of death breaks the power
of the devil, who uses the fear of death to hold people under his sway.
Christ's victory over Satan is both "legal" and ontological. It did not just
occur decisively at the cross but continues to be applied in his high
priestly work, where he is now seated at God's right hand and continues
to exercise his full authority over the principalities and powers.[64]

The victory of Christ can perhaps be better appreciated in light of the
shame-honor culture of the New Testament, as noted in the previous
chapter. It is not surprising that the Colossians passage treats Christ's
victory over the devil as an honor issue. Death on the cross was utter
humiliation from a human standpoint, but in reality it had the very opposite effect: it was the devil who was stripped bare and publicly disgraced. For Christians the cross was no shame but the way to true glory.
For out of a death that was freely embraced in obedience to God's will,

---

[64]Moo thinks that the last phrase of Col 2:15, "triumphing over them in it" (*en autō*), should
be better understood as masculine: "in Christ" rather than in the cross, in which case it
refers to Christ's triumph through the resurrection and ascension (Moo, *Colossians*, p. 215).
But the overall meaning of the verse is not affected, whether the last phrase is "in it" or "in
him." The victory was effected at the cross but the full and continuing display of the victory
is at Christ's resurrection and ascension.

Jesus was raised from the dead and given a name of supreme honor, above every other name (Phil 2:8-9). Or, as Anselm would see it, the death of the sinless God-man accumulated infinite value that is more than adequate to satisfy the divine honor. In honoring the Father in this way, the Father in turn bestows supreme honor on the Son (see also Jn 17:1). The death and resurrection of Christ can therefore be said to provide an objective basis for an alternative system of honor that stands in direct antithesis to how shame and honor are understood by the world. It is on that basis that the writer to the Hebrews can appeal to Christians under persecution to look "to Jesus, the founder and perfecter of our faith, who for the joy that was set before him endured the cross, despising the shame, and is seated at the right hand of the throne of God" (Heb 12:2 ESV). He sets the supreme example for his followers to live by a radically redefined set of honor values.[65] Christians, therefore, must be prepared to be dishonored in the world's eyes, for when they carry the cross of shame for Christ's sake, they too will be exalted. The central Christian message redefines the nature of shame and honor and in so doing creates a new community that transcends the ways of this world.

In primal religious contexts the felt need that the *Christus Victor* teaching addresses is not primarily sociopolitical liberation but liberation from the fear of spirits and the fear of death (Heb 2:15). Fear relating to the spirit world is real for many folk religionists; the gods are capricious and can be easily offended although they can be benevolent if properly appeased. But the good news of the cross is that the once-for-all sacrifice of Christ has removed the need for continuing appeasement of the spirits, and his continuing work as high priest assures believers that the victory over Satan is a present reality. The experience of liberation from bondage to fear and of victory over evil spirits is indeed good news. This is why sociopolitical types of liberation theology do not quite have the impact in primal religious contexts—even in Latin America!

Jesus as mediator-ancestor. In popular Chinese religion, it is common to rely on the mediation of a spiritual medium or fortuneteller in life's

---

[65]David A. deSilva, "Despising Shame: A Cultural-Anthropological Investigation of the Epistle to the Hebrews," *Journal Of Biblical Literature* 113, no. 3 (1994): 439-61.

major catastrophes, such as prolonged illness, or major decisions, such as marriage.[66] Even among Christians at the popular level it is not uncommon to find church members resorting to the "priestly" ministry of the pastor. The priestly ministry is not a subject for theological reflection since it goes against a central Protestant tenet, the priesthood of all believers, yet there are plenty of anecdotal evidences to show that it is implicitly recognized. For example, pastors are popularly perceived as having a "special anointing" that sets them apart from ordinary members. Sometimes dysfunctional pastors are simply tolerated rather than asked to leave for fear of "touching the Lord's anointed."[67] Many African Initiated Churches seem to have similar views about their leaders.[68] They reflect the pervasiveness of priestly mediation in traditional African religions.[69] In Nagaland, a state in northeast India, pastors often complain that their work is overstretched because members insist on their presence to officiate in the dedication of homes, children and even hunting weapons! Members will not settle for a lay leader to do the job.[70] Even though the church is traditionally Baptist, the pastor serves as the de facto mediator; he[71] is regarded as somehow having a special power not accessible to lay people.

This deeply felt need for priestly mediation is often not adequately addressed in Protestantism. The Protestant doctrine of the priesthood of all believers has led ironically to the neglect not only of the priestly ministry of the pastor but the post-ascension priestly ministry of Jesus as well. If Jesus is thought of as priest, it is in relation to his sacrifice at the cross.[72]

---

[66]Ju Shi Huey, "Chinese Spirit-Mediums in Singapore: An Ethnographic Study," in *Studies in Chinese Folk Religion in Singapore and Malaysia*, ed. John Clammer (Singapore: Institute for the Study of Religions and Society, 1983), pp. 21-24.

[67]I have been personally involved in resolving one such crisis in a local church.

[68]Allan Anderson, *Zion and Pentecost: The Spirituality and Experience of Pentecostal and Zionist/Apostolic Churches in South Africa* (Pretoria: University of South Africa Press, 2000), p. 312.

[69]E. Bolaji Idowu, *Olódùmarè: God in Yoruba Belief* (New York: Frederick A. Praeger, 1963), pp. 129-43.

[70]Based on my personal encounters with pastors in more than twenty years of regular visits to Nagaland.

[71]Even though the Baptist Associations of Nagaland ordain women, there are in fact very few ordained women, as most churches prefer a male pastor.

[72]For example, in the popular evangelical systematic theology by Millard Erickson, little is said

But when everyone is a priest, then no one is effectively a priest. If the Asian or African Protestant pastor serves as a de facto priest to the people, we need to rethink the theology of the priesthood. The laicization of priesthood in Protestantism may have suited the Western egalitarian mindset, but in hierarchically ordered societies in Asia and Africa, there is much to be said for maintaining a special order of priests along with the general priesthood of believers.

It is not coincidental that when the priestly ministry of the pastor is not explicitly recognized, the priestly ministry of Christ also becomes marginalized. Any rethinking therefore must begin with the priesthood of Christ. Its significance should become apparent in contexts where the karmic consciousness runs deep, where the endless cycle of rebirths creates resignation and despair, and where fear of the malevolent powers of evil spirits looms large. The general atmosphere in the primal religious world is one of fear. In this context, the teaching of the book of Hebrews concerning Jesus Christ both as victorious over the devil and as high priest takes on a special significance.

Here we learn that Christ is the perfect high priest because he is perfectly human and identifies himself completely with humanity (Heb 2:14-18; 5:7-9); he is also perfectly able to represent humanity before God because of his exalted divinity (Heb 1:1-4), like Melchizedek (Heb 1:13). His once-for-all sacrifice replaces the continuing sacrifices of the Old Testament, which cannot take away sins (Heb 9:9; 10:1). Christ's sacrifice perfects believers (Heb 10:14) and purges the conscience from the need to continually perform sacrifices, which the author of Hebrews calls "dead works" (Heb 9:12-14). This is particularly important in primal religious contexts where the law of karma dictates that one must constantly make amends to offset past mistakes. However, once-for-all does not mean Christians can be complacent. There is no cheap grace. Perseverance and continuing in good works are needed (Heb 13). The Christian life is a continuing journey to the celestial city (Heb 11; see also Heb 12:22; 13:14); it is a race (Heb 12:1-3). The need to persevere is both a demand

---

about the nature of Christ's post-ascension priestly work in contrast to the amount of space given to his atoning work on the cross. *Christian Theology* (Grand Rapids: Baker, 1987).

and a privilege since believers are priests who have the privilege of continuing access into God's presence (Heb 9:14; 12:22-24, 28). Salvation is both present, involving deliverance from the fear of death (Heb 2:15) and future (looking forward to the heavenly Zion). Hebrews, in fact, shifts the focus on faith from personal relationship, as in John and Paul, to faith as faithfulness and perseverance made possible by the priestly ministry of Christ.[73]

Jesus is the effective mediator and high priest because he is one with humanity. Hebrews is careful to note that it was after his resurrection that Jesus identified himself as "our Brother" (Heb 2:11, 12). John's Gospel conveys a similar idea. In his postresurrection appearance, Jesus told Mary, "Go instead to my brothers and tell them, 'I am ascending to my Father and your Father, to my God and your God'" (Jn 20:17 NIV). A new relationship results from Jesus' resurrection and ascension. In his mediatorial role he is our brother, like us and yet unlike us, since he also holds a position of special privilege as "the firstborn among many brothers" (Rom 8:29 NIV). It is in this context that Jesus can be considered our "greatest ancestor."[74] Jesus is at once priest and ancestor. There is a strong christological basis underlying Asian and African Christians' instinctive treatment of their pastor as their bigger brother or "ancestor" and also as priest. This is especially the case among Pentecostal-charismatics, who tend to regard their leaders as "iconic representations of 'the Spirit left by Christ.'"[75] Theologically, this concept of leadership is not very different from that seen in Catholicism and Orthodoxy where the bishop stands in *persona Christi* in relation to the people of God, especially in the eucharistic assembly.[76] In this way the ministry of the ancestor-priest on earth is an extension of the ministry of Christ as ancestor-priest in heaven.

---

[73]I. Howard Marshall, *New Testament Theology: Many Witnesses, One Gospel* (Downers Grove, IL: IVP Academic, 2004), p. 616.

[74]Kwame Bediako, *Jesus in Africa: The Christian Gospel in African History and Experience* (Akropong-Akuapem, Ghana: Regnum Africa, 2000), pp. 21, 27-28.

[75]Karla Poewe, "Rethinking the Relationship of Anthropology to Science and Religion," in *Charismatic Christianity as a Global Culture*, ed. Karla Poewe (Columbia: University of South Carolina Press, 1994), p. 250.

[76]Alexander Schmemann, *The Eucharist: Sacrament of the Kingdom* (Crestwood, NY: St. Vladimir's Seminary Press, 1988), p. 24.

As the big brother the pastor-priest, too, is given a place of special honor. This is but a small step from the practice of ancestral veneration and the veneration of saints. One occurs in the context of the family, the other in the context of the church, the family of God. Both are extensions of the same principle beyond the grave.

Ancestral veneration, like priestly mediation, has a christological basis. Yet despite the prevalence of ancestral veneration in Asia and the practical issues it engenders, it is seldom addressed in relation to Christology (especially among Protestants). Instead, the ancestor problem is usually discussed in relation to New Testament teachings regarding food offerings (1 Cor 10–11), freedom of conscience (Rom 12–14) and idolatry.[77] There is a need to explore the christological foundation of ancestral veneration. In Africa, the deceased ancestors are called the "living dead," a concept that could be given a christological grounding, for Christ is the one "who is, and who was, and who is to come" (Rev 1:4 NIV), the one who was dead and is now alive (Rev 1:18). Those who have died in Christ can be called the living dead. Just as the traditional ancestor is believed to exist in solidarity with the living, the communion of saints includes both saints on earth and saints in heaven united in one church in Christ. In the church, de facto communion exists between the living and the "dead" who are alive in Christ. We shall return to this theme in the final chapter. The serious defect of Protestantism is that its ecclesiology is largely sociologically constructed; it has no doctrine of the church as an ontological reality.[78]

THE IMPORTANCE OF CONVERSION IN ASIA

The grassroots Christology we have been considering shows that issues related to Christology have actually less to do with such grand schemes

---

[77]For example, see Chuck Lowe, *Honoring God and Family: A Christian Response to Idol Food in Chinese Popular Religion* (Bangalore: Theological Book Trust, 2001); Lo Lung-Kwong, "The Nature of the Issue of Ancestral Worship Among Chinese Christians," *Studies in World Christianity* 9, no. 1 (Jan. 1, 2003): 30-42.

[78]But the situation may be changing, as seen in a recent evangelical attempt to ground spiritual practices in a spiritual ontology. See John Jefferson Davis, *Worship and the Reality of God: An Evangelical Theology of Real Presence* (Downers Grove, IL: InterVarsity Press, 2010) and *Meditation and Communion with God* (Downers Grove, IL: InterVarsity Press, 2012).

as sociopolitical liberation as with the day-to-day reality of struggling
with sickness, fear and finance. Poverty is certainly a reality, but in the
minds of most poor Asians it is not associated with unequal distribution
of wealth and unjust social structures. For liberation theologians, this
shows the need for "conscientization" to rid them of "false consciousness."
Yet in places where we would have expected liberation theology to
succeed—such as the Philippines, which has much in common with
Latin America culturally—the poor themselves are hardly attracted to it.
Instead, they flock to charismatic megachurches; to El Shaddai, a popular
Catholic lay-led movement;[79] and to the Iglesia ni Cristo, an indigenous
church considered by traditional churches to be a cult. These movements
have strong social programs but they are also strong conversionist movements with a message of salvation addressing their physical and "spiritual"
needs. It is this message that gives these movements their distinctive
cutting edge. Mansford Prior, in his comprehensive survey of the renewal
movements in the Catholic Church, notes:

> Both the CM [charismatic movement] and BECs [base ecclesial commu-
> nities] are potentially prophetic. Despite its otherworldliness and its re-
> spect for constituted authority, the CM fosters new hope and so a critical,
> non-fatalistic outlook on life. "Baptism in the Spirit" involves a dramatic
> shaking-up of the taken-for-granted world and members embrace of a new
> way of seeing reality itself.[80]

While the gospel is certainly more than the message of conversion, it is
nonetheless true that the message of the gospel as "the power of God for
salvation to everyone who believes" (Rom 1:16 ESV) has always been seen
as central to the church's mission throughout history. When the church
stops reaching out to non-Christians with the message of salvation in
Christ, it stagnates and dies a slow death. Yet for most mainline Protestants,
conversion has become an embarrassment and is largely replaced by dialogue. Dialogue, of course, is an important part of the church's mission but

---

[79]See John Mansford Prior, "Jesus Christ the Way to the Father: The Challenge of the Pentecostals," FABC Paper no. 119, May 2012, Federation of Asian Bishops' Conferences, www
.fabc.org/fabc%20papers/fabc_paper_119.pdf.
[80]Ibid., p. 34.

it cannot be a substitute. The fear of preaching the gospel to non-Christians does not necessarily indicate a better understanding of the nature of our pluralistic world or that the church has grown in the virtue of tolerance; rather, as Newbigin has repeatedly warned the Western church, it is largely the sign of "a tragic loss of nerve" and the loss of faith in the meaning and power of the gospel.[81] Admittedly, the church's preaching has sometimes been intolerant and manifested a crusading spirit instead of love and compassion. But if there is a wrong way of preaching the message of salvation in Christ, there is also a right way. Conversion is not always perceived as a threat. The bold and clear preaching of the gospel done with sensitivity to the needs and concerns of the audience does not generally elicit hostility. The story of the first ordained Protestant minister of the Indian church shows that it is possible to preach to Hindus with a view to their conversion and yet gain their respect.[82]

The conversionist emphasis is also what saves Pentecostalism from being completely assimilated into primal religiosity. We have noted earlier that the phrase "split-level Christianity" has been used to designate certain forms of popular Christianity where an orthodox faith at the rational level sits uneasily with a primal spirituality within the same person. Pentecostalism, with its close affinity with primal religions, is sometimes seen as an example of split-level Christianity. While there are instances of "Christian shamanism,"[83] by and large Pentecostalism has shown a greater capacity of contextualization of the gospel than syncretism with primal cultures.[84] The reason for this is its strong emphasis on conversion. Conversion in Pentecostalism is understood to mean making a conscious decision involving a radical break with the past. In

---

[81]Lesslie Newbigin, *The Gospel in a Pluralist Society* (Grand Rapids: Eerdmans), p. 22. Newbigin has often spoken of the Western loss of nerve except in science and technology. See "A Missionary's Dream," *Ecumenical Review* 43, no. 1 (January 1991): 5. Tragically, some "ecumenical" theologians in Asia seem to be infected by the same Western malaise.

[82]Rajaiah D. Paul, *Chosen Vessels* (Madras: CLS, 1961), pp. 22-24.

[83]Milton Acosta, "Power Pentecostalism," *Christianity Today*, July 29 2009, www.christianity today.com/ct/2009/august/11.40.html.

[84]See my article "Folk Christianity and Primal Spirituality: Prospects for Theological Development," in *Christian Movements in Southeast Asia: A Theological Exploration*, ed. Michael Poon (Singapore: Armour, 2010), pp. 1-18.

this respect it shares much with evangelical Christianity. The strongly felt need for a conversion experience is conspicuous even in paedobaptist churches in Asia. Among those who grow up in Christian families (who ostensibly would not need to break radically with their past), it is quite common to see parents delaying the baptism of their children in order for the children to make their own personal decision. For these parents, the children's personal faith is all-important.

The importance of the conversion experience based on a conscious choice cannot be overemphasized. Conversion radically reorients converts' thinking about God and the world from which they were converted. It is a movement from darkness to light (see Col 1:11-12). The story of the conversion of Sadhu Sundar Singh (1889–1929) from Hinduism to Christianity provides a classic example. Despite his training in the bhakti tradition and in Sikkhism, learning the Bhagavadgita by heart at a young age, Singh continued to experience a deep restlessness until he met Jesus in a vision. His conversion to Christ was unambiguous and overturned everything that he had learned from Hinduism. His relation to God was no immersion in the absolute but "a continuous dialogue . . . in which the distinction between himself and the personal Christ remains clear."[85] Union with Christ does not mean absorption. In short, conversion means the abandonment of the Hindu monistic worldview. In many Asian contexts, conversion is also often experienced as a spiritual encounter in which concrete problems are overcome, such as healing of sickness and deliverance from demon possession. Where the gods failed, the Christian God came and overcame. This *Christus Victor* theme runs through many conversion stories and testimonies.[86] The evangelical conversion experience explains why split-level Christianity, if it exists, cannot be the only explanation.

While there are common features in Christian conversion, there are also a number of distinctive features of conversion experiences in Asia. Conversion in the Asian context is not always like the Western conversion stories that are preceded by intense struggles with a guilt-laden con-

---

[85]Boyd, *An Introduction*, p. 95.
[86]For example, see Tony Lambert, *China's Christian Millions: The Costly Revival* (London: Monarch, 1999), pp. 109-20.

science. The story of St. Augustine has often been presented as a paradigm of Christian conversion, but more appropriately it is a paradigm seen more frequently in the West. In many primal religious contexts of Asia, conversion is more frequently the experience of freedom from bondage to fear, evil powers or the caste system. The patristic experience of *Christus Victor* is perhaps the more dominant paradigm.

In conversion there is an interplay between the individual and the community. Individuals are converted, but they are incorporated into a new community, the church (chapter 6). Thus what makes conversion stories credible is the new set of meaningful interpersonal relationships conversion brings, especially to the family. For example, in a Confucian culture that highly values family solidarity, conversion transforms family relationships from that of domination to that of respect and reciprocity. The following account of the changed behavior of members of an extended family told in a hymn from the house church in rural China says it all:

> Old Granny believes in the Lord, she removes idols and respects the true God. She offers her rice-bowl to thank God and the Heavenly Father gives us a happy household. Peace and joy fill our days, ever moving forward to follow the Lord.
>
> Old Granny believes in the Lord, her temper is much improved. She treats her daughters and daughters-in-law even-handedly. People say she is impartial and the glorious light of the Lord shines on everybody.
>
> Elder brother believes in the Lord, he doesn't smash pots and pans, doesn't curse the chickens and dogs, doesn't lose his temper any more. When people see him they praise him.
>
> Old Auntie believes in the Lord, she loves her husband and respects her relatives. The Gospel educates people to spend their days in joy and peace.[87]

Wingate shows that in India group conversion is just as important as individual conversion. One is sometimes tempted to question the genuineness of such conversions as they seem to be the result of communal pressure. But Wingate also notes that when people convert it is more than for pragmatic reasons. They perceive the religion they convert to as pos-

---

[87]Chan Kim-Kwong and Alan Hunter, *Prayers and Thoughts of Chinese Christians* (London: Mowbray, 1991), p. 40.

sessing "more truth" in terms of giving them direction, purpose and meaning in life. This is true even for the poor Indian villager. We would do them a great disservice if we thought their only motivation was material. As Wingate has rightly observed, "We should not underestimate the good sense of the villager."[88] Group conversion is hardly surprising given the strong communal identity. This can be both a strength and a weakness. It is a strength when the sense of community is transferred to the ecclesial community, but this is not always the case. In some cases, family or caste identity appears to be stronger than Christian identity. In the tribal societies of northeast India where a majority of the tribes are Christian, intertribal rivalry is still very much a reality, leading sometimes to bloody conflicts.[89] The secret Christians of Sivakasi in Tamil Nadu illustrate the complexity of Christian conversion. These are mostly women who want to maintain family unity. Their husbands continue as Hindus for business reasons. The sacraments are important for these secret Christian women and some have taken baptism late in life. But even when the entire family becomes Christian, caste continues to be a decisive factor in the most important decisions involving the family. For example, they would rather give their daughter to a Hindu of the same caste than a Christian of a lower caste.[90]

The complexity and variations of conversion in Asia show that the traditional Protestant concept of conversion, which identifies "being saved" by means of a standard *ordo salutis*, cannot be readily applied. Rather, conversion is a gradual process that may begin with a hazy awareness and understanding of the person of Christ and progress to where certain essential Christian truths are more formed over time. Using the categories proposed by Paul Hiebert, the conversion progresses from a position where no sharp boundaries are discernible between the Christian and the non-Christian ("fuzzy set") to a position where one's

[88] Andrew Wingate, *The Church and Conversion: A Study of Recent Conversions to and from Christianity in the Tamil Area of South India* (Delhi: ISPCK, 1999), p. 281.
[89] Walter Fernandes, ed., *Search for Peace with Justice: Issues Around Conflicts in Northeast India*, (Guwahati, India: North Eastern Social Research Centre, 2008); A. Wati Longchar, ed., *No More Guns! People's Struggle for Justice* (Jorhat, Assam, India: Eastern Theological College, 2006); Yangkahao Vashum and Woba James, eds., *Peacemaking in North East India: Social and Theological Exploration* (Jorhat, Assam, India: Eastern Theological College, 2012).
[90] Wingate, *The Church and Conversion*, pp. 84-85.

faith is more clearly defined by reference to some identifiable core Christian value and to something or someone outside of oneself ("extrinsic centered set"). That is to say, Christianity is now understood as a relationship to another ("extrinsic") rather than just some inner change within oneself, and this relationship is with reference to some central feature of the Christian faith ("centered set"). In the latter state, Christianity takes on a more distinct shape but is not defined by fixed categories such as baptism, saying the sinner's prayer, joining a church, changes in behavior and so on.[91] New *ordines salutis* may be needed to account for distinctly different conversion phenomena.

The progressive nature of conversion is in fact very much in keeping with an older concept of salvation found especially in Eastern Orthodoxy. Their concept of deification highlights the fact that salvation is not an impersonal act. It is not some kind of grand rescue operation associated with certain types of evangelical preaching; rather, salvation is part of a larger process of being united with God and being transformed by that union to become Godlike. Deification points to the ultimate divine purpose of creation, which goes beyond soteriological concerns, namely, communion with the triune God. Salvation presupposes the fall; deification is the process that humans have to pass through with or without the fall. Thus Irenaeus compares Adam before the fall to a child who still needs to grow into Godlikeness.[92] Deification—being "by grace . . . that which God is by nature"—is man's "supreme vocation," to which he is called by God from the beginning of his creation.[93] The distinction between deification and salvation can be explained in this way: If humans had not sinned, the second person of the Trinity would still have to be incarnated. Like Adam in his "infantile" stage, we need to be accustomed first to the hidden glory of Christ as a man before we can fully encounter his "immortal glory."[94] Only in this way can the fullness of communion

---

[91]Paul Hiebert, "The Category Christian in the Mission Task," in *Anthropological Reflections on Missiological Issues* (Grand Rapids: Baker, 1994), pp. 107-36.

[92]Irenaeus, *Against Heresies* 3.22.4; 4.38.1-2.

[93]Vladimir Lossky, *Orthodox Theology: An Introduction*, trans. Ian and Ihita Kesarcodi-Watson (Crestwood, NY: St. Vladimir's Seminary Press, 1989), pp. 71-72.

[94]Irenaeus, *Against Heresies* 4.38.1.

within the Godhead be communicated to humanity and our human participation in God be fully actualized.

According to Lossky, following the tradition begun by Maximus the Confessor, the very nature of God's creation *ex nihilo* involves a separation between the Creator and creation. This separation or division runs through the entire creation itself: between celestial and terrestrial, between the intelligible and the sensible; in the sensible creation, between heaven and earth; on earth, between Paradise and the rest of the world; and within Paradise, between male and female. The "vocation" of Adam was to bring these natural divisions into a deeper union and communion: between God and humanity, among humanity (a growth in love), and even between human and nonhuman creation. "Thus in the overcoming of the primordial separation of the created and uncreated, there would be accomplished man's deification, and by him, of the whole universe."[95] Redemption is only the way of God to put us back on the original trajectory that Adam failed to realize. Communion is always a union of difference, perhaps closer to the Taoist concept of harmony of opposites than the Hindu concept of absorption into Brahman.

But however conversion is defined, certain changed patterns of behavior must be evident if the term "conversion" is to mean anything. This change goes beyond individual transformation and includes new patterns of ordering church life. Failure of the church to live out its faith as a redeemed community constitutes the most serious stumbling block to conversion and the retention of new converts. Wingate notes repeatedly that part of the failure of mission in India is the failure of the church's practical witness leading to reversion to Hinduism or Islam. When the church proclaims full equality in Christ but fails to demonstrate it in its practice, its proclamation becomes unconvincing. When caste and tribal loyalties continue to divide the church it is small wonder that some who have joined the church with the hope of a different way of life became deeply disappointed and reverted to their former religion.[96]

---

[95]Lossky, *Orthodox Theology*, p. 74.
[96]Wingate, *The Church and Conversion*, p. 291.

THE PARTICULAR AND UNIVERSAL CHRIST

One of the distinctive marks of Christianity is its belief that while divine revelation was originally communicated in Hebrew and Greek, it is not confined to these languages. Along with preaching the gospel, Christian mission has also engaged in translating the Bible into local languages. Underlying this impulse is the incarnation and the Pentecost event. Incarnation underscores the truth of particularity. God became man—a male Jew in the land of Judea in the days of King Herod. The gospel is about the person of Jesus Christ, whose unique life, death and resurrection affects every person on earth and even the entire cosmos. It cannot be reduced to a christic principle. But the Pentecost event universalizes that particularity by making the gospel message infinitely translatable into any language. The speaking in tongues on the day of Pentecost reverses the confusion of tongues at the Tower of Babel and makes all languages translatable.[97] The church, which is the communion of the Holy Spirit, is not united by one language but by a multiplicity of languages from every nation, tongue and tribe (Rev 7:9).

It is not coincidental that early Pentecostals regarded glossolalia as the language of the Spirit. The one language of the Spirit is to be found in its diversity. The gospel, Lamin Sanneh has pointed out, is infinitely translatable;[98] it can be translated into any language without loss. At the same time, its translatability poses one of the greatest challenges in the church's mission: how does the church discover its larger unity transcending language and culture without destroying its unique local identities? One of the greatest challenges to the development of local theologies in Asia is the sheer diversity and multiplicity of ethnic and tribal groups. They are a constant source of real and potential conflicts both in the church and society at large. This raises a serious problem of contextualization: how local should local theologies be? To develop local the-

---

[97]See the insightful essay by Daniela C. Augustine, "The Empowered Church: Ecclesiological Dimensions of the Event of Pentecost," in *Toward a Pentecostal Ecclesiology: The Church and the Fivefold Gospel*, ed. John Christopher Thomas (Cleveland, TN: CPT, 2010), pp. 157-80.
[98]Lamin Sanneh, *Translating the Message: The Missionary Impact on Culture*, rev. ed. (Maryknoll, NY: Orbis, 2009).

ologies along strictly tribal lines would only accentuate the tribal divide.[99] In the end the universality of the church is undermined. This is the age-old issue of the tension between the local and universal. Here, Christology can play a significant role: Christ is both the universal Christ who is over all (Colossians) and who never ceases to be the particular Christ who uplifts individual personhood and dignity. The resurrected Christ who transcends space and time is also the Christ who appears to his disciples, eats fish with them, and challenges Thomas to put his hands on his pierced side. This is made possible by the gift of the Spirit who, as the "other Paraclete," communicates both Christ's real presence to particular persons as well as throughout his church in the Eucharist.

CONCLUSION

Christology in Asia reveals a number of contrasts. First, there is the contrast between the elite and the grassroots. Elitist Christology tends to focus on the sociopolitical dimension of life, while the grassroots tends to highlight the ethnographic. For elite theologians liberation is freedom from poverty and political oppression; for the grassroots liberation is physical and psychospiritual: healing of bodies and freedom from the fear of evil spirits and fatalism. The Christ of elite theologians is encountered in dialogues with religion, culture and the poor; the Christ of grassroots Christianity is encountered in Christophanies, healings and deliverance from demonic spirits, big and small instances of answered prayers, and special providences. Second, there are broad dissimilarities in soteriological emphases between popular forms of Christianity in Asia and their Western counterparts, such as evangelical Protestantism. Asian Christianity stresses the cosmic, corporate and progressive nature of salvation, while Western evangelicalism tends to emphasize the juridical and individual nature of salvation and salvation as a crisis event. The former prefers the soteriological motifs of Hebrews and Colossians while the latter favors Romans and Galatians.

Perhaps the most distinctive contribution from Asian grassroots

---

[99]The problem has been highlighted by Schreiter, *Constructing Local Theologies* (Maryknoll, NY: Orbis, 1985), pp. 37-38.

Christianity is the understanding of Jesus as the ancestor-mediator. This offers a theological basis for addressing one of the most intractable issues, namely, ancestral veneration, and with it the doctrine of the communion of saints. Tracing the practice of ancestral veneration to its christological foundation has also bequeathed to the wider church a more catholic ecclesiology. This will be taken up in the final chapter.

5

THE HOLY SPIRIT
AND SPIRITUALITY

THE SPIRIT IS THE Spirit of communion (2 Cor 13:14). The Christian tradition refers to the Holy Spirit, following Augustine, as the bond of love between the Father and the Son and by extension the bond of love between the church and its head, Christ. As Pannenberg puts it, the Holy Spirit is the "condition and medium" of the fellowship between the Father and the Son and "only on this basis may the imparting of the Spirit to believers be seen as their incorporation into the fellowship of the Son with the Father."[1] Or, as Ratzinger would put it, if somewhat more strongly, if the Spirit who is love and unity is God's gift to the church, then the statement "the church is love" is a dogmatic statement.[2]

But how are we to understand the relation of the Spirit to the world? Given the multireligious context of Asia, the question takes on a special urgency. The issue is simply this: If God is truly the Lord of the whole world, what are we to make of the differing spiritual quests? In much contemporary discussion pneumatology has become the primary means of framing this question.[3] While the pneumatological highlights im-

---

[1]Wolfhart Pannenberg, *Systematic Theology* (Grand Rapids: Eerdmans, 1991), 1:316.
[2]Joseph Ratzinger, "The Holy Spirit as *Communio*: Concerning the Relationship of Pneumatology and Spirituality in Augustine," *Communio* 25, no. 2 (Summer 1998): 334-35, 339.
[3]We see this, for example, in Pentecostal theologian Amos Yong, who has sought to develop a theology of religions based on the universal presence of the Spirit. In fact, for Yong, pneumatology has become the foundational principle. See *The Spirit Poured Out on All Flesh: Pentecostalism and the Possibility of Global Theology* (Grand Rapids: Baker, 2005).

portant problems that were not adequately addressed in the past, a more crucial question is how the pneumatological dimension of this question is to be related to the whole trinitarian economy.

Traditionally, God's relation to the world outside of his special covenantal relationship with Israel and the church has not been understood in primarily pneumatological terms. These older attempts have tended to focus on God's role as the Creator. If the world was created by God it must in some ways reflect the divine glory (Ps 19:1). Humans in particular reflect God in a greater way by virtue of their being made in God's image. In spite of the fall, the *imago Dei* is not completely erased; otherwise, humans would cease to be humans. There remain in creation the imprints of God (*vestigia Dei*), and in the case of human beings, they retain some true knowledge of God (*prisca theologia*). These imprints are often explicated in terms of conscience and natural law based on such texts as Romans 2:14-15. They are predicated on God's covenants with Adam and Noah, which cover the whole creation.[4] Nowadays, the concept of the *vestigia Dei* has generally fallen out of favor as being too static. It implies that the point of contact between the Creator and the creation is based on a work that occurred in the past. It seems to preclude God's continuing operation in the world, both in humans and in nonhuman creation.

The concept of the cosmic Christ is offered as a way to move beyond the static conception. As we have already noted in the previous chapter, it was popular in mainline Protestant theology in Asia in the 1970s and continues to be employed in certain inclusivist theories of religion.[5] First, Christ is the one through whom God made the world and therefore can be said to be more immediately connected with creation. Furthermore his coming into the world reestablishes God's relationship with the world. But advocates of the cosmic Christ take it a step further by identifying certain processes in the world as signs of Christ's continuing "incarnation." It is not just the historical Christ who came at a point in history but the continuing presence of the cosmic Christ that accounts

---

[4]See above pp. 62-63.
[5]For example see Jacques Dupuis, *Toward a Christian Theology of Religious Pluralism* (Maryknoll, NY: Orbis, 1997).

for the salvific work of Christ outside the church. Certain "christic" principles manifested in movements and religions promoting peace, justice and freedom are instances of the presence of the cosmic Christ.

In yet more recent times God's relationship with the world has been understood in terms of the sending of the Spirit. As the *Creator Spiritus* the Spirit is the active agent ordering the affairs of the world in order to realize God's redemptive purpose, not just for humans but also the whole creation. The Spirit is conceived as actively at work in movements that promote liberation, justice and peace. God's relation to the world cannot be confined to what he has done at creation (*vestigia Dei*) or to certain common principles or aspirations that Christians and people of other faiths share (cosmic Christ); God is actively working by his Spirit to accomplish his purpose in the world. What we see in Christianity is only one instantiation of the Spirit's activity throughout the world, both in creation and in human beings. It is also thought that a pneumatological approach to understanding God's relation to the world would address the ecological question more adequately.

There are different ways of understanding the Spirit's relation to the world.[6] One form conceives of the Spirit in almost pantheistic terms. The Spirit is the life force animating all of life, human and nonhuman equally. Driven by a deep ecological concern, it rejects all forms of anthropocentric understandings of the Spirit in favor of "biocentrism."[7] Others, while affirming the presence of the Spirit in the world, have sought to give a more critical role to the presence of the Spirit in the Christian tradition. Michael Welker, for example, rejects as inadequate pneumatologies based on the Enlightenment paradigm that looks for truth in universal principles ("old European metaphysics," "dialogical personalism" and "social moralism")[8] and instead offers a "realistic the-

---

[6]For more examples, see Simon Chan, *Pentecostal Ecclesiology: An Essay on the Development of Doctrine* (Blandford Forum, Dorset, UK: Deo, 2011), chap. 1.

[7]For example, see Mark I. Wallace, *Fragments of the Spirit: Nature, Violence, and the Renewal of Creation* (New York: Continuum, 1996), esp. pp. 162-68. Wallace calls his approach "ecological pneumatology" (9).

[8]Michael Welker, *God the Spirit*, trans. John F. Hoffmeyer (Minneapolis: Fortress, 1994), pp. 41-44.

ology" that essentially modifies the universal principles of modernity in the light of the ongoing work of the Spirit in the Christian traditions and in human cultures,[9] which he identifies as justice, mercy and the knowledge of God in their interconnections.[10] While Welker's approach may have given more specific content to the criteria for discerning the Spirit's work in the world, the basis of discernment is still broad principles rather than the particularity of the Christian tradition.[11] On such a basis Welker can make such sweeping statements as "The Spirit is seen in worldwide religious movements. The Spirit universally establishes justice, mercy, and knowledge of God."[12] It also has led him to confidently affirm that various liberation and feminist movements are the diverse works of the Spirit.[13]

For many churches in Asia God's relation to creation, especially through the presence of the cosmic Christ and the *Creator Spiritus* forms the basis for the church's threefold task of inculturation, dialogue and liberation.[14] There is, however, a difference in the way this threefold task is understood in relation to the proclamation of the gospel. Liberal Protestants and Catholics regard the threefold task as basic to and definitive of the mission of the church. In their view, proclamation and evangelization are incompatible with genuine dialogue. For example, some Asian Catholics have questioned the Asianness of the Apostolic Exhortation of John Paul II *Ecclesia in Asia*, since it sees the relation of the Asian religions and Christianity primarily in terms of preparation and fulfillment, respectively.[15] In point of fact, *Ecclesia in Asia* presents a view that is perhaps closer to the scriptural trajectory on a number of theological issues, including Christology, mission and the relationship of Christi-

---

[9]Ibid., pp. 46-49.
[10]Ibid., chap. 3.
[11]Welker's method, for all its nuances and caveats, is essentially not very different from the Tillichian method of correlation.
[12]Welker, *God the Spirit*, p. 40.
[13]Ibid., pp. 16-17.
[14]Luis Anthony G. Tagle, "Ecclesiologies, Asian," in *Dictionary of Third World Theologies*, ed. Virginia Fabella and R. S. Sugirtharajah (Maryknoll, NY: Orbis, 2000), pp. 74-76.
[15]For example, see Michael Amaladoss, *"Ecclesia in Asia:* An Asian Document?" in *The Future of the Asian Churches: The Asian Synod and Ecclesia in Asia*, ed. James H. Kroeger and Peter C. Phan (Quezon City, Philippines: Clarentian, 2002), pp. 115-17.

anity and other religions, which Christians in the Catholic, Orthodox and evangelical churches would have no trouble accepting. We will have to return to this issue later, after we have clarified the link between Christ, the Spirit, the church and creation. For it is out of a proper understanding of their relationships that a more coherent pneumatology vis-à-vis the religions can be developed.

CHRIST AND THE SPIRIT

More immediate to our present concern, *Ecclesia in Asia* propounds an evangelical or gospel-centered pneumatology. Repeatedly John Paul II stresses that the role of the Spirit is to lead the world to Christ while affirming what is true in other religions and nonreligious movements. The Spirit's work in the world and in other religions serves as a preparation for the gospel of Jesus Christ. This is essentially a reaffirmation of what he taught in his encyclical *Redemptoris missio*:

> The action of the Spirit in creation and human history acquires an altogether new significance in his action in the life and mission of Jesus. The "seeds of the Word" (*semina verbi*) sown by the Spirit prepares the whole creation, history and man for full maturity in Christ.
>
> [The Spirit] is not an alternative to Christ, nor does he fill a sort of void which is sometimes suggested as existing between Christ and the Logos. Whatever the Spirit brings about in human hearts and in the history of peoples, in cultures and religions serves as a preparation for the Gospel and can only be understood in reference to Christ, the Word who took flesh by the power of the Spirit "so that as perfectly human he would save all human beings and sum up all things."[16]

John Paul II's understanding is clearly in line with Johannine pneumatology. In all the five Paraclete sayings (Jn 14:15-17, 25-26; 15:26-27; 16:7-11, 12-15), the Spirit's basic identity is revealed as the "Spirit of truth" sent from the Father, and his primary role is to point to, testify, and glorify Jesus, the way, the truth and the life (Jn 14:15-17, 25-26; 15:26-27; 16:12-15). Even in his work of convicting the world of sin, righteousness and judgment, the main

---

[16]*Ecclesia in Asia* §16; *Redemptoris missio* §28.

focus is on his work as "advocate or legal advisor" in securing a conviction in order to vindicate Jesus.[17] The sin the Spirit convicts the world of is the sin of not believing in Jesus (Jn 16:9; see also Jn 1:11; 3:19; 15:22). The righteousness the Spirit convicts the world of concerns Jesus' returning to the Father (Jn 16:10); that is, Jesus' resurrection and ascension is God's way of reversing the evil verdict of the Sanhedrin and openly declaring that Jesus is indeed the righteous one (see also Acts 2:23-24; 3:13-15). He convicts the world of judgment because the prince of this world is judged. This judgment took place when Jesus was lifted up on the cross (Jn 12:31).[18] For it was at the cross that Christ "disarmed the powers and authorities" and "made a public spectacle of them, triumphing over them" (Col 2:15 NIV). The Spirit is the "person without a personal face" whose chief concern is to shine the spotlight on Jesus. He "mediates the presence of the Father and of the glorified Son to the disciples (14.16-26)."[19] Thus, we cannot speak of the Spirit's role in the world and the created order apart from his work of preparing men and women for the gospel of Jesus Christ. The church's "triple dialogue" with religions, cultures and the poor, therefore, must be carried out in such a way that Christ is revealed "explicitly as the one and only Savior." John Paul II makes this point in no uncertain terms:

> The presence of the Spirit in creation and history points to Jesus Christ in whom creation and history are redeemed and fulfilled. The presence and action of the Spirit both before the Incarnation and in the climactic moment of Pentecost point always to Jesus and to the salvation he brings. So too *the Holy Spirit's universal presence can never be separated from his activity within the Body of Christ, the Church.*[20]

As the above quote makes clear, the cosmic Christ cannot be reduced to a christic principle, nor the *Creator Spiritus* reduced to movements of liberation, nor can the two be separated from each other or from the church. This is very much in accordance with the scriptural trajectory. Even in the

---

[17]G. R. Beasley-Murray, *Gospel of Life: Theology in the Fourth Gospel* (Peabody, MA: Hendrickson, 1991), p. 72.
[18]Ibid., p. 77.
[19]Max M. B. Turner, *The Holy Spirit and Spiritual Gifts* (Peabody, MA: Hendrickson, 1996), pp. 80-81.
[20]*Ecclesia in Asia* §16; *Redemptoris missio* §29. Emphasis added.

locus classicus on the cosmic Christ in Colossians (Col 1:15-20), his universal presence is understood in relation to his being "the head of the body, the church" (Col 1:18 NIV). The cosmic Christ comes to his own only in relation to the Spirit. The ascension of Christ to assume his universal role corresponds exactly to the descent of the Holy Spirit to the church to actualize Christ's universal presence. Jesus' "departure" through the cross, resurrection and ascension back to the Father is the precondition of the Spirit's coming as the "other Paraclete" (Jn 16:7). This point is repeatedly emphasized in John Paul II's encyclical *Dominum et Vivificantem*.[21] Through the Spirit the particular Christ is universalized in and through the church.

The Spirit who, like the wind, blows where he wills, is at once the agent who universalizes the particular in its concreteness rather than reduces the particular to general and abstract principles. We encounter the first particularization at the incarnation, where the Spirit who "rests" eternally on the Logos rests on and indwells Jesus, in time making him the incarnate Christ.[22] At Pentecost the Spirit rests upon and indwells the church to communicate Christ in all his particularity to the church, making the church the "corporate" Christ, existing in its concrete particularity as the church catholic. Through the church the Spirit continues to communicate the particular Christ to the world through the church's mission. The renewal of the whole creation is possible through the church, as Boris Bobrinskoy has well put it:

> It is through the sacraments of the church, or rather, the "totally sacramental character" of the church as extension of the Saviour's divine humanity, that the life-giving energies of God permeate the world. The whole "natural" life of humanity is marked with the sign of the cross, with the breath of the Spirit, by the church's many "blessings" of the natural elements, times, places. The church's prayer upholds the world, exorcises it by freeing it from dark forces hidden in its depths.[23]

---

[21]*Dominum et Vivificantem* 11, 13, 14, 22, 27, 30, 61, 64.

[22]The "rest" of the Spirit is especially highlighted by Eugene Rogers Jr., *After the Spirit: A Constructive Pneumatology from Resources Outside the Modern West* (Grand Rapids: Eerdmans, 2005).

[23]Boris Bobrinskoy, "The Holy Spirit—in the Bible and in the Church," *Ecumenical Review* 41, no. 3 (July 1989): 361.

The cosmic Christ, then, is essentially his eucharistic presence in the Church. This is not to say that he cannot be present outside the Eucharist, but if he is present elsewhere, it is to lead men and women—indeed the whole creation—into eucharistic communion in the church. It is in and through the church that the Spirit's operations in the world find their ultimate consummation. Thus with Nissiotis we can say that "the pneumatological transubstantiates the Christological," but also the ecclesiological, making the church no longer just a sociological-functional community but an ontological-spiritual koinonia.[24]

SPIRIT AND THE CHURCH

In short, the church, through the indwelling Spirit mediating the cosmic Christ (that is, his eucharistic presence), experiences the particular Christ universally. But what is the relationship between the Spirit and the church? The Christian tradition has been quite unequivocal that the Spirit's basic identity is defined by his relationship to the church. The Spirit is the Spirit of God, sent from the Father through Jesus Christ primarily to the church and therefore the Spirit is the Spirit *of the church.* This is why not only in the Nicene-Constantinopolitan Creed is the church understood as part of the third article, but also in some early baptismal creeds the question posed to catechumens was: "Do you believe in the Holy Spirit in the holy church?" Their intimate relationship can even be described as a mutual conditioning. I have touched on this elsewhere and so will not repeat it here.[25]

This experience of the Spirit, as we have said, achieves its sharpest focus in the Eucharist. Again, the major Christian traditions have been quite unequivocal on this: the real presence of Christ is his eucharistic presence.[26] The Eucharist realizes the cosmic presence of Christ since it is where both the anamnetic and epicletic events take place. As an anamnetic event the church looks back and remembers the history of Jesus

---

[24]Nikos Nissiotis, "Spirit, Church, and Ministry," *Theology Today* 19 (1963): 488.
[25]Simon Chan, *Pentecostal Ecclesiology,* pp. 22-25.
[26]For example, see Douglas Farrow, *Ascension and Ecclesia: On the Significance of the Doctrine of the Ascension for Ecclesiology and Christian Cosmology* (Grand Rapids: Eerdmans, 1999).

Christ. In the Western church the anamnesis not only connects the church to her past but also her continuing transformation where Christ's real presence is actualized in the bread and wine through the words of institution. In the East, the anamnesis is followed by the epiclesis as the culmination of the eucharistic prayer, thus giving the eucharistic event, besides its christological basis, an equally strong pneumatological grounding. In the epicletic event the church calls on God the Father to send the Spirit again and again upon the church and upon "these gifts of bread and wine" that they may be transfigured to become the body and blood of Christ—his eucharistic presence—in anticipation of the Marriage Supper of the Lamb. The Spirit in a continuing Pentecost transforms the history of Jesus into "Pentecostal-charismatic" events transcending space and time.[27] The Spirit especially in the Eucharist unites Christ to the church, making the church the body of Christ, the "extended" Christ on earth.[28] The major Christian traditions are quite clear on this point: There is no cosmic Christ except the Christ who is embodied in the church through the Spirit. The church in the power of the Spirit in turn communicates this Christ to the world.

INTERRELIGIOUS DIALOGUE

The Spirit leads the church to Christ who leads to the Father. The Spirit is not satisfied with some "general revelation" in the world, or some hazy notion of divinity; his work is to lead the world to find its fulfillment in the church where the Trinity is acknowledged and glorified. If this particular understanding of Christ, the Spirit and the Church is in fact the Christian way of understanding the world, the question we must now squarely face is, how then should the Christian engage in dialogue with people of other faith traditions?

For John Paul II, the dialogue that the church engages with people of other faiths must always be governed by a Christology and pneumatology finding their fullest expression in the church. But can genuine dialogue

---

[27]John Zizioulas, *Being as Communion* (Crestwood, NY: St. Vladimir's Seminary Press, 1985), p. 130.
[28]See Chan, *Pentecostal Ecclesiology*, pp. 67-73.

be conducted on explicitly Christian terms? Before we answer the question, we might note that the pope's understanding of other religions in terms of *praeparatio evangelica* and fulfillment did not stop him from calling the leaders of other faith traditions to pray together at Assisi in October 1986.[29] It shows that serious engagement between people of different faith traditions can be undertaken without compromising their respective uniqueness. In fact, as Milbank has argued, it is only as we begin with "the truth-of-difference" that dialogue can be undertaken with integrity.[30] For an Asian pluralist like Michael Amaladoss, however, such a position smacks of Western imperialism and is an indication of a lack cultural sensitivity.[31] But as we have seen in chapter 1, the question about the "Asianness" of a theology often hides a deep theological divide; it is less about cultural integrity as it is about differences in basic theological orientation. Calling another person's position "un-Asian" is a convenient way of debunking a view one does not share. It may be an effective way of silencing opposing views but it is neither accurate nor helpful in assessing its merits or demerits.

The dialogue advocated by pluralists assumes that all religions can be subsumed under a common religious genus. It presupposes some kind of neutral ground or universal truth on which all particularities of the various religions can be temporarily set aside so that the dialogue partners can arrive at a common goal. These assumptions reflect the Enlightenment myth of a universal rationality. It is a myth because no one (not even John Hick!) have been able to define what that common truth is. In the end, the one common goal turns out to be the goal set by the dominant culture, namely, Western secular culture. The fact that many Asian

[29]D'Costa notes that the prayer is "multi-religious prayer" and not "interreligious prayer." In the former, each religion maintains its own distinctiveness in the presence of the other faith traditions, whereas the latter is "an occasion when people of different faith traditions plan, prepare, and participate in a prayer which all those who come can or may claim as their prayer." Gavin D'Costa, *Theology and Religious Pluralism* (Oxford, UK: Basil Blackwell, 1986), p. 149, citing *Findings of an Exploratory Consultation on Interreligious Prayer* §1, a joint statement by the Pontifical Council for Interreligious Dialogue and the Office on Interreligious Relations of the World Council of Churches.
[30]John Milbank, "The End of Dialogue," in *Christian Uniqueness Reconsidered: The Myth of a Pluralistic Theology of Religions*, ed. Gavin D'Costa (Maryknoll, NY: Orbis, 1990), p. 177.
[31]Amaladoss, "*Ecclesia in Asia*," pp. 115-17.

theologians have been sold on this idea of dialogue shows the extent to which the Enlightenment paradigm has shaped the Asian elite.[32] Even the idea that there is a commonly shared concept of justice and liberation in the religions is due to the fact that many religious elite in Asia have accepted the concept of justice and liberation defined by modernity.[33]

Thus, rather than seeing the preparation-fulfillment paradigm as incompatible with dialogue, one needs to begin with the question: How does the traditional doctrine of God's revelation in Christ affect our practice of dialogue? In other words, a theology of dialogue cannot begin with some preconceived notion of what dialogue ought to be; rather, if one begins with the givenness of the gospel, then it follows that a different definition of dialogue ensues. This is what another Catholic theologian, Gavin D'Costa, has done. Using the documents of Vatican II, especially *Gaudium et Spes* and other post-Conciliar documents such as *Crossing the Threshold of Hope* and *Redemptoris Missio*, D'Costa argues that a tradition-specific—in other words, a trinitarian—approach to interfaith dialogue in fact allows for more genuine openness, tolerance and equality than the approach of pluralists, although the meanings of these three terms are transformed in the process.[34]

D'Costa basically follows the pneumatological trajectory of John Paul II but faults the latter's interpretation for being too unilateral. It only sees other religions as finding their fulfillment in the church but does not seem to recognize that the truths found in other religions (*semina verbi*) could also enrich Christianity.[35] But D'Costa's view at this point poses a problem. If the Spirit's work in the other religions could enrich Christianity, does this mean that there is something the Spirit does in the other religions that he is not doing in Christianity? If so, what is to prevent one from concluding with the pluralist that some parts of God's revelation can be found in other religions that are not found in Christianity? D'Costa

---

[32]See the trenchant critique by Milbank, "The End of Dialogue," pp. 174-91.

[33]Ibid., p. 181. Similar critiques have been advanced by S. Mark Heim, *Salvations: Truth and Difference in Religion* (Maryknoll, NY: Orbis, 1995).

[34]Gavin D'Costa, *The Meeting of the Religions and the Trinity* (Maryknoll, NY: Orbis, 2000), pp. 99-101.

[35]Ibid., p. 141.

circumvents the problem by stating that what the Spirit does in other religions must bear some analogy with what he is doing in the church.[36] Specifically, since the Spirit does not bring new revelation but always points to Jesus and his teachings, bringing newness from the old, what the Spirit does in other religions cannot be new revelations either.[37] "Hence, all truth, goodness and grace wherever they are found outside the church can never in any sense contradict the reality of God's transformative life inaugurated in Jesus, and when they are incorporated into the practice and articulation of the church, their new context will transform them radically—as well as transform the church."[38]

Further, in a carefully qualified endorsement of interreligious prayer, D'Costa concedes that any overlap between Christianity and other religions is at best "fragmentary"; it does not apply to religions as "wholes."[39] It is clear from D'Costa's careful qualifications that if the Christian faith is to be further enriched by other faith traditions, these faith traditions need to be set within a distinctively trinitarian template. In the last chapter we will notice many examples of Christianity's own enrichment when the church in Asia deepens its understanding of the faith by its interaction with religions at the grassroots level. For example, in the matter of ancestral veneration, the practice of inculturation by the Japanese indigenous Christian movements not only helps Christians attend to neglected texts of Scripture but also opens up a deeper understanding of the meaning of the communion of saints. In Christianity's adaptation of folk religious values in China, the process of incorporating certain concepts and rituals from Confucianism allows the concepts and rituals to acquire a new meaning as much as the Christian doctrine of the communion of saints is further developed. Another example we shall look at below is Sadhu Sundar Singh.

Quite clearly, D'Costa is pushing the boundary beyond what is explicitly taught in *Redemptoris Missio,* which affirms the fulfillment of

---

[36]Ibid., p. 116.
[37]Ibid., p. 129.
[38]Ibid., p. 126.
[39]Ibid., p. 161.

other religions in Christ in a more unilateral fashion. D'Costa wants to see a more dialogical relationship where Christianity also finds some form of fulfillment in the interaction with other religions. His endorsement of interreligious prayer is predicated on this dialogical relationship. Be that as it may, the explicit teaching of New Testament on the Spirit, especially the Johannine pneumatology, is quite clearly on the side of John Paul II's understanding as seen in *Ecclesia in Asia* and *Redemptoris Missio*, whereas the scriptural evidence for a dialogical relationship may be (in D'Costa's own words) as "extremely thin" as the evidence for interreligious prayer.[40]

Given these qualifications, dialogue not only benefits non-Christian religions, it can benefit the church as well. We can begin with some practical benefits to the Christian. Dialogue is valued for its ability to clarify the Christian's misconceptions about the religious "other." Even for those who believe in the finality of God's revelation in Christ, their perception of that revelation may still stand in need of correction.[41] Furthermore, there is more to dialogue than formal engagements between religious elites; sometimes more effective dialogues may be occurring at the grassroots level between faithful practitioners of different faith traditions.[42] This is because while faith traditions as whole belief systems are irreducible to a common denominator, practically, in actual personal contact, people of different faith traditions often discover that they are not totally incommensurable. First, different faith traditions are inhabited by human beings who are capable of "the willing suspension of unbelief" and imaginatively "indwelling" another community. Second, most people of faith do inhabit more than one community. They are not only members of their respective religious bodies but also of nations, tribes and social institutions (the army, schools and so on). Each has its own ground rules,

---

[40]Ibid., p. 149.
[41]These practical benefits are recognized by both pluralists as well as exclusivists. See Bob Robinson, *Christians Meeting Hindus: An Analysis and Theological Critique of the Hindu-Christian Encounter in India* (Carlisle, UK: Regnum, 2004), pp. 164-65.
[42]Geoffrey Wainwright, *Lesslie Newbigin: A Theological Life* (New York: Oxford University Press, 2000), p. 227. For examples of such dialogues and their effects see Robinson, *Christians Meeting Hindus*, pp. 41-53.

grammar and logic.[43] To be sure, these entities are not equally important to the individuals who inhabit them, but each person is usually able to negotiate between them and move (though not always effortlessly) from one to the other. People can indeed discover common things within different traditions that can become the basis for dialogue.[44]

Certain common experiences—for example, deriving from being common citizens—might be the beginning for further explorations involving deeper matters of faith. To cite a case in point, when the Singapore government decided to legalize casino gambling, many leaders of different religions reacted with a common aversion. There was something from their respective traditions that told them something was deeply amiss. The Christian would see this as a concrete instance of the *vestigia Dei* or of the presence of the Spirit, but this understanding is derived from a distinctively Christian perspective. A Buddhist or Muslim might interpret it differently, but that is to be expected. Their reasoning might be different; still, what was it that made them share a common feeling that it was ethically wrong? That is a good basis to begin a dialogue.

HOLY SPIRIT AND THE CHRISTIAN LIFE

The above assertion that the basic identity of the Spirit is to be found in his relation to the church is confirmed in the experience of grassroots Christianity, especially in its evangelical and Pentecostal modes. They demonstrate in their practice that the basic identity of the Spirit is as Spirit of the church. Even if their imperious attempts to convert the world through the preaching of the gospel in the power of the Spirit and their modus operandi in church-building and church growth may leave much to be desired, there can be no doubt that these activities reflect an understanding of the mission of the church that is basically sound, namely, that the basic mission of the church is to point people to a personal knowledge of Jesus Christ as Lord and Savior, that evangelization cannot be replaced by inculturation, dialogue and liberation. In this respect, Pentecostals, evangelicals and Catholics share a similar ethos, if not theology, con-

---

[43]I'm thinking here of Wittgenstein's concept of language games.
[44]See Milbank, "The End," p. 185.

cerning the Spirit's orientation to Christ and the church.[45]

The theology underlying their practice can perhaps be better expressed in the Orthodox language of "hypostatization." The work of the Spirit is essentially to "hypostatize," to make humans more uniquely the distinct persons they are meant to be, to be a distinct "other" yet existing in communion with other persons, or to be in communion without abrogating personal identities. The advantage of the language of hypostatization is that it allows for its extension beyond the human to other rational beings and even nonrational beings. We have difficulty conceiving these relationships "hypostatically" because we tend to view their existences as somehow incompatible with each other: what do humans have in common with nonhumans and inanimate things? But as Bulgakov reminds us, there is a reason for the church in its final glorified state to be pictured as "the holy city" with all its physical details intricately described. "This directly indicates that this heavenly-earthly glorified Jerusalem contains the sum-total of universal history as well as the matter of the creaturely world." It is so because "the world has its center in man. . . . It is essentially human."[46]

The Spirit who "hypostatizes" human beings hypostatizes the nonhuman creation as well through human beings; that is, through the church the Spirit "transfigures" nonhuman creatures by sustaining them in their unique "otherness" or particular "mode of being." This is already anticipated in the Eucharist where bread and wine are "transfigured" by the operation of the Spirit.[47] We may not be able to conceptualize the way the nonhuman creation is hypostatized, but it is equally inconceivable that the new creation, the new heavens and new earth, will in any way lack the richness, variety and beauty of created things that we know of now. There was a prelapsarian creation with all the animals and

---

[45]For example, on the question of the salvation of those who have not heard the gospel, there is remarkable convergence between the view of John Paul II and the conservative Calvinist Terrence Tiessen.

[46]Sergius Bulgakov, *The Bride of the Lamb*, trans. Boris Jakim (Grand Rapids: Eerdmans, 2002), pp. 521, 520.

[47]On the hypostatization of the Spirit in the Eucharist and creation, see John Zizioulas, *Communion and Otherness*, ed. Paul McPartlan (London: T & T Clark, 2006), pp. 87-98 *passim*.

plants on land and who knows what variety of creatures in the dark depths of the seas! If the new creation is more than the restoration of fallen creation to its Edenic state but attains a state of full maturity in Christ that surpasses Adam before the fall, then the new creation can only have more, not less, of the best that we can possibly imagine now. Difficult though it is to imagine, since it belongs to the realm of "meta-history,"[48] it is not without basis in Scripture when it refers to the resurrection of the body, the renewal of the creation (Rom 8:19-21), the new heavens and the new earth (Rev 21–22).

THE EXPERIENCE OF THE SPIRIT AS PERSONAL INDWELLING

We have seen that the predominant understanding of the Spirit's presence in the world and other religions is that he is there to prepare people for their full encounter with the triune God and only in such an encounter can they be said to find their fulfillment. But the Spirit is present in the church in a distinctively different way. Only in the church is the Spirit present in his own person. Here we begin to see a realignment of the various Christian traditions. We see a parting of ways between Pentecostals and evangelicals on the one hand, and a convergence between the Pentecostals and the Orthodox on the other.

Orthodox theologians have been quite emphatic on the personal indwelling of the Spirit. The following statement from Nikos Nissiotis is representative of Orthodox teaching on this point:

> The communion of the Holy Spirit is not merely the actions, the charismata, the enthusiastic elements of the community life of the Christians but the personal "hypostasis" of the Holy Spirit. Church communion is not a category of the action of the Holy Spirit but the visible reference to his presence among men. The Holy Spirit is *koinonia* because in him and through him, the Father and the Son are One and present in the church. The communion of the Holy Spirit is his personal revelation as the Creator of the church in time in the grace given by the redeeming act of Jesus and the love of the Father.[49]

---

[48]Bulgakov, *The Bride*, p. 520.
[49]Nikos Nissiotis, "Spirit, Church, and Ministry," *Theology Today* 19 (1963): 485.

Vladimir Lossky goes further to assert that the uniqueness of the Pentecost is the coming of the Spirit to indwell each person:

[The Spirit] appeared as a Person of the Trinity, independent of the Son as to His hypostatic origin, though sent into the world "in the name of the Son." Then He appeared under the form of divided tongues of fire which rested upon each one of those who were present. This is no longer a communication of the Spirit to the Church considered corporately. . . . The Holy Spirit communicates Himself to persons, marking each member of the Church with a seal of personal and unique relationship to the Trinity, becoming present in each person.[50]

This Orthodox understanding of the Spirit's personal presence in the Church and with each baptized Christian seems to find a strange coincidence in the spirituality of grassroots Pentecostalism. This spiritual affinity can perhaps be better appreciated if we juxtapose Pentecostal experience of the Spirit with the spirituality of their nearest spiritual kinsmen, the evangelicals. They differ quite significantly in the way the Spirit is experienced in the Christian life. The evangelical tends to speak in terms of the operations of the Spirit rather than the personal presence of the Spirit. Calvin refers repeatedly to the "secret operation of the Spirit,"[51] and this seems to be the way evangelicals have understood and experienced the Spirit's work. In relation to the Spirit, they speak of being illuminated or sanctified by the Spirit; only in relation to Christ do they speak of a personal relationship. The emphasis is on the work of the Spirit leading people to a personal relationship with Christ; there is little or no consideration of the Spirit's personal relation to the believer and the church. Evangelical spirituality is clearly Jesus-centered. As one evangelical puts it, "Evangelical prayer is directed particularly to Jesus. Evangelical spirituality ultimately is obtained through Christ and into

---

[50]Vladimir Lossky, *The Mystical Theology of the Eastern Church* (London: James Clarke, 1957), p. 168. Lossky sees the communication of the Spirit to the church corporately in the Johannine Pentecost in Jn 20:19-23 (pp. 166-68). Lossky is perhaps correct if the first communication is to the *ecclesia congregans* while the second (Pentecost in Acts) is to the *ecclesia congregata*.

[51]Calvin, *Institutes of the Christian Religion* 3.1.

Christ."[52] Evangelical spirituality recognizes the distinctive work of Christ (Christ's proprium) but fails to consider the Spirit's own personal relationship to the believer (the Spirit's proprium). The Spirit's proprium is seen in the way Pentecostals refer to the Spirit as the active personal agent in their lives while acknowledging his work in directing the Christian's attention to Jesus Christ.

We see this repeatedly affirmed in Pentecostal testimonies. Pentecostals often use language that suggests a more direct working of the Spirit that impinges upon their senses. The Spirit is referred to not only in terms of powerful and supernatural activities; he is often spoken of as the subject of those activities. The Spirit guides, speaks, empowers, restrains and so on. This is the language used in the book of Acts (see Acts 13:4; 16:6-7; 20:22-23, 28) but is conspicuously absent in evangelical spirituality. For example, in Pentecostal ecumenist David du Plessis's classic *The Spirit Bade Me Go* (see Acts 11:12 KJV) we read, "I suddenly felt a warm glow come over me. I knew this was the Holy Spirit taking over." "I knew that the Holy Spirit was in control."[53] Dennis Bennett, one of the early Episcopalian charismatics, has something similar: "I feel peaceful. I don't understand why. . . . Quick as a flash, the Holy Spirit said in my heart: 'Of course you don't. This is the peace that passes understanding.'"[54] There is no question that what clearly distinguishes Pentecostal spirituality is the experience of the Spirit, not as an impersonal force but as personally present and active, carrying out certain actions as an active, personal agent. This was what Bennett noticed when he first encountered two Pentecostals who made a deep impression on him: "They seemed to know God—to be so sure of Him."[55] The language of personal agency is even more pronounced in the work of Korean Pentecostal David Yonggi Cho. Not only is the work of the Holy Spirit strongly affirmed, there is sometimes the tendency to conceive of the Spirit as a separate individual with

---

[52]Evan Howard, "Evangelical Spirituality," in *Four Views on Christian Spirituality* (Grand Rapids: Zondervan, 2012), p. 164.

[53]David du Plessis, *The Spirit Bade Me Go: The Astounding Move of God in the Denominational Churches* (Oakland, CA: David du Plessis, 1960), p. 16.

[54]Dennis J. Bennett, *Nine O' Clock in the Morning* (London: Coverdale House, 1974), p. 80.

[55]Ibid., p. 20.

whom the Christians can cultivate fellowship just like they do with the Father and the Son:

> Nowadays I always force myself to recognize the Holy Spirit, to welcome the Holy Spirit and to worship the Holy Spirit, because He is a person. . . . Dear Holy Spirit, I welcome you, I recognize you and I love you. I depend upon you. . . . Dear Holy Spirit, now I'm starting. Let's go. Supply all the knowledge and wisdom and discernment, and I'm going to give it out to the people. . . . Dear Holy Spirit, we did a wonderful job together, didn't we? Praise God![56]

Although in speaking of the Spirit in this way there is a real danger of fixation on the third person divorced from the trinitarian relationship, what is clearly highlighted is the Spirit's proprium—something not fully appreciated in evangelical theology.

The way in which evangelicals distinguish themselves from Catholicism might explain why evangelicals lack a robust understanding of the Spirit's proprium. Like their Protestant forebears, evangelicals tend to define themselves against what they perceive to be abuses in Catholicism. This defining-against becomes one of the hallmarks of evangelical self-identity: "The Protestants broke with the scholasticism of Catholic theology, the hierarchy of Catholic ecclesiology, the mechanics of late medieval spirituality, and the basic structure of late medieval Catholic ascetic and mystical consciousness."[57] The things that evangelicals are opposed to in Catholicism—scholasticism, hierarchy, a too-mechanical way of cultivating the Christian life, and mysticism—at first appear quite unconnected to each other, but on closer examination, they are built on the Catholic (and, we may add, Orthodox) theology that understands the union between the Trinity and the church in ontological terms.

In the West, scholasticism provides the language for explicating this ontological connection between God and his creatures. The church is not "caused" by God in the same way as a house is made by a builder (efficient cause), nor is the church caused by God in the same way as a cat produces

---

[56]David Yonggi Cho, *The Holy Spirit, My Senior Partner* (Altamonte Springs, FL: Creation House, 1989), p. 124.
[57]Howard, "Evangelical Spirituality," p. 162.

kittens (formal cause). In Rahner's view it is somewhere in between.[58]
The relationship could be called "quasi-formal causality."[59] God is not the
formal cause of the church; otherwise the church would be of the same
essence as God. By calling the relationship quasi-formal Rahner is
seeking on the one hand to emphasize the close identity between God
and the church and also to distinguish the church from God. There is a
close semblance and unity between God and his church when "God communicates himself *in his own person* to the creature," yet the church is
distinguished from God in essence.[60] In Orthodoxy, especially in its
Palamite expression, this close relationship is understood in relation to
the doctrine of deification: the church becomes Godlike, partaking of the
uncreated "energies" of God without being identified with God's "essence."
God reveals himself wholly in his energies while remaining unknowable
in his essence.[61] It is out of this Catholic-Orthodox understanding of the
ontological relationship between God and humanity that we can understand its mysticism, which goes beyond ethical union, and a hierarchy
that is more than functional. The church's hierarchy is parallel to the
order (or *taxis* in Orthodoxy) of the Trinity, founded on the monarchy
of the Father.

What evangelicals reject in Catholicism are precisely the things that
derive directly or indirectly from the close identification between the
church and God—an ontological unity effected by the personal presence
of the Spirit in the church. Furthermore, for evangelicals, personal relationship tends to be focused almost exclusively on the person of Jesus
Christ because of a shared human nature. But even here, the personal
relationship with Jesus has its limits: it tends to be restricted to Christ in
his humanity (his life on earth, death and resurrection) rather than to

---

[58]For some of its ramifications, see Ralph Del Colle, *Christ and the Spirit: Spirit-Christology in
Trinitarian Perspective* (New York: Oxford University Press, 1994), p. 74; David Coffey, "Did
You Receive the Holy Spirit When You Believed?" Some Basic Questions for Pneumatology (Mil-
waukee: Marquette University Press, 2005), pp. 28-34.

[59]Karl Rahner, "The Concept of Mystery in Catholic Thought," *Theological Investigations*, vol.
4 (London: Darton, Longman and Todd, 1974), pp. 65-67.

[60]Ibid., p. 67. Emphasis mine.

[61]John Meyendorff, *St. Gregory Palamas and Orthodox Spirituality* (Crestwood, NY: St. Vladimir's Seminary Press, 1974), pp. 122-29.

Christ in his post-ascension glory. This is why there is very little in evangelical spirituality that develops out of Christ's priestly ministry in heaven. It is also the reason that evangelicals have not developed a spirituality of communion between the saints in heaven and the saints on earth, even though the doctrine of the communion of saints is an article of faith. The post-ascension story of Christ is particularly important for pneumatology because it includes the story of the sending of the Spirit from the Father through Christ. The ascension of Christ corresponds to the descent of the Holy Spirit. The ministry of the ascended Christ coincides with the coming of the Spirit in his own person to indwell the church. This personal indwelling is what grassroots Pentecostalism instinctively recognizes in its experience. It is within the context of the Spirit's own distinctive work, his personal presence in the church that we can better deal with issues such as extraordinary phenomena and contact with the world of spirits—in short, matters covered in the study of mystical theology.

THE SPIRIT AND CONTACT WITH THE SPIRITUAL WORLD

The Spirit unites the church to its head Christ and unites all believers in a communion that transcends space and time. This implies that through the Spirit believers on earth and those who have departed this world are in fact in communion. It is not coincidental that those who are most acutely aware of the personal presence of the Spirit are also most open to the extraordinary world of dreams and visions. Most Pentecostals may not have such experiences themselves but are quite open (sometimes naively so) to those who have. Those with claims to extraordinary experiences of the spiritual world are more likely to find a ready audience among Pentecostals than any other group of Christians. Yet in a context where a theology of extraordinary phenomena is most sorely needed, it is most sorely lacking. A common mistake is for Pentecostals to read their own visions too literally, as if they picture exactly the realities in the spiritual world. A lot of visions are actually rearrangements of previous images already implanted in the mind. As Underhill puts it, "If we would cease . . . to regard visions and voices as objective, and be content to see in them forms of symbolic expressions, ways in which the subconscious activity of the spiritual self reaches the surface-mind, many of the disharmonies noticeable in visionary experience . . . would fade away."[62]

This does not mean that visions are merely the result of unexplained mental processes. It is still possible that God can use those very processes to communicate his truth, which is in fact how the visions that are judged genuine are often understood.[63] Visions require discernment and interpretation, which are best supplied by the Christian community. This is where the Catholic tradition has a distinct advantage. Over a long history of engagement with "enthusiastic" movements, together with its doctrine and practice of the canonization of saints, it has developed a body of literature, a meticulous process, and a tradition for the discerning of spirits.[64] Protestantism, lacking a comprehensive doctrine of the communion of saints and a controlling magisterium, has left the work of the discerning of spirits very much to individual visionaries. A common mistake is to think that somehow having received a special vision gives one an inherent authority to teach. But if the Christian tradition is any guide, it shows that even the soundest mystics have their moments of "temporary loss of balance."[65] Even saints made mistakes, and the true mystics themselves would be the first to admit this possibility.[66] One of the greatest visionaries of the church, St. John of the Cross, gives this warning:

> And I am appalled at what happens in these days—namely, when some soul with the very smallest experience of meditation, if it be conscious of certain locutions of this kind in some state of recollection, at once christens them all as coming from God, and assumes that this is the case, saying: "God said to me . . ."; "God answered me . . ."; whereas it is not so at all,

---

[62]Evelyn Underhill, *Mysticism: A Study of the Nature and Development of Man's Spiritual Consciousness* (New York: E. P. Dutton, 1961), p. 271.

[63]Augustin Poulain, *The Graces of Interior Prayer* (1910; repr., Whitefish, MT: Kessinger, 1996), chap. 20.

[64]See R. A. Knox, *Enthusiasm: A Chapter in the History of Religion* (Notre Dame, IN: University of Notre Dame Press); Benedict Groeschel, *A Still Small Voice* (San Francisco: Ignatius, 1993), esp. chaps. 5–8; Thomas Dubay, *Fire Within* (San Francisco: Ignatius, 1989); John Paul II, *Wonders and Signs* (Boston: Daughters of St. Paul, 1990). The classic work is probably Augustin Poulain, *The Graces of Interior Prayer.*

[65]Underhill, *Mysticism,* pp. 270-71.

[66]Poulain, *The Graces* 21.2.

but, as we have said, it is for the most part they who are saying these things to themselves.[67]

Pentecostal visionaries need not be left to their own devices. They can at least learn from those who have studied extraordinary phenomena, especially those accompanying a revival, such as Jonathan Edwards.[68]

THE VISIONS OF SADHU SUNDAR SINGH

The visions of Sadhu Sundar Singh may serve as an important case study. What is remarkable about the man is the unique place he occupies in relation to the broad theological spectrum within Protestantism. He was accepted by both conservative evangelicals as well as liberal Protestants with almost equal measures of enthusiasm. Evangelicals have produced a number of hagiographies of the Sadhu,[69] while mainline Protestants were enthused over him as a near perfect specimen of a Protestant mystic.[70] But Sundar Singh also attracted severe criticisms especially from the Roman Catholics of his day. A more recent historical study by Eric J. Sharpe rightly cautions both his admirers and critics against the danger of approaching the Sadhu from their respective preconceptions.[71] Sharpe was perhaps right when he said, "The main issue was perhaps not so much the credentials of the Sadhu himself, as the reputations of some of those who had backed him."[72]

The portrait that emerges from Sharpe's careful analysis is of someone who was highly enigmatic and controversial. Yet one must be careful not to give Sharpe's work more weight than what any historical study *qua* history is expected to yield. A historian living some years after the events

---

[67]St. John of the Cross, *Ascent on Mount Carmel* 2.29.4, trans. E. Allison Peers, Jesus Army, www.jesus.org.uk/vault/library/stjohn_of_the_cross_ascent.pdf.

[68]Jonathan Edwards, *Treatise Concerning Religious Affections* (1746), www.ccel.org/browse/bookInfo?id=edwards/affections.

[69]For example, see Cyril James Davey, *The Story of Sadhu Sundar Singh* (Chicago: Moody Press, 1963); Rebecca J. Parker, *Sundar Singh: Called of God* (Madras: Christian Literature Society, 1968); Janet Lynch-Watson, *The Saffron Robe: A Life of Sadhu Sundar Singh* (London: Hodder and Stoughton, 1975).

[70]Frederick Heiler, *The Gospel of Sadhu Sundar Singh* (Delhi: ISPCK, 1996); A. J. Appasamy, *Sundar Singh: A Biography* (Madras: Christian Literature Society, 1966).

[71]Eric J. Sharpe, *The Riddle of Sadhu Sundar Singh* (New Delhi: Intercultural, 2004), p. 20.

[72]Ibid., p. 136.

may not experience the deep emotions that come with direct contact with a charismatic and magnetic personality. It is easy to highlight the preconceptions with which both Sundar Singh's staunch admirers and equally staunch critics treated their subject. But historical distancing does not necessarily make the analysis more objective than that of those who knew the Sadhu directly. The people who knew him personally might be able to capture the deep nuances of their personal encounter while a historian writing many years later cannot. A good historical study, however, does provide a third alternative with its own limitations, shaped by the historian's own context and perspective. Our interest, however, is neither phenomenological nor historical but theological.

Sundar Singh's theology is basically evangelical at its core, which explains his wide acceptance in evangelical circles. But it also pushes beyond the boundary of evangelical teachings of the early twentieth century. This is particularly apparent in his visions of the spiritual world. The basic outline of his eschatology is remarkably similar to C. S. Lewis's. For instance, his *Visions of the Spiritual World* is highly reminiscent of Lewis's *The Great Divorce* as far as its substance is concerned, except that Sundar Singh portrays the goings on in the world of spirits as actual states of affairs, while *The Great Divorce* is a fantasy in the same genre as Dante's *Divine Comedy*. To cite a case in point, the Sadhu's account of the death of a German philosopher[73] bears a striking parallel with the artist in *The Great Divorce*.[74] One is obsessed by science, the other by art. In another vision a sincere seeker after truth, even though an idolater on earth, is given the opportunity to see Christ.[75] The story is very similar to the story of Emeth in C. S. Lewis's *The Last Battle*. When Emeth is welcomed by the Lion in the heavenly Narnia, he is confused:

> "Alas, Lord, I am no son of thine but the servant of Tash." He answered, "Child, all the service that thou hast done to Tash, I account as service done to me."

---

[73]T. Dayanandan Francis, ed., *The Christian Witness of Sadhu Sundar Singh: A Collection of His Writings* (Madras: The Christian Literature Society, 1989), pp. 257-59.
[74]C. S. Lewis, *The Great Divorce: A Dream* (Glasgow: Fount, 1991), pp. 72-76.
[75]Francis, *The Christian Witness*, pp. 261-62.

In response to whether Tash and Aslan are same, the Lion has this to say:

> I take to me the services which thou hast done to him. For I and he are of such different kinds that no service which is vile can be done to me, and none which is not vile can be done to him. Therefore, if any man swear by Tash and keep his oath for the oath's sake, it is by me that he has truly sworn, though he know it not, and it is I who reward him. And if any man do a cruelty in my name, then, though he says the name Aslan, it is Tash whom he serves and by Tash his deed is accepted.[76]

Sundar Singh's understanding of the nature of hell, like Lewis's, contains nothing like the divine despot dragging unbelievers screaming into the lake of fire. In his conversations with B. H. Streeter and A. J. Appasamy, he was recorded as saying:

> The heavenly light shows the wicked to themselves; they see at once that they cannot live in that fellowship of saints and angels. They feel so out of place there, they find everything so uncongenial, that they ask to be allowed to go away from Heaven. Men are not turned out of Heaven by God, Heaven is not a place with walls and gates where you have to ask for a ticket of admission. The ticket of admission is the life a man has led.[77]

He even seems to entertain a form of universalism, although according to Streeter and Appasamy, the Sadhu was reticent to speak about it in his public preaching.[78]

> I was also told that the love of God operates even in Hell. God does not shine in His full light, because those there could not bear it, but He gradually shows them more and more light and by and by brings them on and moves their conscience towards something better, although they think that the desire is entirely their own. Thus, what with God's work within and the Light without, almost all those in Hell will ultimately be brought to Christ's feet.[79]

---

[76]*The Chronicles of Narnia* (New York: HarperEntertainment, 2008), p. 757.
[77]Burnett Hillman Streeter and A. J. Appasamy, *The Sadhu: A Study in Mysticism and Practical Religion* (London: Macmillan, 1921; Kessinger Legacy Reprints), p. 126.
[78]Ibid., p. 130.
[79]Ibid., p. 128.

His doctrine of the communion of saints moves beyond the typical evangelical view and reflects an openness to the larger Christian tradition:

The "Communion of Saints" was a fact so real in the experience of the early Church, that it is given a place among the necessary articles of its faith, as stated in the "Apostles Creed." Once, in a vision, I asked the saints, and was told that it was to be found clearly given in Zachariah 3:7-8, where "those that were standing by" were not angels, nor "men" of flesh and blood, but saints in glory; and God's promise, on condition of Joshua fulfilling His command, is that he will be given "a place of access to walk among them (saints) that stand by," and these are his "fellows"—the spirits of men made perfect with whom he could commune.[80]

His teaching of an "intermediate state" in which "spirits" are being purified and made ready for the fuller life as "saints" in heaven is reminiscent of the Catholic doctrine of purgatory.

When people earnestly desire to live lives pleasing to God, the readjustment of their views and the renewal of their lives begin in this world. Not only does the Spirit of God teach them directly, but in the secret chamber of their hearts they are helped by communion with the saints, who, unseen by them, are ever at hand to assist them towards the good. But, as many Christian believers, as well as non-Christian seekers after truth, die while still holding false and partial views of truth, their views are corrected in the world of spirits, provided that they are not obstinately welded to their opinions, and are willing to learnt [sic], because neither in this world, nor in the next, does God, or any servant of His, force a man to believe anything against his will.[81]

His idea of hell is that it is essentially the assertion of human self-will: "God neither cast any one into hell, nor will He ever do so, but man himself, by being entangled in sin, creates hell for himself. God never created any hell."[82] See Lewis: "I willingly believe that the damned are, in one sense, successful, rebels to the end; that the doors of hell are locked on the *inside*."[83]

---

[80]Francis, *The Christian Witness*, p. 242.
[81]Ibid., pp. 260-61.
[82]Ibid., p. 266.
[83]C. S. Lewis, *The Problem of Pain* (New York: Macmillan, 1970), p. 127. Emphasis author's.

AN ASSESSMENT

Sundar Singh's theology could be described as a generous orthodoxy. It explains why he is accepted by both evangelicals and the more liberal Christians in the West, although, as would be expected of a person who stands at the boundaries of both traditions, he is also not fully accepted by both.

One difficulty for many Protestants who are otherwise sympathetic to Singh's theology is his indebtedness to Emmanuel Swedenborg. Sharpe notes that in the earlier years Singh and Swedenborg were sufficiently different for the Swedenborgians to conclude that he was "an unreliable witness," but in his later life, after his return from Europe, when he had more leisure to read some of Swedenborg's works, his visions were more readily accepted by the Swedenborgians. Singh specifically acknowledged his indebtedness to Swedenborg's writings and claimed to have seen Swedenborg in his vision.[84]

The story of Sundar Singh reveals the woeful lack of a tradition of interpretation and system of checks for dealing with revelations, visions and other extraordinary phenomena in Protestantism. The words of Sharpe are well worth noting:

> If the word "mystic" is to have any meaning at all, there must be control, evaluation, communication to a community having the collective experience to grasp what is being told. Protestantism of the early twentieth century variety had lost almost the whole of the experience it had had once. Whatever may have happened to the Catholic tradition since the 1920s, at that time it still knew how to guide, by precept, example and such just correction as might be necessary, the way of the mystic. Sundar Singh had no one to guide him. Eventually he was to take Emanuel Swedenborg as his guide.[85]

If Singh's visions had been subjected to the same magisterial rigors with which the Catholic Church assesses its saints, much of the "riddle" and the few theological ambiguities in Sundar Singh could have been

---

[84]Sharpe, *The Riddle*, pp. 148, 150-56.
[85]Ibid., p. 99.

cleared up. To be sure, evangelicals might still have had difficulty with some of his teachings regarding the communion of saints and hell, but there is very little he said that had not been said by others in the larger Christian spiritual tradition. We should not be surprised that this godly man made some mistakes; rather, we should be surprised that given the lack of a Protestant magisterium, he made so few.

CONCLUSION

In Asia the world of spirits is very much a part of everyday life. But how the church is to engage this world depends very much on its doctrine of the Spirit. In this chapter we have focused primarily on the Spirit as the bond of unity of the Trinity, between the church and the Trinity, and between the church and creation. But it is important to see how the bond of unity is achieved. Through the Spirit's indwelling the church, the church is united to Christ as his body and ultimately to the Father, the source of all things; through the Spirit-indwelled church the rest of the created order is hypostatized, brought into relation with the triune God in such a manner that it retains its distinctive "otherness." Thus only in and through the church does creation find its true meaning and fulfillment. Through the same Spirit the church on earth is united with the church in heaven as the communion of saints. It is in this ecclesial context created by the Spirit that we properly understand the place of "extraordinary" phenomena involving contact with the spiritual world, a world in which dreams and visions have their own place. The nature of the communion of saints will be further explored in the next chapter.

6

THE CHURCH

In Asia, theological anthropology with its emphasis on inter-personal relationships morphs easily into ecclesiology. If previously an individual's self-identity was defined by his or her network of family re-lationships, as a Christian he or she is now defined primarily by relation to the ecclesial community. If previously self-understanding took place primarily in the home, as a Christian self-understanding takes place pri-marily in the church as the communion of saints. Christianity, by intro-ducing a new eschatological community that claims one's ultimate (though not exclusive) allegiance, relativizes all other social relationships, including marriage and home. Thus, "those who have wives should live as if they do not. . . . For this world in its present form is passing away" (1 Cor 7:29-31 NIV). The tension between continuity and discontinuity is perhaps the chief ecclesiological issue in Asia. Different proposals on how to be church in Asia revolve around this tension.

Elitist Ecclesiologies

The so-called ecumenical perspective on ecclesiology is generally quite predictable. The one recurrent feature is the emphasis on the church's mission understood largely in terms of liberation, inculturation and dia-logue. This is true of mainline Protestantism and Catholicism. The Catholic perspective is perhaps best summed up at the First Bishops' In-stitute for Missionary Apostolate of the Federation of Asian Bishops'

Conferences (FABC) in 1979.[1] It spells out what each of these concerns entails. Liberation from poverty and oppression calls for the church to be on the side of the poor, not to create "a confrontation between rich and poor" but to bring "them together in love, in sharing, in service."[2] Dialogue is not opposed to evangelization since "the ideal form of dialogue is also the ideal form of evangelization, for it carries on the dialogue of salvation in which God speaks His word in the world." Nor does dialogue impugn the uniqueness of Christ since it presupposes the presence of the "Cosmic Christ in whom the uniqueness of Jesus of Nazareth is fully and finally manifested."[3] Inculturation is not merely an anthropological and sociological matter, but "a truly theological issue." It "brings the Good News into the heart of people in the concrete life-situation in which they are; it also challenges people to a change of heart."[4] Basically, the church engages these concerns through a "triple dialogue" with "cultures and traditions," "religions and spiritualities," and "people in need of liberation from poverty and oppression."[5]

Subsequent papers show that these three concerns continue to occupy the FABC to this day with dialogue as the means to engaging the other concerns.[6] In the early formulation on the church's mission an intricate balance is sought between the church as the "sacrament of Christ" in *Lumen Gentium* and "sacrament of mankind" in *Gaudium et Spes*.[7] But in some subsequent FABC papers the focus seems to have shifted to the latter. One result is a significant shift from the church's universal, hierarchical and institutional life to "basic ecclesial communities" or "the local church."[8] This shift is by no means uniform but reveals the unhappiness among some Asian theologians toward the official teachings emanating

---

[1]"First Bishops' Institute for Missionary Apostolate of the Federation of Asian Bishops' Conferences," FABC Paper no. 19, 1979, www.fabc.org/fabc%20papers/fabc_paper_19.pdf.
[2]Ibid., p. 7.
[3]Ibid., p. 8.
[4]Ibid., p. 9.
[5]Ibid., p. 5.
[6]Felix Wilfred, "The Federation of Asian Bishops' Conferences: Orientations, Challenges and Impact," FABC Paper no. 69, 1995, www.fabc.org/fabc%20papers/fabc_paper_69.pdf.
[7]Ibid., p. 5.
[8]For example, see C. G. Arevalo, "The Church in Asia and Mission in the 1990s," FABC Paper no. 57b, 1990, www.fabc.org/fabc%20papers/fabc_paper_57b.pdf.

from the Vatican. This is seen especially in the Asian Bishops' Synod called by John Paul II in 1998 as part of the preparation for Jubilee Year 2000. Before the synod Rome presented a series of proposals (*Lineamenta*) to which the bishops gave their responses.[9] The proposals in the *Lineamenta* seek to "address the question of evangelization according to the particular situation and needs of each continent."[10] The way the questions in the *Lineamenta* are framed presupposes the priority of evangelization, as seen in the following questions: "What specific areas should receive attention and what specific approaches should be taken by the church in Her evangelizing mission in Asia?"[11] "To what extent can the specific aspects of Asian religions be used and developed in the fulfilment of the Church's mission of bringing salvation to all peoples in Asia?"[12] "Describe the ways in which the Church can maintain the centrality of the proclamation of Jesus Christ in very difficult political, social and cultural situations. In what ways can the Church present Jesus Christ as the one and only Savior as well as the universality of salvation in Him?"[13]

The Asian bishops and theologians' responses are mixed. The Singapore-Malaysia-Brunei Conference appears to accept the official line of approach and responds accordingly. But the Japanese and Indian bishops are highly critical. The Asian bishops generally favor dialogue as the starting point rather than evangelization and proclamation. Some fear that if proclamation is made too explicit it will be perceived as proselytization and triumphalism. For the Indians, the basis for dialogue is the cosmic Christ,[14] while the Japanese bishops find the *Lineamenta* too

---

[9]See Peter C. Phan, ed. *The Asian Synod: Texts and Commentaries* (Maryknoll, NY: Orbis, 2002).

[10]*Ecclesia in Asia*, §2. *Ecclesia in Asia* is the post-synodal apostolic exhortation of John Paul II based on the Asian bishops' responses to the *Lineamenta*. The responses to *Eccelsia* are mixed. Some, such as Peter Phan and Jonathan Tan, see it as an imposition from Rome on the Asian churches; others see it as genuinely reflecting the Asian concerns. For an account of the diverse reactions see Nick Chui, "On Being Catholic and Singaporean in the Third Millennium: Identity and Mission with Reference to *Ecclesia in Asia*" (master's thesis, John Paul II Institute for Marriage and Family, 2011), pp. 12-19.

[11]*Lineamenta*, in Phan, *Asian Synod*, chap. 1.

[12]Ibid., chap. 3.

[13]Ibid., chap. 4.

[14]Phan, *Asian Synod*, p. 22.

Western and in its Christology "a certain defensiveness and apologetic attitude."[15] The responses of the more "progressive" bishops bear a striking resemblance to the Reconstruction of Theological Thought in China in the late 1990s. Both insist that their respective approaches do not undermine orthodoxy but seek to give meaningful expression to it in a different context.[16] Like its Protestant counterparts, the theological divide is framed as a difference between East and West. This is a form of self-legitimation. By presenting the difference not as a shift in dogmatic content but as a change in approach necessitated by culture, it can then be argued that the new approach represents a legitimate development of the Catholic tradition.

In mainline Protestantism, the ontological nature of the church such as seen in *Lumen Gentium* is almost totally absent. This is readily borne out by an examination of the documents from the Ecumenical Association of Third World Theologians (EATWOT). What we see is the church understood in largely functional terms. Further, of the three concerns that define the mission of the church that mainline Protestantism shares with Catholicism, the Asian theologians in EATWOT seem to focus almost exclusively on the liberation motif.[17] Even where the subject is Christian spirituality or indigenous peoples, it is understood largely in sociopolitical terms.[18] On the whole, the ecumenical perspective on ecclesiology is mostly focused on the church's mission in the world. Tagle's assessment, therefore, is hardly surprising: "Apart from the ecumenical perspectives arising from dialogue between mainline Christian groups, there is not much 'ecumenical ecclesiology' in Asia."[19]

---

[15]Ibid., p. 30.

[16]See the evaluation of Jonathan Y. Tan, "The Responses of the Indonesian and Japanese Bishops to the *Lineamenta*," in Phan, *Asian Synod*, pp. 59-72.

[17]K. C. Abraham, ed., *Third World Theologies: Commonalities and Divergences* (Maryknoll, NY: Orbis, 1990).

[18]Virginia Fabella, Peter K. H. Lee and David Kwang-sun Suh, eds., *Asian Christian Spirituality: Reclaiming Traditions* (Maryknoll, NY: Orbis, 1992); "Indigenous Peoples' Struggle for Justice and Liberation in Asia," statement of the Asian Theological Conference VII, *Voices*, vol. 34, no. 3 (July–September 2011), p. 67-74, http://internationaltheologicalcommission.org/VOICES/VOICES-2011-3.pdf.

[19]Luis Anthony G. Tagle, "Ecclesiology: Asian," in *Dictionary of Third World Theologies*, ed. Virginia Fabella and R. S. Sugirtharajah (Maryknoll, NY: Orbis, 2000).

One wonders if this paucity of ecclesiological reflection might not be due to an elitist approach that tends to exclude other forms of theological reflection. But an elitist approach is increasingly recognized to be unsatisfactory not only because of its tendency to ignore the contribution of grassroots Christianity but also the failure to assess grassroots Christianity on its own terms. As one Catholic scholar has pertinently asked, "While Pentecostalism is truly a faith *of* the poor, has the FABC simply produced a vision *for* the poor?"[20] Consequently, a shift is discernible in the way popular religious movements like Pentecostalism are being assessed. An example of this shift can be seen in more recent approaches to *minjung* theology.[21] A number of Pentecostal scholars have risen in Korea to challenge the *minjung* theologians' claim to represent the minjung. Yoo Boo-Woong points out that sociopolitical *minjung* theology is not quite the theology of the *minjung* but the theology of the elite about the *minjung*.[22] The *minjung* are, in fact, better represented by the Pentecostals as the latter's largely implicit theologies are more readily received by the ordinary people.[23] Pentecostalism impacts society in its own way, but not according to the expectation of a particular sociopolitical theology.[24]

Similarly, the study of Kim Dongsoo shows that *minjung* theology and Pentecostalism adopt different ways of dealing with the problem of *han*.[25] While *minjung* theology locates the cause of *han* in sociopolitical structures, the Pentecostal preacher, who is often seen by the people as the Christian shaman, "unravels" their *han* by dealing directly with its immediate cause, namely, poverty and sickness.[26] Yet while incorpo-

---

[20]John Mansford Prior, "Jesus Christ the Way to the Father: The Challenge of the Pentecostals," FABC Paper no. 119, 2006, www.fabc.org/fabc%20papers/fabc_paper_119B.pdf, p. 32.

[21]Paul S. Chung, Kim Kyoung-Jae and Veli-Matti Kärkkäinen, eds., *Asian Contextual Theology for the Third Millennium: A Theology of Minjung in Fourth-Eye Formation* (Eugene, OR: Pickwick, 2007).

[22]Yoo Boo-Woong, *Korean Pentecostalism: Its History and Theology* (Frankfurt: Peter Lang, 1988), p. 206.

[23]Koo D. Yun, "*Minjung* and Asian Pentecostals," in *Asian Contextual Theology*, p. 100.

[24]Ibid., p. 98.

[25]Kim Dongsoo, "The Healing of *han* in Korean Pentecostalism," *Journal of Pentecostal Theology* 15 (1999): 123-39.

[26]Ibid., pp. 130-33 *passim*.

rating shamanistic practices, they also distance themselves from shamanism.[27] Pentecostalism adopts a nonelitist approach to social
problems and as a result has been more successful in addressing issues
that directly affect the lives of ordinary people. The two approaches represented by *minjung* theology on the one hand and Korean Pentecostalism on the other can be seen in other parts of Asia. John M. Prior,
speaking of the impact of the Pentecostal movement on the Catholic
Church in Asia, echoes the same sentiments of a Latin American theologian: "The Catholic Church has opted for the poor while the poor has
opted for Pentecostalism."[28]

THE CHURCH AND OTHER RELIGIOUS COMMUNITIES

Asia is the continent of the great world religions with their comprehensive visions integrating the "cosmic" (this-worldly) and "metacosmic"
(otherworldly) dimensions of existence.[29] It is hardly surprising,
therefore, to find the major ecclesiological issue revolving around the
church's relation to these Asian religions. The problem arising from this
relationship is further complicated by the fact that Christianity differs
significantly from other Asian religions with respect to the nature of
religious communities.

In Asia, the primary locus of religious life is the home. For example,
"Chinese religion," a phrase referring to a form of religious practice commonly found among the diaspora Chinese of Southeast Asia and con-
sisting of a mixture of popular Taoism, Buddhism and Confucianism, is
largely home-based. In Confucianism, even the ruler-subject relationship
is modeled after the family, which "has always been the centre of Confucian life and ethics." It finds its most conspicuous expression in ancestral veneration.[30] In Hinduism, too, most ritual expressions occur

---

[27]Yun, "*Minjung*," p. 99.
[28]Prior, FABC Paper no. 119, p. 30. The phrase was first cited by Miller and Yamamori quoting
an unnamed Latin American theologian. Donald E. Miller and Tetsunao Yamamori, *Global
Pentecostalism: The New Face of Christian Social Engagement* (Berkeley: University of California Press, 2007), p. 215.
[29]Aloysius Pieris, *An Asian Theology of Liberation* (Maryknoll, NY: Orbis, 1988), pp. 74-81.
[30]Julia Ching, *Confucianism and Christianity: A Comparative Study* (New York: Kodansha International, 1978), pp. 96-98.

daily at home. Devotees go to the temple only on special occasions such as on the feast day of a particular deity.[31] Thus in Asia religion blends seamlessly with family and social life. This close relationship between religion and family reflects the value that Asians place on traditional family structure and corporate life. This Asian value also forms a solid substructure of many an Asian church and explains why denominational churches in Asia, with their inherited beliefs and practices, tend to be more conservative than their parent bodies. The gay issue that splits the Anglican Communion is a poignant illustration of this: Global South Anglicans generally see it as a serious challenge to the basic structure of the family.

In Christianity, however, the community called "church" is essentially eschatological, as seen in the two major documents on the church in Vatican II.[32] The church exists not only as "the historical community of Christ" but also "the eschatological creation of the Spirit," which transcends history and points to the new creation.[33] Thus entrance into the new community may at times require severing natural family ties (Mt 10:34-37; Lk 14:26). This is why the chief marks of the church are baptism, which incorporates one into the new community, and the Eucharist, the eschatological family meal. While early Christians worshiped in homes, their worship enacted a new reality that transcends home and social relations. As Schmemann puts it, the church is formed in the liturgical gathering around word and sacrament, which begins with Christians leaving the world to "constitute the church" or "be transformed into the church."[34] The new community created by the Spirit at the very least distinguishes itself from the social and familial bonds that have shaped Asian religions for millennia. Frequently it detaches the Christians from their kin and loosens familial and social bonds. This does not mean that the church is a collectivity of individuals; rather, it brings families into a new network

[31]Eric J. Sharpe, *Thinking About Hinduism* (London: Lutterworth Educational, 1971), p. 38.
[32]*Gaudium et Spes* 45; *Lumen Gentium* chap. 7.
[33]Jürgen Moltmann, *The Church in the Power of the Holy Spirit* (New York: Harper & Row, 1977), pp. 33-35.
[34]Alexander Schmemann, *For the Life of the World: Sacraments and Orthodoxy*, 2nd ed. (Crestwood, NY: St. Vladimir's Seminary Press, 1973), p. 27.

of relationship.[35] The existence of such a community is both a threat and a promise. For some, chafing under the iron law of karma, it is the promise of a new beginning; for others, it threatens to undo cherished institutions built from time immemorial. Such is the nature of the church. While Christianity's Western trappings may pose a problem for the church in Asia, the greater problem by far is its eschatological orientation. It explains why Christianity appears so foreign to a world where the (extended) family forms the basic structure of society and where religion is coopted to support it. We see this especially in Muslim societies where "family honor" is everything, and there is no end to which one is prepared to go to defend it.[36] A religion that radically disrupts the existing family structure will inevitably be viewed as a serious threat to society.

The various ecclesiological reconfigurations in Asia are ways of addressing the tension that Christianity's eschatological vision inevitably creates. Basically, they seek to answer the question, what is the place of the family and other religious communities vis-à-vis the church? The question can be approached from different perspectives. Pastorally, some urban churches in Southeast Asia promote themselves as family-friendly and develop strong social services aimed at strengthening family bonds.[37] Toward the same end, others seek stronger liturgical affirmation for children in the church. For example, Indian Orthodox bishop Geevarghese Mar Osthathios appeals to Protestants and Catholics to consider admitting children to the Eucharist (which is practiced in the Orthodox church) since "children in Asia are among the most neglected children in the world."[38] But underlying these pastoral concerns is the highly contested theological question of the relationship between the church and the

---

[35]Stanley Hauerwas, *A Community of Character: Toward a Constructive Christian Social Ethic* (Notre Dame, IN: University of Notre Dame Press, 1986).

[36]Mohamad K. Yusuff, "Honor Killings in the Name of Religion," Islamic Research Foundation International, Inc., March 1999, www.irfi.org/articles/women_in_islam/honor_kill ings_in_the_name_of_re.htm.

[37]Michael Nai-Chiu Poon, ed., *Christian Movements in Southeast Asia: A Theological Exploration* (Singapore: Genesis, 2010), pp. 108-10.

[38]Geevarghese Mar Osthathios, "Ecclesiological Issues Emerging from Asian Manifestations of the Life, Worship and Witness of the Church," in *Tradition and Innovation: A Search for a Relevant Ecclesiology in Asia* (Singapore: Christian Conference of Asia, 1983), pp. 29-30.

world. Some believe that the way to resolve the tension is to develop a church with porous boundaries. Others, however, feel that precisely because of the challenge posed by other religious communities, the church needs to present a clear witness to its essential identity as an eschatological community. This intraecclesial debate is well illustrated in the exchanges between M. M. Thomas and Lesslie Newbigin.[39] Although the debate occurred in the 1970s, the issues they raised are still relevant today.

Thomas wants to create a church that is part of the larger Hindu community. Thomas's strategy is understandable given the history of Christianity, especially in the colonial period when it was perceived not only as a foreign religion but a tool of imperialism. Thomas argues that there is a "new humanity" that is larger than the church. There are two loci where this new humanity can be found. First, it is found in "struggles of societies for a secular human fellowship" that goes beyond shared ideologies.

> There are some struggles in which the men involved have come to realise the frustration of the path of self-righteousness of principle, law and ideology, and are looking for a new path beyond it, and open themselves up to the reality of transcendent forgiveness in the secular experience of mutual forgiveness which makes love and community real at the I-Thou level.[40]

In this secular fellowship, Thomas goes on to observe, there may not be "the full acknowledgement of Christ as Person" but "a partial but real acknowledgement of Him."[41] The problem with such a fellowship where Christ is not explicitly acknowledged is how Thomas can avoid reducing Christ to a christic principle.[42] The problem is exacerbated by the fact that Thomas does not sufficiently clarify the substantial difference between the two loci with respect to the person of Christ. The first acknowledges Christ only implicitly, while the second does so explicitly.

The second locus where the new humanity is found is in the "churchless

---

[39]M. M. Thomas and Lesslie Newbigin, "Baptism, the Church, and Koinonia," *Religion and Society* 19, no. 1 (March 1972): 69-90.
[40]Ibid., p. 72.
[41]Ibid.
[42]Ibid., p. 82.

Christianity" represented by people like Keshub Chander Sen and Subba Rao. Here Christ is explicitly acknowledged, but they stop short of identifying themselves with the existing institutional churches through baptism. The problem with churches is that they are perceived as "socio-political-religious" communities tending toward separation from the larger Hindu community. Thomas is open to the idea of a "church" of word and sacrament "linked explicitly and decisively with Jesus but remaining religiously, culturally and socially part of the Hindu community."[43] For Thomas the "minimum" at which a fellowship can be considered in historic continuity with the church is when it acknowledges "the centrality of the Person of Jesus Christ for the individual and social life of mankind."[44]

Thomas's second locus of the "new humanity" is perhaps less problematic than the first. Since Thomas acknowledges that it is still open to further development into the plentitude of Christ, it could be understood as an example of *prisca theologia*, a preparation for the gospel.[45] But it is not without its problem if it stops short of becoming fully a church. As Newbigin points out, a fellowship that is "explicitly linked to Jesus Christ" yet remains "culturally and socially part of the Hindu community" is a docetic church.[46] Historically, the church's very existence necessarily involves a break with the sociocultural-religious element that challenges the lordship of Christ. For Newbigin, the issue is not whether the Christian faith can exist without a community with its "forms, structures, practices, beliefs" (it cannot); rather, it is whether the community's structures are "congruous with the Lordship of Jesus Christ."[47] Newbigin believes that if the church is to bear witness in a secular society, it does so not so much as a corporate entity, but by its members' faithfulness in their witness and suffering in the world. To do so, the church needs to strengthen its religious life through worship, prayer, word and sacrament. This can happen only by maintaining strong ecclesial communities.

---

[43]Ibid., p. 74.
[44]Ibid.
[45]See above pp. 62, 130.
[46]Thomas and Newbigin, "Baptism," p. 78.
[47]Ibid., p. 80.

Thomas in his response to Newbigin explains his preference for the Christian fellowship remaining within the Hindu religious community rather than creating a separate Christian "religious-communal body" (a church). For only in this way can the Hindu community be transformed from within. Newbigin, however, questions the viability of such a "fellowship" as it would require "disowning the existing churches and starting something wholly new." One ends up creating another sect. Newbigin's warning of what Thomas's ecclesial program might end up as a century down the road could well be prophetic:

> It would be very easy to envisage—round about the year 2,100 A.D.—a litter of small Indian sects embodying in a fossilised form the particular ideas about secularisation, dialogue etc. which happen to be fashionable just at the moment, comparable to the litter of American sects which are the fossilised reminders of the living religious ideas of the mid-19th century.[48]

CHURCHLESS CHRISTIANITY

Leaving aside Thomas's idea of the secular fellowship, his proposal of a "Christ-centred fellowship" relates to a pervasive phenomenon in Asia, namely, "churchless Christianity." The phrase is used to describe a range of phenomena ranging from individual practices to more organized movements. It sounds like a contradiction in terms that a study on ecclesiology should include a phenomenon distinguished by the explicit repudiation of the church. The reason for its inclusion is that churchless Christianity, however amorphous it may be, coheres around a number of discernible characteristics and acknowledged leaders so that, phenomenologically, it can be considered a kind of church. Hoefer calls such Christians "non-baptized believers in Christ" (NBBCs).[49] He estimates that there may have been as many as two hundred thousand NBBCs in the city of Madras (Chennai) alone in the 1980s.

These NBBCs are mostly educated but poor. The majority are women, for whom, not surprisingly, the place of greatest significance is the home.

---

[48]Ibid., p. 81.
[49]Herbert E. Hoefer, *Churchless Christianity* (Madras: Asian Program for Advancement of Training and Studies India, 1991).

They have a personal relationship with Jesus Christ but do not belong to any Christian church. Many have come to experience Jesus personally through answered prayer and miraculous healing but they want to remain within a Hindu or Muslim cultural setting.[50] Baptism for them means entering into a different cultural community—a step they are not prepared to take. It is perhaps worth noting that some reject baptism over issues that could be considered adiaphora: holiness taboos such as cinema-going and wearing jewelery. Others do so over certain ritual practices such as the covering of the head for women in church. For Hindu women the rite conveys a very different meaning: heads are covered when one is going to a funeral.[51] Since in Hinduism one is free to worship a god of one's choice, for the NBBCs, Jesus is their chosen God. Usually the God who answers prayer is the God to be served.[52]

In Japan a movement with a wide following stemming from similar impulses is the No-Church (*Mukyokai*) movement founded by Kanzō Uchimura. Mullins calls it "the fountainhead of Japanese Christianity" as it was the major inspiration for other indigenous churches that followed.[53] Uchimura was strongly opposed to institutional Christianity, which he accused of trivializing the faith by keeping to a form without content. The No-Church movement should be better termed the "non-churchism" movement since *Mukyokai* is not opposed to church as such, but to church being dominated by its organizational life, formal assent to doctrines and so on.[54] Joining a church often means being isolated from family and community. *Mukyokai* seeks to cultivate in the individual what Uchimura believes to be the essence of Christianity without isolating him or her from the community: "Christianity is God's grace appropriated by man's faith," which provides the inner power to enable a person to keep the law—something that heathen religion cannot do.

---

[50]Ibid., p. 13.

[51]Ibid., pp. 14-15.

[52]Ibid., p. 14.

[53]Mark R. Mullins, *Christianity Made in Japan: A Study of Indigenous Movements* (Honolulu: University of Hawaii Press, 1998), pp. 54-67.

[54]Raymond P. Jennings, *Jesus, Japan, and Kanzo Uchimura* (Tokyo: Kyo Bun Kwan Christian Literature Society, 1958).

"Christianity is Christ, and Christ is a living person"; more precisely, it is Christ crucified:

> When, as at present, many things pass for Christianity, which are not Christianity—such for instance as Social Service, Ethical Evangelism and International Thinking—it is very desirable that we should call Christianity by a new name. I propose Crucifixianity as such; and when it too shall have been abused and vulgarized by new theologians, I will coin another.[55]

Mukyokai is decidedly nonsacramental in its worship since it is institutional Christianity expressed in certain rites in a church that is seen as opposed to Japanese religion and its rituals found in the home.[56] As Uchimura puts it,

> To me . . . [ceremonies] are not only not helps for worship, but positive hindrances. . . . I worship God inwardly in spirit and serve him outwardly in ordinary human conduct. This formless Christianity is called *mukyo-kaishugi-no-Kirisutokyo*, Christianity of no-church principle. . . . It is not a negative faith but positive.[57]

But Jennings also notes that Uchimura was not opposed to sacraments per se, but only insofar as they represented a form of Christianity that lacked inner life and content. Uchimura was open to baptism if he thought that it would help a person.[58]

AN ASSESSMENT

How is churchless Christianity to be assessed practically and theologically? Three responses may be given. First, churchless Christianity has other problems besides the ones Newbigin highlighted. Wingate notes that compared to baptized believers, NBBCs do not last very long in their faith.[59] Attempts to create loose fellowships of unbaptized believers such

---

[55]Cited by Jennings, *Jesus*, pp. 47-49.

[56]Jennings, *Jesus*, p. 77.

[57]Cited by John F. Howes, "Christian Prophecy in Japan: Uchimura Kanzō," *Japanese Journal of Religious Studies* 34, no. 1 (2007): 127-50.

[58]Jennings, *Jesus*, p. 50.

[59]Andrew Wingate, *The Church and Conversion: A Study of Recent Conversions to and from Christianity in the Tamil Area of South India* (Delhi: ISPCK, 1999), p. 204.

as the Hindu Church of Jesus Christ, or *Natu Sabai*, and the movement inspired by Subba Rao have no grassroots appeal and tend to be confined mostly to the elite.[60] Elitism is not the only reason for its failure; there is also a theological reason: the church is not only a new community of the Spirit, it is also a community of the incarnation, finding expression in a visible structure. Churchless Christians may relish a spiritual experience with Jesus, but in repudiating the incarnational dimension of the Christian faith, they fall short of its fullness.[61]

Second, while not minimizing the centrality of the incarnation for ecclesiology, we must also acknowledge that the present institutional church does not exhaust the meaning of the church as the body of Christ since it is still *in via*. If the present church has not yet attained its fullness, it therefore ought to be a little more humble and work toward becoming the one holy catholic and apostolic church. There are individuals, loose fellowships and informal ecclesial bodies that are not formally associated with the church, but that does not make them any less a true part of the body of Christ. What is remarkable is that other than their rejection of the visible church, churchless Christianity is basically orthodox.[62] Paraphrasing Irenaeus, if it is the case that where the Spirit of God is and where Christ is explicitly acknowledged as Lord and Savior there is the church and every kind of gift, then churchless Christianity in its various expressions must be understood as manifesting in some real way the church of Jesus Christ and may in fact have something valuable to teach the traditional churches, notwithstanding its inherent weaknesses already noted in the Newbigin-Thomas debate. As Emil Brunner urges, after his contact with churchless Christianity in Japan, *Mukyokai* and *Kyokai* need one another.[63]

Third, if conversion is understood as a continuing process along a continuum ending in perfection in Christ, could not unbaptized indi-

---

[60]Ibid., p. 194.
[61]Ibid., p. 205.
[62]Jennings, *Jesus*, p. 46.
[63]Emil Brunner, "Ecclesia and Evangelism : A Message to the General Assembly of the United Church of Christ in Japan, Oct 27, 1954," *Japan Christian Quarterly* 21, no. 2 (April 1, 1955): 154-59.

viduals, those in Christ-centred fellowships, and baptized Christians be seen as inhabiting different points on the ecclesial continuum? The concept is suggested in Vatican II, where the church is said to "subsist in" the Catholic Church. The phrase "subsist in" implies that though the one true church of Christ "continues to exist fully only in the Catholic Church," the Catholic Church does not exhaust the total reality of the church, since "outside of her structure, many elements can be found of sanctification and truth."[64] Roman ecclesiology can be pictured as a series of three concentric circles with the Catholic Church at the center, followed by Orthodox "churches" and Protestant "ecclesial communities."[65] Without necessarily agreeing with the particular Roman Catholic identification of these circles, it is possible to accept the concept of church comprising a number of overlapping communities moving toward greater concreteness, visibility and final unity as the holy city, the center of the new creation.[66] The difficulty with Protestantism in assessing churchless Christianity is that its ecclesiology consists of one big circle where people are either in or out.

INDIGENOUS CHURCHES IN ASIA

Churchless Christianity is not the only alternative to institutional Christianity. As Wingate notes, there are Pentecostal churches that appeal to the masses while making a clear distinction between Christianity and Hinduism.[67] They exemplify a way of being church that is replicated in indigenous churches throughout Asia. In India alone it is estimated that there are more than a hundred indigenous denominations.[68] Unlike churchless or nonchurch Christianity, indigenous church movements recognize the need for church structure and organization. They reflect a serious attempt to live out the Christian faith in a particular social

---

[64]*Dominus Iesus* 16; *Lumen Gentium* 8.
[65]*Dominus Iesus* 17.
[66]See *Lumen Gentium* 51.
[67]Wingate, *The Church*, p. 194.
[68]Paul G. Hiebert, "The Christian Response to Hinduism," in *Missiology for the 21st Century: South Indian Perspectives*, ed. Roger E. Hedlund and Paul Joshua Bhakiaraj (Madras: ISPCK, 2004), p. 332.

context; at the same time they seek to be identified with the church universal. Theologically, they do not differ greatly from denominational churches; what distinguishes them is a combination of emphases reflecting their peculiar context and their strongly independent character stemming from their charismatic founders. An example is the Mukti Church founded by Pandita Ramabai (1858-1922), which combines Pentecostal fervor with outreach to abused women and children.[69]

There are usually some distinctive features that set indigenous churches apart. The Ceylon Pentecostal Mission (later named the Pentecostal Mission) was formed in 1924 by two leaders, Paul Ramankutty, a Dalit, and Alwin R. de Alwis, an English college teacher. It insists that ministers embrace celibacy and wear white. This outfit not only comports with Buddhist practice in Sri Lanka but is also believed to come from Scripture: "Let thy garments be always white" (Eccles 9:8 KJV).[70] Another unique feature is the founding of "faith homes." These are places for worship and training but also serve as a communal home for pastors and church workers. Possessions are held in common and hospitality is extended to all, especially the destitute.[71]

Indigenous churches reflect in various degrees the eschatological orientation of Christianity. Needless to say, Ceylon Pentecostal Mission teachings are much more so.[72] Hiebert notes that while indigenous churches maintain a strong Indian identity and character, their links with the global church are weak. This has tended to result in suspicion, leading to the charge of syncretism.[73] However, among the Indian-initiated churches are Pentecostal groups that are clearly Indian in identity, but their Pentecostal faith at once links them to the worldwide Pentecostal movement.[74] Among them, the Ceylon Pentecostal Mission again stands

---

[69]Roger E. Hedlund, "Indigenous Christianity," in *Missiology for the 21st Century*, pp. 375-77.
[70]G. P. V. Somaratna, *Origins of the Pentecostal Mission in Sri Lanka* (Mirihana-Nugegoda, Sri Lanka: Margaya Fellowship of Sri Lanka, 1996).
[71]Ibid., pp. 35-36.
[72]Hedlund, "Indigenous Christianity," p. 377.
[73]Hiebert, "The Christian Response," p. 333.
[74]Roger E. Hedlund, "Indigenous Pentecostalism in India," in *Asian and Pentecostal: The Charismatic Face of Christianity in Asia*, ed. Allan Anderson and Edmond Tang (Oxford, UK: Regnum, 2005), pp. 215-44.

out. Not only is it international in reach, it manifests a rare ecumenical ethos. It has 848 branches in nineteen countries with 3,984 full-time ministers. Pulikottil describes it as "the first Dalit Pentecostal denomination in India . . . which integrated Dalits and non-Dalits in its membership and leadership."[75] In the South Asian context, its ability to transcend caste, race and social status is unprecedented when compared with other churches.[76] Another remarkable achievement is that it suffered no major division for nearly eighty years.[77] Paul Ramankutty was very much influenced by the Ezhava reformer Sri Naryana Guru (1854–1928), who "created an alternative public sphere" for the low-caste Ezhavas. The Pentecostal Mission too was an alternative public to those created by missionaries and Christians from the higher castes.[78]

JAPANESE INDIGENOUS CHRISTIAN MOVEMENTS (JICMs)

Like other Asian indigenous churches, JICMs are concerned about Christianity's alienation from culture, and within Confucian cultures of East Asia a major issue is ancestral veneration. Adherents develop a theology of the dead and appropriate Christian rituals to honor them. In so doing they challenge mainstream Christianity's culturally restricted interpretations.[79] For instance, Mullins notes that the JICM interpretation of salvation beyond the grave may provide fresh insights into the phrase "descent into hell" in the Apostles' Creed and neglected passages of Scripture such as 1 Peter 3:18-22; 4:6. It is perhaps not coincidental that some of the founders of JICMs were Pentecostal, and their movements still retain distinctively classical Pentecostal doctrines such as Spirit-baptism and glossolalia.[80]

---

[75]Paulson Pulikottil, "Ramankutty Paul: A Dalit Contribution to Pentecostalism," in *Asian and Pentecostal*, p. 246.

[76]Somaratna, *Origins*, p. 36.

[77]Hedlund, "Indigenous Christianity," p. 220; Pulikottil, "Ramankutty Paul," p. 246.

[78]Pulikottil, "Ramankutty Paul," pp. 253-55.

[79]Mark R. Mullins, "What About the Ancestors? Some Japanese Christian Responses to Protestant Individualism," *Studies in World Christianity* 4, no. 1 (1998): 41-64.

[80]Mark R. Mullins, "Japanese Pentecostalism and the World of the Dead: A Study of Cultural Adaptation in Iesu no Mitama Kyōkai," *Japanese Journal of Religious Studies* 17, no. 4 (1990): 354-74.

Mullins further observes that while the rites following from JICM belief, such as evangelism of and prayer and baptism for the dead, may strike traditional Christians as novel, underlying these rites is a basically orthodox Christian belief that salvation for all can come only from a personal encounter with Jesus Christ, who died and rose again.[81] It is precisely because of their strong conviction in the necessity of salvation through Christ that a major contextual concern (namely, ancestors who did not know Christ while they were one earth) needs to be adequately addressed. In terms of contemporary theologies of religion, the JICM approach can be seen as a specific form of the postmortem theory of salvation—a view to which some Catholics and evangelicals are favorably disposed.[82] The main difference between JICMs and other Christians is that the former have devised appropriate rites to address their peculiar concerns. This is important because in Confucian culture, as in many other traditional Asian societies, proper rites or *li* are crucial in embodying the Confucian way.[83] In popular Chinese religion rites are often observed as an unquestioned tradition ("It has always been done this way"), but they are regarded as no less important for it.[84] Further, the response of JICMs to ancestral veneration challenges Protestants to take a fresh look at their doctrine of the communion of saints. Protestants generally tend to confine the communion of saints to those who are alive on earth because its conception of the church is essentially sociological. A doctrine of the communion of transcending space and time presupposes an ontological understanding of the church as a spiritual, universal body of Christ united to Christ the head.

---

[81] Mullins, "What About the Ancestors?" p. 60.

[82] J. A. DiNoia, *The Diversity of Religion: A Christian Perspective* (Washington, D.C.: Catholic University Press of America, 1992), pp. 103-8; Donald Bloesch, *Essentials of Evangelical Theology* (San Francisco: Harper & Row, 1987), 2:227. For DiNoia, a postmortem salvation for non-Christians could be based on a slightly revised doctrine of purgatory since traditionally purgatory is meant for Christians in further need of purification (pp. 104-5).

[83] Julia Ching, *Chinese Religions* (Maryknoll, NY: Orbis, 1993), p. 74; see also Mathias A. H. Zahniser, *Symbol and Ceremony: Making Disciples Across Cultures* (Monrovia, CA: World Vision, 1997).

[84] See Tong Chee Kiong, *Rationalizing Religion: Religious Conversion, Revivalism and Competition in Singapore Society* (Leiden: Brill, 2007), p. 113.

THE CHURCH AS CONTRAST COMMUNITY

In the face of the great axial religions of Asia, Christianity as a minority faith could respond in the following ways: It could join forces with the majority to advance the welfare of the larger society by engagement in dialogue with other religions, liberation movements and cultures. This approach stresses Christianity's continuity with culture. Most mainline churches including Catholicism tend to adopt this approach. Others, however, believe that beyond continuity, there is a need also to highlight Christianity's discontinuity. The church is "in the world" but also "not of the world." It should not only exemplify the incarnational principle as the body of Christ on earth but also the pneumatological principle as the temple indwelled by the Spirit and as the firstfruits of the new creation. It exists on earth but comes originally from heaven: it is a divine humanity. Such a view of the church is found not only in traditional Catholicism, it is also elaborately developed by Watchman Nee (see below). The church is, therefore, irreducibly a contrast community in its present existence straddling two worlds. We will look at the works of two churchmen who exemplify this vision of the church.

Wang Ming Dao. Though not a theologian, Wang is nevertheless deeply conscious of the vast implications of the gospel for the church. And within the peculiar historical situation in which he found himself, he sought to create a contrast community that would indirectly challenge the absolutist claims of a totalitarian regime. Wang Ming Dao (1900–1988), the name he took after his conversion, means understanding the truth. Wang did not write theology, but in his many sermons there is a consistent theological ethics. Wang lived in a period of history when China was going through vast changes socially and politically. The impact of Western science and technology on China beginning with the May Fourth Movement in 1919 led to radical rethinking and self-questioning among Chinese intellectuals. Why had China been lagging so far behind? Such soul-searching led to the question of the role that religions had played in Chinese society. Inevitably Christianity came up for questioning. The Western educated elite saw Christianity as a superstition and a hindrance to progress. Many Chinese Christian apologists rose up to defend the faith. But Wang was seemingly unconcerned about these developments. This has led some scholars of this period to regard him as an escapist who was concerned only with spiritual matters.[85] But this is really to misunderstand Wang. Part of the problem is that Wang has been evaluated by a particular theory of social engagement—what Hauerwas calls the "Constantinian" model[86]—where the only recognizable form of social engagement is one that subsumes the church within a supposedly larger public sphere. Wang's approach is far more subtle, less direct, but no less threatening to a totalitarian regime.[87]

Wang was primarily concerned about the church and what it ought to be. He directed his messages to and at the church, but always with an eye on the way the church would affect the world. Even in his earlier sermons, when conflict with the Three Self Patriotic Movement was not on the horizon, Wang was consciously seeking to mold the church into a contrast community. In "Dangers of the Present-Day Church" he warned of the enemies inside the church, namely, the worship of wealth, conformity to the world and toleration of sin. His idea of holiness was not formed by the typical Holiness list of dos and don'ts: smoking, drinking, the cinema and so on. Rather, he castigated social evils that had crept into the church:

> The strongest evidence of this "Mammon Worship" is the prevalent attitude of attaching weight to wealth and of despising poverty. Vast amounts of money are in the hands of wealthy men. To get money, by following human methods, involves going to these wealthy man [sic] "cap in hand" and playing the sycophant. Wealthy people are invited to occupy the best seats in the church building and to fill the important offices in the church. Board members, Board chairmen, Committee members, Committee chairmen, Elders, Deacons, Presidents, Honorary pastors—these seats are largely occupied by people with money. . . . So long as you have money you can occupy the best seats in the church building . . . even when it is known

---

[85]Lam Wing Hung, *Chinese Theology in Construction* (Pasadena, CA: William Carey Library, 1983), pp. 22-23, 75-76.
[86]Stanley Hauerwas and William H. Willimon, *Resident Aliens: A Provocative Christian Assessment of Culture and Ministry for People Who Know That Something Is Wrong* (Nashville: Abingdon, 1989).
[87]Thomas Alan Harvey, *Acquainted with Grief: Wang Mingdao's Stand for the Persecuted Church in China* (Grand Rapids: Brazos, 2002), pp. 36-37.

that the wealth of these people has [*sic*] amassed by dealing in opium and trading in tobacco, or by using an official position to squeeze money out of people.[88]

His call to the church became even clearer between 1949 and 1955, the year he was imprisoned. In sermon after sermon he spoke out against compromise and for the need to be faithful and obedient to God. In "Nitty Gritty Faithfulness," based on Luke 16:10, he warned of the danger of making small compromises that in the long term undermined one's integrity and made one completely powerless. This was obviously a reference to the leaders of the Three Self Patriotic Movement:

> Suppose a piece of white paper is laid before us and most people declare, "It is black," but I insist that it is white. That will surely disturb those others and invite their ill feelings. Some friends might advise, "Don't make an issue of it. What does it matter if everyone is saying that the paper is black; go ahead and agree with them and keep peace.... Why not peacefully coexist with others and gain greater opportunities to serve them and witness for the Lord? ... If you persist in saying that the piece of paper is white, you will not only irritate others, you will disrupt all harmony with them and lose the chance to help them...." This kind of argument or logic may sound quite reasonable and attractive, but if you analyse it carefully you will know it is based on a principle which looks right but is completely wrong.[89]

Wang recognized that these seemingly inconsequential actions were deadening because they arose from fear:

> Today, because you are afraid to offend another person over such a seemingly small matter, and agree to lie, someday many people may say that a certain innocent person is evil—and will you have the courage to say that he is innocent when you know that he truly is?[90]

Wang's implicit hermeneutics is quite "postmodern"; it is a process of indwelling the gospel story. This is a feature he shares with many other

---

[88]Wang Ming Dao, "Dangers in the Present-Day Church," in *Spiritual Food* (Southampton, UK: Mayflower Christian Books, 1983), p. 39.

[89]Wang Ming Dao, *A Call to the Church*, trans. Theodore Choy, ed. Leona F. Choy (Fort Washington, PA: Christian Literature Crusade, 1983), p. 18.

[90]Ibid., p. 20.

Asian preachers. Their sermons are mostly taken from biblical narratives, especially the Gospels, and filled with anecdotes and testimonies. The truth is not an abstract principle but a concrete reality that is either confirmed in the daily lives of Christians or repudiated by unbelievers. For example, when Wang challenged his congregation to obey God rather than men in the face of the pressure of the Three Self Patriotic Movement to capitulate to the Chinese Communist Party, he did not launch into a discussion of ethical principles, dilemmas or casuistry. In the sermon "Obey God or Men," the example of Peter before the Sanhedrin clinched the argument.[91] For him, the biblical story had the ring of truth that needed to shape the story of the present-day church.[92] Wang's underlying "narrative theology" carries vast sociopolitical implications. As Harvey has rightly pointed out, "This was a war to decide whose rhetoric, drama, and sacred text would define the church in China: the ideology of the state or the dramatic narrative of the Bible."[93]

Wang knew what was really at stake. The line must be clearly drawn between truth and falsehood, between the church and the world. The choice between God and the world always comes as an either/or: "Anyone who works for God should make an irrevocable decision whether he intends to please God or to please men. There is only one choice—a person cannot have it both ways."[94] Only by remaining a contrast community can the church maintain integrity in the midst of incessant assaults from a godless ideology.

Vishal Mangalwadi. Vishal Mangalwadi is an Indian Christian and founder-director of the Association for Comprehensive Rural Assistance (ACRA), an organization dedicated to helping the poor villagers who are often the victims of exploitation and injustice perpetrated by their high-caste landlords with the connivance of a corrupt bureaucracy. Mangalwadi discovered early in his work among the poor that the problem of poverty was not a matter of backwardness in technology; it was part of a

---

[91]Ibid., pp. 23-28.
[92]Harvey, *Acquainted*, p. 74.
[93]Ibid., pp. 77-78.
[94]Wang, *A Call*, pp. 68-69.

system of ordering society based on religious sanctions going back thousands of years. When the rich and high-caste believe it is their right to be rich and powerful and the poor and oppressed also believe that it is their lot to live in poverty and servitude because the all-pervading law of karma so dictates, the only way to change this unjust structure is by changing people's basic outlook. Mangalwadi sees three possible options. First, one can minimize the injustices inherent in the caste system by enacting laws, but this will not fundamentally change the structure of a caste-based society. One can also try to change people at the top, that is, by removing those who are responsible for the injustices. Again, this will not do in India where the perpetrators of oppression of the lower castes number in the hundreds of thousands. The only option is the third, which requires a two-pronged approach: first, "to change the oppressed" by freeing them "from mental or ideological slavery" through gospel proclamation, and second, having them "opt out of the socio-religious systems" by joining a community that practices the gospel.[95]

Common to Mangalwadi and Wang is the central place of the church. Both see the church as a counterculture. But Mangalwadi is more explicit. He describes the church as a "power structure" that provides the antidote to structural evil.[96] Structural evil can be effectively dealt with only by a counterstructure that is the church Christ built, against which the gates of Hades will not prevail.[97] Mangalwadi chides modern theologians who "dismiss the very concept of the church as irrelevant to the struggle against injustice and the struggle for the weak."[98] For him, evangelism and church planting must go together: The church is "an inseparable part of the Good News."[99] His concern for the church reminds us of what D. T. Niles, the Sri Lankan ecumenical theologian, once said: "The answer to the problems of the world is the answer that Jesus Christ provided, which is the Church."[100]

---

[95]Vishal Mangalwadi, *Truth and Social Reform* (London: Spire Books, 1989), pp. 36-37.
[96]Ibid., pp. 106-23.
[97]Ibid., p. 109.
[98]Ibid., p. 101.
[99]Ibid., p. 107.
[100]D. T. Niles, *The Message and Its Messengers* (Nashville: Abingdon, 1966), p. 50.

THE UNIVERSAL AND LOCAL CHURCH: WATCHMAN NEE

While Watchman Nee can be considered as belonging to the tradition of building contrast communities, his unique contribution to ecclesiology is that he did not only successfully implement a peculiar indigenous church principle throughout China and among diaspora Chinese; he also developed one of the most elaborate theologies of the church as its basis. His concept of the "local church" will remain controversial, but there is no denying that it was based on a well-thought-out ecclesiology. For this reason his theology of the church merits more extended treatment.

To understand Nee's rather radical ecclesiology, we need to appreciate the profound impact the Christian faith had on him. Grace May notes that Nee's spiritual experience freed him to do very unconventional things in defiance of deeply rooted Chinese traditions as long as the actions were thought to be biblical.[101] He was as equally prepared on the same basis to part ways with those he deeply respected, such as the Plymouth Brethren, whose teaching on closed communion he could not accept.[102]

The church as the corporate Christ. Central to Nee's ecclesiology is his concept of the church as a spiritual reality. Using typological interpretation, he argues that just as Eve was "the constituent of Adam," so the church is a constituent part of Christ: "Only that which is out of Christ can be the church."[103] And just as "Eve was not made from clay but from Adam," the "material" of the church is Christ.[104]

The church has its beginning even before creation, according to Nee: it exists as God's plan from eternity.[105] As Nee puts it, "Heaven is both the origin and abode of the Church, but not her destination."[106] That is to say, the church is not so much going to heaven but made in heaven and

[101]Grace Y. May, "Watchman Nee And the Breaking Of Bread: The Missiological and Spiritual Forces That Contributed to an Indigenous Chinese Ecclesiology" (DTh diss., Boston University School of Theology, 2000), pp. 101, 102.
[102]Ibid., p. 100.
[103]Watchman Nee, *The Collected Works of Watchman Nee*, vol. 34, *The Glorious Church* (Anaheim, CA: Living Stream Ministry, 1993), p. 27.
[104]Ibid., p. 29.
[105]Ibid., pp. 32, 40-41.
[106]Nee, *Collected Works*, vol. 40, *What Shall This Man Do?* p. 164.

therefore "perfect beyond any possibility of improvement."[107] "To see eternal reality in Christ is to cease to differentiate between what the Church is potentially and actually."[108] The church is so linked to Christ that it can be called the "corporate Christ":

> In the New Testament there are two ways to look at Christ. On the one hand, He is Jesus Christ the Nazarene—this is the individual Christ. On the other hand, He is Christ plus the church—the corporate Christ. First Corinthians 12:12 refers to the second aspect when it says, "All the members of the body, being many, are one body, so also is the Christ." Anything apart from Christ is not the church. There is only one thing in a Christian that forms a part of the church—Christ. The church is the corporate Christ. In the church there is only Christ. During the bread-breaking meeting, the portion that we break off from the whole still signifies the Body of Christ, the church. The church is not what is added to Christ but what issues out from Christ.[109]

Nee's strong emphasis on the church leads naturally to an equally strong emphasis on corporate spirituality. Christian living is essentially living in the body of Christ.[110] This corporate spirituality is expressed in bearing the cross. To live in the body means to carry the cross, dying to the natural life so that the life of Christ might be revealed. Practically, bearing the cross in the body requires one to be limited by the weaknesses of another member.[111] In the body there is no "direct communion with another." Fellowship must always be through the head, without which fellowship turns into little cliques.[112]

The Lord's Supper. The central act of the church that expresses its corporate spiritual life is the Lord's Supper. Drawing from 1 Corinthians 10:17—"Seeing that there is one bread, we who are many are one Body"— Nee makes the following comment:

---

[107]Ibid., p. 165.
[108]Ibid., p. 166.
[109]Nee, *Collected Works*, vol. 44, *Conferences, Messages, and Fellowship (4)*, p. 787. See also Nee, *The Glorious Church*, pp. 29-33.
[110]Nee, *Conferences*, p. 808.
[111]Ibid., p. 805.
[112]Ibid., p. 812. See also Bonhoeffer's view of Christian communion: It is never direct, but Christ always stands between people. *Life Together*, trans. John W. Doberstein (New York: Harper Brothers, 1954), p. 35.

When we remember the Lord, I take a little piece from the loaf, you take a little piece from the loaf, and others do the same. For many centuries throughout the world, all Christians have taken a little portion of this loaf and eaten it! If you could take all the pieces they have eaten and put them together, they could become the whole church. The church is not an individual "I" plus an individual "you." It is not Mr. Smith plus Mr. Jones or even all the Christians in the whole world put together. The church is the Christ in you, the Christ in him, and the Christ in all the Christians around the world throughout all the centuries put together.... The only part of us which is related to the church is the portion of the loaf which we have eaten.[113]

For Nee the breaking of bread is about a spiritual-ontological reality. Had he known, he probably would have affirmed with Henri de Lubac that the Eucharist makes the church.[114] The Lord's Supper is also no mere ritual but a profound religious experience for Nee.[115] The Chinese have a deep appreciation of the family meal. Just as the family meal epitomizes the traditional Chinese family, the Lord's Supper for Nee is a spiritual family meal that epitomizes the church as a spiritual family. Nee regards the Supper even more highly than preaching since church membership is based on the number of persons breaking bread, which is the first action in the assembly. Thus Nee prefers the Supper to be observed in the evening service where a smaller group of committed Christians come together.[116] Nee is no sacramentalist, at least not explicitly, but his understanding of the Lord's Supper resonates generally with traditional teachings. He also has a profound sense of the meal as a deep symbol. The meal declares the death of Christ by presenting the bread (body) and wine (blood) as separate. It is also the meal that binds Christians together at table fellowship (1 Cor 10). Nee is open to having Christians from anywhere participate at the table.[117]

---

[113]Nee, *The Glorious Church*, p. 29.
[114]Henri de Lubac, *Corpus Mysticum: The Eucharist and the Church in the Middle Ages, Historical Survey*, trans. Gemma Simmonds with Richard Price and Christopher Stephens; ed. Laurence Paul Hemming and Susan Frank Parsons (Notre Dame, IN: University of Notre Dame Press, 2006), p. 88.
[115]May, "Watchman Nee," p. 100.
[116]Ibid., pp. 334-35.
[117]Nee, *Collected Works*, vol. 48, *Messages for Building Up New Believers (1)*, pp. 261-72.

Out of the central practice of the breaking of bread Nee develops a church order in which every member is expected to be active. He abolishes the clergy-laity distinction, preferring a church led by lay elders who function as fathers in the spiritual family.

The key to becoming the church is new birth; not even repentance and confession of sin make us the church. Only through new birth do we share the life of Christ.[118] Nee believes that the creation of the church involves a "nonredemptive" aspect of Christ's death that results in the giving of his life to form the church. This is typified in the creation of Eve (the church) out of Adam when he slept, and also at the cross. After his death, his side was pierced and water flowed out (Jn 19:31-37). The latter refers to the water of life, which Christ imparts by his death.[119] These two aspects of the church are imaged by the body and the bride. The church as the body of Christ refers to its present existence, in which it needs to be constantly cleansed and nourished by Christ (Eph 5). The church as the bride of Christ refers to its eschatological perfection realized only in the new heavens and new earth.[120]

The "local church." One of Nee's most controversial teachings is his doctrine of the local church. It is often regarded as exclusive and authoritarian.[121] Roberts thinks that it is incompatible with his earlier doctrine of the universal church.[122] The local church, however, cannot be properly understood apart from his doctrine of the eternal church. The church eternal is concretely realized in the local church. The local church is where the real action of the body of Christ is taking place. This gives rise to a concept of the church as a divine humanity: "The church is partly heavenly and partly on earth. The heavenly part concerns the authority of the Holy Spirit; the earthly part concerns the boundary of locality." One is just as necessary as the other: "The church absolutely belongs to a locality."[123]

---

[118]Nee, *The Glorious Church*, p. 131.
[119]Ibid., pp. 35-38.
[120]Ibid., pp. 44-66.
[121]Dana Roberts, *Understanding Watchman Nee* (Plainfield, NJ: Haven, 1980), pp. 131-38.
[122]Ibid., p. 131.
[123]Watchman Nee, *Further Talks on the Church* (Los Angeles: Stream, 1974), p. 19.

Historically, Nee notes, churches are distinguished by time, place of origin, personality and doctrine, but the only valid distinction is the locality or city.[124] There can be only one true church in one locality.[125] The church cannot be smaller or bigger than the locality and must be named after the locality, not after a person, doctrine, system or place of origin— for example, the Church of England.[126]

The actualization of the eternal church in the local church is brought about by the Holy Spirit. Nee's pneumatology develops directly out of his doctrine of the corporate Christ. Reading Psalm 133 typologically and correlating it with Ephesians 4, Nee believes that just as Christ is anointed by the Spirit, the same anointing extends to the whole body. Christ is the anointed one; we as members of his body are "little anointed ones." But we are not anointed individually, only "in Christ."[127] The anointing of the Spirit links the body to the head and to one another. Again and again Nee brings out the spiritual implications of his teaching. The anointing is translated into an "inner feeling of life" that must guide our action. Without the anointing everything becomes dead letter, mere doctrine.[128] Our part is to "consecrate and yield ourselves [so] that the authority of the Holy Spirit might come out continuously."[129]

Authority. Nee is no bleary-eyed idealist. He knows all too well that for a church to function effectively, it has to address the issue of authority. Here again it is hard to gainsay Nee's concept of ecclesiastical authority. The problem with denominations, according to Nee, is that they have substituted the authority of the Holy Spirit (which is the mark of the eternal church) with human authority. Leaders are selected based on social status and natural abilities rather than on vital faith and relationship with God.[130] "In the Body of Christ authority is a matter of life, not of position."[131] This is a further reason that denominational churches

---

[124]Nee, *Messages for Building Up*, p. 94.
[125]Nee, *Further Talks*, pp. 20-23.
[126]Ibid., p. 96.
[127]Nee, *Conferences*, p. 816.
[128]Ibid., pp. 816-20.
[129]Nee, *Further Talks*, p. 17.
[130]Nee, *Conferences*, p. 822.
[131]Ibid., p. 825.

cannot form the true church. All church authorities are derived from the head. Apostles, prophets and so on do not have authority in themselves; they represent Christ's authority on earth. Leaders who are given Christ's authority will be recognized as leaders by the people rather than ratified by the people through an election. An elder of the church cannot be made an elder by the people anymore than a father can be made a father. A father is one by virtue of having a son.[132]

This is the context in which Nee understands the practice of the laying on of hands. At baptism the "representative authority established by God," such as an apostle, lays his hand on the baptizand signifying that the person is joined to the body of Christ and the blessing of God is transmitted to him. It also means that the person is now under the authority of Christ the head. The laying on of hands ensures that the blessing of God's anointing on the head continues to flow to each member of the body on whom hands are laid.[133]

It is easy to see Nee's insistence on male headship as reflecting an authoritarianism derived from Chinese culture.[134] Two things must be said by way of qualification. First, we have noted that Nee is a thoroughgoing biblicist who is prepared to jettison anything from culture that he deems unbiblical. Second, he has a theology of authority that is seldom appreciated, namely, authority is to be exercised in mutual dependence between leaders and people. Mutuality is the character of the body of Christ.[135] The pulpit needs the help of the congregation just as the congregation needs the help of the pulpit.[136] Mutuality is needed even in the matter of elders anointing the sick (Jas 5:14-16). Nee believes that sickness here is no ordinary sickness but brought on by the sin of breaking away from the body of Christ (see 1 Cor 11: 29-30). Mutual confession between the elders and the sick is needed. The sick confesses to having broken fellowship, while the elders confess that they have failed in love and

---

[132]Ibid., pp. 825-27.
[133]Nee, *Messages for Building Up*, pp. 99-111.
[134]Joseph Tse-Hei Lee, "Watchman Nee and the Little Flock Movement in Maoist China," *Church History* 74, no. 1 (2005): 68-96.
[135]Nee, *Conferences*, p. 805.
[136]Ibid., p. 806.

watchfulness.[137] Mutual confession is followed by mutual prayer: the elders praying for the sick and the sick for the elders![138] But beyond the biblical horizon lies the Confucian principle of reciprocity. Nee's local church may look like a macrocosm of the Confucian family,[139] but underlying it is a rather sophisticated theology of ecclesial authority.

AN ASSESSMENT

Nee is often accused of sectarianism, but theologically, Nee's ecclesiology is no more exclusive than the Roman Catholic Church's claim that the true church "subsists" in the Catholic Church.[140] What Nee has done is transfer the Roman exclusiveness to the "local church." But unlike the Catholic understanding, the charge of sectarianism will not go away as long as Nee questions the legitimacy of nonlocal churches. Yet for all the problems Nee's local church doctrine entails, it has several advantages. First, it encourages the development of strong indigenous churches that are not dependent on foreign mission support. Nee was a master strategist, using the same methods as the communists to establish many indigenous churches even in the remotest parts of China.[141] It involves encouraging several families to migrate to a new area to form a local church. The result is the creation of strong family-based local churches well-suited to survive under severe trials.[142] Second, it encourages strong corporate life at the local church level. Over and over again Nee spoke in the strongest possible terms against individualism: "Therefore, even though we have God's life within us, we still need God to work upon us to break our individualism. God must break down the thought that I myself am enough. We need to be one with all the rest of God's children. . . . [God] must crush us day after day until we come to know the life of

---

[137]Ibid., p. 833.

[138]Ibid.

[139]Lee, "Watchman Nee," p. 76.

[140]*Lumen Gentium* 8.

[141]Lee, "Watchman Nee."

[142]Chua Wee Hian, "Evangelization of Whole Families," in *Perspective on the World Christian Movement: A Reader,* ed. Ralph D. Winter (Pasadena, CA: William Carey Library, 2009), pp. 653-56.

the Body."[143] "Individualism is hateful in the sight of God. . . . I must allow the other members of the Body to minister to my needs. We must avail ourselves constantly of the fellowship of the Body, for it is our very life."[144] Finally, it encourages local churches to be kept at a reasonable size. A church should be big enough for the full complement of ministries to be undertaken but small enough for adequate discipline to be exercised and meaningful fellowship to be realized, especially at the Lord's Table.[145]

Nee's theological vision of the church is far more traditional and "catholic" than perhaps he himself realized. His concepts of the corporate Christ and the distinction between the body and bride bear close resemblance to the Catholic idea of *totus Christus* seen in Pope Pius XII's encyclical *Mystici Corporis Christi* and in other Catholic writers.[146] His understanding of authority as a reciprocal relationship between the elders and people is not very different from that of Orthodoxy.[147] Even the laying on of hands is surprisingly close to the traditional understanding of the sacrament of confirmation.

Nee's vision of the universal church when juxtaposed to his rather eccentric concept of the local church at first seems baffling. But there is an underlying logic that runs from one to the other. For Nee, doctrines are not abstract ideas but truths that have far-reaching implications for living. Repeatedly Nee consciously seeks to link doctrine to living. The doctrine of the corporate Christ is "a reality and not a doctrine or a theory" and entails a spirituality of cross-bearing and self-abnegation.[148] Nee probably derives this peculiar understanding of spirituality from Keswick sources. Basic to Keswick spirituality is the belief that all that is possible for Christian living has already been accomplished by Christ. All that the

---

[143]Nee, *The Glorious Church*, p. 32.
[144]Nee, *Conferences*, p. 801.
[145]May, "Watchman Nee," p. 329.
[146]Emile Mersch, *The Theology of the Mystical Body* (St. Louis: B. Herder, 1951); *The Whole Christ: The Historical Development of The Doctrine of The Mystical Body in Scripture and Tradition* (London: Dennis Dobson, 1962).
[147]Nicholas Afanasiev, *The Church of the Holy Spirit* (Notre Dame, IN: University of Notre Dame Press, 2007); Alexander Schmemann, *The Eucharist* (Crestwood, NY: St. Vladimir's Seminary Press, 1987).
[148]Nee, *Conferences*, pp. 805-8.

Christian needs to do is appropriate the reality through a process of self-surrender and "reckoning" that it is so.[149] Nee's understanding of the church as both an eternal reality and a human reality conforms to this Keswick pattern. The purity of the eternal church must be appropriated and lived out concretely in the local church.

THE COMMUNION OF SAINTS (SANCTORUM COMMUNIO)

The third article of the Apostles' Creed brings together the Holy Spirit, the church, the communion of saints, resurrection of the body and life everlasting. It links pneumatology and ecclesiology, communion and eschatology. In the previous chapter we considered the relationship of the Holy Spirit and the church; we must now examine the relation between the communion of saints and eschatology. But underlying this exposition is a concern of far-reaching implication. The doctrine of the church as the communion of saints if properly understood can offer the best answer to one of the greatest challenges facing the church in Asia for much of its history, namely, the practice of ancestral veneration. Traditional responses have been varied depending on social location. Chuck Lowe identifies three social locations, each with a different interpretation of the practice. At the grassroots level, ancestral veneration tends to be given a strongly supernaturalistic interpretation. In contrast, the religious elite, both Christian and non-Christian, tend to reinterpret the practice as a purely cultural expression of filial piety. The bureaucratic elite, like their religious counterparts, prefer a more rational understanding shorn of "superstitions" but also seek to commend the sanitized practices as useful for promoting social cohesion.[150] Most Christians, however, recognize that there are both cultural and religious elements in the practice—a position supported by sociological and anthropological studies.[151] Attempts at either reinterpreting the rites or distinguishing between the cultural and religious have turned out to be unsatisfactory. The first ap-

---

[149]Hannah W. Smith, *The Christian's Secret of a Happy Life* (Old Tappen, NJ: Fleming H. Revell, 1970), p. 44; Nee, *The Collected Works*, vol. 33, *The Normal Christian Life*, pp. 41-56.
[150]Chuck Lowe, *Honoring God and Family: A Christian Response to Idol Food in Chinese Popular Religion* (Bangalore: Theological Book Trust, 2001), pp. 27-29.
[151]Ibid., p. 26, citing sociologist Tong Chee Kiong.

proach tends to be dismissive of grassroots beliefs and practices while the second has not been met with any broad consensus on what are cultural and what are religious elements.

Ancestral veneration underscores the unsurpassed value placed on the family in Asia. Christians have responded to the challenge by presenting the church as family-friendly, placing special emphasis on ministry to the family.[152] The church is conceived as the family of God in which earthly families find their true fulfillment. But could the Christian church in Asia do it in a convincing way? One of the constant complaints of Japanese indigenous Christian movements is that traditional Christianity has not addressed issues relating to dead ancestors: if they did not know Jesus while on earth, can they still become Christians? Can the living bring the gospel to the dead? If so, how? These questions not only express a crying need, but underlying them is a belief in the solidarity of the family that extends beyond the grave. It is a belief that can be adequately understood only if given a christological grounding; that is to say, in Christ, all the saints throughout the ages, in heaven and on earth, are united as one organic, living church by the power of the Holy Spirit.

Full communion is an embodied communion that is consummated at the final resurrection of the body. Thus in Scripture, the final state of the church's communion with God is pictured as the eschatological marriage supper of the Lamb, of which the eucharistic meal is only a foretaste. The Christian tradition has also taught that between death and the final resurrection, the saints enjoy an imperfect communion in the "intermediate state." The concept of the intermediate state is the church's way of stating its belief that communion with God cannot be broken even at death. This is the logic of dichotomy, as we have noted in chapter two. Dichotomy may not adequately explain what the nature of the person is or how the person continues to enjoy communion with God after death while awaiting the final resurrection, but it seeks to make the best sense of the state of human existence between these two defining moments. Humans

---

[152]Charles E. Farhadian, "A Missiological Reflection on Present-Day Christian Movements in Southeast Asia," in *Christian Movements in Southeast Asia*, ed. Michael Nai-Chiu Poon (Singapore: Genesis, 2010), pp. 108-110.

are complex beings open to continuing transfiguration or metamorphosis by the Spirit of God from one state of existence to another. Eternal life begins with their incorporation into Christ through baptism, and henceforth that God-given life continues to be transfigured until it is perfected in the resurrection of the body.

The belief in an afterlife is something Christianity shares with primal religions, as evidenced by the elaborate ritual practices relating to the "living dead" and ancestral veneration in Africa and Asia. In fact, venerating dead ancestors reveals more than just some vague belief in life after death; it anticipates the Christian doctrine of the communion of saints transcending space and time. Protestantism, however, falls far short in practice what it acknowledges in theory. It acknowledges one holy catholic and apostolic church, but in practice the communion of the church does not extend to its diachronic dimension. Here is where a juxtaposition of the doctrine of the communion of saints with the Asian practice of ancestral veneration could become mutually enriching.

For the family in East Asia, family solidarity is experienced not just with those present but with those who are dead. So significant is this concern that failure to address it adequately is a main reason why Christianity has not had strong appeal among the masses in Confucian societies. Historically, Christians have been deeply divided over the issue. Even within the Catholic Church the rites controversy ran for more than three centuries, pitting different religious orders against each other.[153] But with greater emphasis placed on "inculturation" since Vatican II, and coupled with its doctrine of the communion of saints, Catholicism is perhaps better placed to deal with the issue compared to Protestants. In Asia, the Japanese indigenous Christian movements have given the issue the most sustained attention. The key doctrine the Asian church needs to revisit, therefore, is the communion of saints and the ramifications arising from it. The crucial issue, however, is whether the doctrine can

---

[153]The papal bull *Ex quo singulari* (1742) simply put a gag on the controversy but did not quite end it. The end came with the decree *Instrucio circa quasdam caeremonias super ritibus sinensibus* on December 8, 1939. For a history of the rites controversy see George Minamiki, *The Chinese Rites Controversy from Its Beginning to Modern Times* (Chicago: Loyola University Press, 1985).

be nuanced in such a way that practices related to ancestral veneration like those seen in popular Japanese indigenous churches can be meaningfully incorporated.

In Latin, the word *sanctorum* can be understood either as masculine or neuter. *Sanctorum communio* can mean either communion of saints or communion of holy things. Stephen Benko in his study on the question has argued for the neuter as the original and primary meaning. His basic argument is the observation that the phrase *sanctorum communio* appeared in the creeds in the West for the first time around A.D. 350 at a time when the current form of the creed in the East at that point had "baptism for the forgiveness of sins." This led Benko to conclude that *sanctorum communio* was the equivalent of "baptism for the forgiveness of sin." Thus, "*communio* and *sancta* referred respectively to participation and sacraments."[154] *Sancta* (holy things) would be equivalent to the Eastern *hagia*, which refers to sacraments, especially the Eucharist. But over time the personal interpretation of *sanctorum* (of saints) from the ninth century came to dominate Western interpretations of the creed, so much so that the phrase is now generally understood as standing in apposition to *ecclesia sancta* (the holy church) rather than to the sacraments.[155]

A proper doctrine of the communion of saints must begin with the primacy of the sacramental interpretation.[156] This is in fact reaffirmed in the catechism of the Catholic Church:

> The Church is a "communion of saints": this expression refers first to the "holy things" (*sancta*), above all the Eucharist, by which "the unity of believers, who form one body in Christ, is both represented and brought about."[157]

---

[154]Stephen Benko, *The Meaning of Sanctorum Communio* (London: SCM Press, 1964), pp. 64-65.

[155]Ibid., pp. 109-38.

[156]Major Protestant theologians have recognized the sacramental interpretation but have tended to give both the sacramental and personal equal emphasis. Barth says that "the *sancti* belong to the *sancta* and vice versa" (*Dogmatics in Outline* [London: SCM Press, 2007], p. 135). Similarly, Wolfhart Pannenberg insists that both interpretations should be given "equally primal force" (*The Apostles' Creed in the Light of Today's Questions* [Philadelphia: Westminster Press, 1972], p. 145).

[157]*Catechism of the Catholic Church* §960, citing *Lumen Gentium* 3.

The Catechism also affirms the personal interpretation:

> We believe in the communion of all the faithful of Christ, those who are
> pilgrims on earth, the dead who are being purified, and the blessed in
> heaven, all together forming one Church; and we believe that in this com-
> munion, the merciful love of God and his saints is always [attentive] to our
> prayers.[158]

This sequence and their relationship is, interestingly, one of the points of
agreement in the German Catholic-Lutheran Dialogue:

> [The communion of saints] relates first to the holy gifts that God gives to
> the church, especially in the Eucharist. Only on the basis of this compre-
> hensively foundational gift do those who receive it become "saints": the
> participation (*koinonia, communio*) in the holy gifts (*sancta*) founds the
> communion (*koinonia, communio*) of sanctified Christians (*sancti*) with
> Christ and among each other.[159]

The primacy of the sacramental interpretation affirms that there is no
communion of saints without first their common participation in holy
things, especially baptism and the Eucharist. Baptism is into Christ and
Eucharist is communion of the body and blood of Christ. This brings us
back to the christological foundation of ancestral veneration, which is
but a specific contextual expression of the communion of saints.[160] It is
holy things that make holy people. This is vividly portrayed in Eastern
rites where before the distribution of the bread and wine the celebrant
declares: "Holy things for holy people" (*sancta sanctis*). Only in feeding
on the body and blood of Christ can the saints grow in communion.[161] It
is perhaps for this reason that the final consummation of communion
between God and the church is pictured as a wedding and a wedding
supper (Rev 19:7-9).

If indeed the communion of holy things constitutes the foundation of

---

[158]*Catechism* §962, citing Paul VI's *motu propio* "Credo of the People of God" §30.
[159]*Communio Sanctorum: The Church as the Communion of Saints*. Official German Catholic-
Lutheran Dialogue, trans. Mark W. Jeske, Michael Root and Daniel R. Smith (Collegeville,
MN: Liturgical, 2004), §4.
[160]See chapter four.
[161]Cited in *Catechism* §948.

the communion of saints, we can begin to understand why the sacramental dimension of church life has played a critical role among the early Pentecostals and in some of the indigenous churches in Asia.[162] For example, the Japanese indigenous Christian movements' creation of elaborate rituals relating to evangelizing of and communion with the dead clearly implies a sacramental foundation of the communion of saints.[163] Mullins' description of the special memorial services practiced by the Holy Ecclesia of Jesus is one example:

> During these services members hold the photograph of the deceased family member on their lap until they are instructed to bring them forward and place them on a table at the front of the sanctuary for a pastoral prayer. The service concludes with a "vicarious mass" or Lord's Supper on behalf of the dead. The names of the deceased are read and the living receive the bread and wine on their behalf. This is a concrete manifestation of the "communion of saints," and it is understood that the dead are receiving this communion spiritually in heaven.[164]

The sacraments that unite the church to Christ are the basis of the communion of saints; that is to say, the Christ who reconciles all things in heaven and on earth (Col 1:20) is the foundation of communion between saints on earth and in heaven. But what is the nature of the communion between saints on earth and saints in heaven? Perhaps a good place to begin would be the German Catholic-Lutheran Dialogue since it represents a measure of consensus between Catholics and Protestants that on the whole seems to advance the Protestant understanding of the subject.

Both sides agree that since the church exists both in heaven and on earth, communion cannot be restricted to just saints on earth. Two key points of agreement are noted in this connection. First, the communion of saints includes the honoring of saints in heaven for their exemplary character.[165] The saints are honored and praised not for their own spir-

---

[162]See my discussion in *Pentecostal Ecclesiology: An Essay on the Development of Doctrine* (Blandford Forum, Dorset, UK: Deo, 2011), pp. 115-18.
[163]Mullins, "What About the Ancestors?" pp. 41-64.
[164]Mullins, *Christianity Made in Japan*, p. 142.
[165]Lutheran-Catholic Dialogue, §229.

itual accomplishments but because of what Christ has made them to be so that "the praise of the saints is the praise of the goodness of the Triune God."[166] Second, the Dialogue also mentions several ways in which saints are venerated: naming of church buildings after a saint, naming a child after a saint at his or her baptism, pilgrimages to places associated with particular saints, veneration of relics of saints. Protestants are, in principle, not averse to the "loving preservation of signs of remembrance" of people they hold dear,[167] but generally they do not develop an elaborate *cultus* associated with some of these forms of veneration as Catholics do.

Catholics and Lutherans, however, differ on whether veneration includes invocation of the saints. Lutherans fear that this would undermine the sole mediatorship of Christ.[168] A more intractable problem is praying for the dead, yet this much is agreed upon:

> Together we are convinced that it corresponds to the communion in which we are bound together in Christ beyond death with those who have already died to pray for them and to commend them in loving memory to the mercy of God. All people—including those who have led a Christian life—remain sinners who fall short of God's demand and have need for the accepting love of the merciful God.[169]

The point at which a sharper difference emerges is whether commending the dead to the mercy of God includes "a process of a purification . . . of the dead." Lutherans reject the need for such purification but agree on another kind of purification: the perfecting of communion when "through the pain over failure in earthly life, persons come with their love to give the perfect response to the love of God."[170] The church on earth can pray for the dead for their communion with God to be perfected.

Closely linked to the veneration of the saints is the invocation and intercession of the saints. On this matter there is no disagreement. After all, we request fellow Christians to pray for us; how much more should

---

[166]Ibid., §235.
[167]Ibid., §252.
[168]Ibid., §231.
[169]Ibid., §223.
[170]Ibid., §228. The language here is somewhat obscure.

we ask those whose "lives of faith and love" are "a living interpretation of the message of the gospel" to do the same, since Christians on earth are united with the saints in heaven in the one body of Christ, the church?[171]

The Dialogue shows that while there is considerable agreement on the doctrine of the communion of saints between Catholics and Protestants, there are still significant differences in their respective practices. For example, Protestant liturgies are not likely to have a place for the invocation of a specific saint during the intercessory prayer, whereas the invocation of saints forms a regular part of Catholic and Orthodox liturgies. Their difference may be traced partly to their different traditional understandings of sainthood. For Protestants, saints refer to all the people of God who are sanctified regardless of their actual level of personal sanctity,[172] whereas the Catholic side has tended to stress continual development of personal sanctity even beyond this life. There is something to be said for the Catholic view. We have noted in previous chapters that some form of contiguity that exists between Christianity and other religions, especially primal religions, has been explained by some as an ancient knowledge of God that serves as preparation for the gospel.

But implied in such a theology is the need for further growth in the knowledge of Christ if one is to attain full salvation, that is, full communion. Their salvation will still be incomplete if by salvation we mean more than being rescued from some impending disaster but communion with the triune God. There is still the need to grow into a fuller and more explicit knowledge of God through Jesus Christ, which, for those who have never heard or heard only imperfectly, can only be attained beyond death. It is against this backdrop that we can better assess the Japanese indigenous Christian movements' practice of praying for, and even preaching to, the dead. It can be understood as a further extension of a general principle expressed in the Catholic-Lutheran Dialogue on the communion of saints. Through the church on earth, deceased ancestors who did not hear the gospel in life are

---

[171]Ibid., §240.
[172]For example, the Second Helvitic Confession, chap. 17.

given the opportunity to hear it, but continuing growth to a fuller knowledge of God is also needed for the perfecting of communion with the triune God. This communion is possible because of Christ the ancestor-priest whom we honor and through whom both the dead in Christ are also honored and those not yet in Christ are prayed for by their descendants on earth.

The only objection that could be raised against the JICM view is that it goes against a commonly held view that the offer of salvation is given only in this life, based on texts such as Hebrews 9:23-28 and Luke 13:23-30.[173] This direct proof-texting approach, however, fails to consider the larger context of Scripture. The idea of the finality of judgment after death must be rejected for the same reason that we reject an immediate resurrection at death. It goes against the biblical teaching and the overwhelmingly received view of all the major Christian traditions that final resurrection and judgment occur only at the end of history.[174] It is to account for this "lapse" between death and final resurrection-judgment that the doctrine of the intermediate state is introduced. But the intermediate state also implies that death does not seal the soul in its final condition until the final judgment. If this is so, then the Hebrews 9 passage cannot be taken to mean that the state of the soul is settled with finality at or after death. The argument from Luke 13 is even more tenuous. There is nothing in the text to suggest that the closing of the door of opportunity (Lk 13:25) occurs at death.

Besides Scripture, there are two other considerations from the Christian tradition that support a theology of postmortem salvation and continuing development. One is the traditional teaching of Christ's descent into Hades derived from 1 Peter 3:19-20. Although the Scripture passage refers originally to those who died during the flood, the Christian tradition has expanded its meaning to include "a guarantee of the recon-

---

[173]See Terrance L. Tiessen, *Who Can Be Saved? Reassessing Salvation in Christ and World Religions* (Downers Grove, IL: InterVarsity Press, 2004), p. 221. This is also the traditional Catholic view. See DiNoia, *The Diversity*, pp. 104-5.

[174]To cite but two influential examples: Wolfhart Pannenberg, *Systematic Theology* (Grand Rapids: Eerdmans, 1991), 3:577-78; N. T. Wright, *Surprised by Hope: Rethinking Heaven, the Resurrection, and the Mission of the Church* (New York: HarperOne, 2008), p. 168.

ciling power of the death of Christ even for those who died before he came."[175] In the Eastern Church's iconography the "harrowing of Hades" pictures Christ laying hold of Adam and Eve, symbolizing the entire human race.[176] The implication is that none is excluded from the benefits of Christ's salvific work, including those who had had no opportunity to encounter him during their earthly life.

A second consideration is the teaching that no one is eternally damned against his or her own will. Hell is the deliberate, persistent and final rejection of God's grace.[177] As C. S. Lewis has aptly noted, "The doors of hell are locked on the *inside*."[178] Hell is the final reality at the final judgment, just as the new creation is the final reality that is realized at the final resurrection. That is to say, if it is conceivable that saints continue to receive divine grace for the perfecting of their communion with God before its final consummation at the resurrection, it is not inconceivable to suppose that sinners are being offered divine grace before the final judgment. Given the broad consensus in the doctrine of the communion of saints and its ramifications with regard to those who have not heard the gospel or are in need of further growth in communion, the ritual practices of the JICMs relating to deceased ancestors may not appear so far-fetched after all. It could, in fact, contribute toward a fuller understanding of the communion of saints.

The Consummation of Communion

Two images stand out in the New Testament concerning the consummation of the communion of saints with the triune God. One is the image of adoption. Romans 8:23 speaks of adoption as a future event corresponding to the redemption of the body. The freedom from bondage to sin that the redeemed receive from the Spirit of life, who is the foretaste of the new creation, will be consummated as freedom from bodily decay.

---

[175]Pannenberg, *Systematic Theology*, 3:616.

[176]Vigen Guroian, *The Melody of Faith: Theology in an Orthodox Key* (Grand Rapids: Eerdmans, 2010), pp. 37-38.

[177]For a fuller account see Simon Chan, "The Logic of Hell: A Response to Annihilationism," *Evangelical Review of Theology* 18, no. 1 (January 1, 1994): 20-32.

[178]C. S. Lewis, *The Problem of Pain* (New York: Macmillan, 1970), p. 127. Emphasis author's.

In this full freedom, each "son of God" is also fully in communion with each other in the church as the consummated family of God. There is no longer the tension that currently exists between the individual and the community.[179] This is the situation that the whole creation awaits with eager anticipation, for it too will be liberated when the children of God are revealed in their full glory as children of the heavenly Father (Rom 8:21), when they partake fully of the divine nature and are fully conformed to the image and likeness of the Son of God. "Dear friends, now we are children of God, and what we will be has not yet been made known. But we know that when Christ appears, we shall be like him, for we shall see him as he is" (1 Jn 3:2 NIV).

The second image is the marriage between the church as the bride and Christ as bridegroom (Rev 19:7-9; 21:1–22:21). There is a long history in the church of employing the marriage metaphor for the mystical union between Christ and his church,[180] thus providing further confirmation that communion is the ultimate goal of human existence. Marriage is the most poignant symbol of the relationship between Christ and his church. Or should it be said that it is the spiritual union of Christ and his church that sets the normative pattern for earthly marriages?[181] This is how Paul understands the mystery of marriage in Ephesians 5:25-33. The love of Christ for his church forms the basis of Paul's appeal to husbands and wives regarding their own respective responsibilities in marriage (Eph 5:32). The whole Christian life can be said to be a continuing growth in nuptial union as well as a continuing preparation for its final consummation. Already Christ's first coming to earth was seen by John the Baptist as the coming of the bridegroom for the bride (Jn 3:29). His second coming can be said to consummate the marriage.

---

[179]See Pannenberg, *Systematic Theology*, 3:128-30.

[180]From Origen's commentary on the Song of Songs in the third century to Teresa of Avila in the seventeenth. See Origen, *The Song of Songs Commentary and Homilies,* Ancient Christian Writers, vol. 26 (New York: Newman, 1953); Teresa of Avila, "The Interior Castle," in *The Collected Works of St. Theresa of Avila,* 2 vols., trans. Kieran Kavanaugh and Otilio Rodriquez (Washington, D.C.: ICS, 1980). Teresa describes the highest level of mystical union, the prayer of *transforming* union, as a mystical marriage (7.2).

[181]James E. O'Mahony, "Espousals of Christ and His Church," *Orate Fratres* 3, no. 10 (August 11, 1929): 311-14.

The final chapters of Revelation imply such a progression in three stages. There is first the bride's preparation for the wedding where she adorns herself with clean clothing and the banquet is prepared (Rev 19:7-9). Then comes the wedding itself when she "descends as the New Jerusalem 'prepared as a bride adorned for her husband' [Rev 21:2]." Finally, having been fully united with Christ, her full glory is finally displayed (Rev 21:9-27).[182] She is revealed as the centerpiece of the entire creation, thus fulfilling God's original purpose for her to be his "work of art" (Eph 2:10, Jerusalem Bible), displaying "to the rulers and authorities in the heavenly realms" the "manifold wisdom of God" (Eph 3:10 NIV). It is important to note how familial imagery continues to dominate the vision of eschatological communion—a vision that is readily appreciated in many traditional cultures. For example, in Chinese tradition the Lunar New Year is ushered in by scattered members of an extended family gathering at the ancestral home for a grand reunion dinner.

The final vision of the church brings us full circle to the beginning of time. Just as the end of a good story ties up the loose ends, resolves the tensions and clears up the mysteries, the end of the story of the triune God clarifies the mysteries of the beginning. In the New Testament the communion of saints with and in the Trinity is consummated in the new heaven and new earth (Rev 21–22). Its fulfillment in the new creation shows that it has something to do with the old creation. Many Old Testament scholars are of the view that the Genesis creation account reflects the thought pattern of the ancient world, which sees the whole creation as God's temple, that is, the place where God dwells and where sacrifices and worship are rendered. The six-day creation is not a scientific account of cosmogony but a theological account of God's ordering of the world to become his dwelling place, while God's resting on the seventh day is the inauguration of the cosmic temple, of which the tabernacle and temple in Israel's history is but a microcosm.[183]

---

[182]Jan Fekkes III, "'His Bride Has Prepared Herself': Revelation 19-21 and Isaian Nuptial Imagery," *Journal of Biblical Literature* 109, no. 2 (1990): 269-87, esp. 283.
[183]John H. Walton, *The Lost World of Genesis One: Ancient Cosmology and the Origins Debate* (Downers Grove, IL: IVP Academic, 2009).

This is further corroborated by the fact that there are unmistakable priestly and liturgical elements in Genesis 1–3: terms used to describe Adam's work ("till" and "keep") are used of priestly work as well (Num 3:7-8; 8:25-26; 18:5-6; 1 Chr 23:32; Ezek 44:14), the repeated use of the liturgical number seven, the close correlation of the creation account with the building of the tabernacle and so on.[184] The whole history of creation can be described as a history of temple building: from the cosmic temple of Genesis 1–3 to the tabernacle in the wilderness and temple on Mount Zion, to the incarnation as the coming of the temple in human flesh (Jn 1:14), to Pentecost as the inauguration of the church as the temple of the Holy Spirit, and finally to the new creation as the realization of the cosmic temple of Genesis 1. The implication is clear: God's ultimate intention in creating is to enter into communion with humanity and through humanity, with the whole created order. This cosmic communion, this meeting of God and all his creatures, is primarily expressed in worship and achieved in worship. Not only does the church on earth join the "angels and archangels and all the heavenly hosts" to render unending praise to the Trinity, singing, "Holy, holy, holy"; it is also joined by a host of lesser earthly creatures for the same purpose (Ps 148:7-12 NIV):

> Praise the Lord from the earth,
>> you great sea creatures and all ocean depths,
> lightning and hail, snow and clouds,
>> stormy winds that do his bidding,
> you mountains and all hills,
>> fruit trees and all cedars,
> wild animals and all cattle,
> small creatures and flying birds,
> kings of the earth and all nations,

---

[184]For example, see Gordon J. Wenham, "Sanctuary Symbolism in the Garden of Eden Story," in *"I Studied Inscriptions From Before the Flood": Ancient Near Eastern, Literary, and Linguistic Approaches to Genesis 1–11*, ed. Richard S. Hess and David Toshio Tsumura (Winona Lake, IN: Eisenbrauns, 1994), pp. 399-404; Jon D. Levenson, *Creation and the Persistence of Evil: The Jewish Drama of Divine Omnipotence* (Princeton, NJ: Princeton University Press, 1988), pp. 66-77; Jeff Morrow, "Creation as Temple-Building and Work as Liturgy in Genesis 1–3," *Journal of the OCABS* 2, no. 1 (2009): ocabs.org/journal/index.php/jocabs/article/viewFile/43/18.

you princes and all rulers on earth,
young men and women,
old men and children.

The eternal liturgical celebration is where all creatures—angelic, human
and nonhuman—find their own unique voices; it is where they actualize
their distinct hypostases.

CONCLUSION

The chief ecclesiological problem in Asia is how to be church in the midst
of more ancient family-based religious communities. One answer to the
problem is churchless Christianity. In India and Japan churchless Christianity arises from a situation in which the person of Christ is warmly
received but not the church as a visible community. Churchless Christianity, however, raises some serious theological questions, not just practical ones: what is the nature of the ecclesial community into which a
believer is baptized? Can the church be a "religious" community without
being a sociocultural community? Can Christianity exist without the
church? Putting it theologically, what would the church be like without
its eschatological orientation? These questions touch on not only the
function but the ontology of the church. The exchanges between Thomas
and Newbigin highlighted these issues that are still being contested.

The challenge that churchless Christianity poses is perhaps more acute
for established church bodies with their rigid structures. Outside of
mainline church establishments, the more fluid structure of Pentecostal
churches appears better equipped to address the concerns of nonbaptized
believers in Christ (NBBCs).[185] Pentecostal churches are less enamored
of issues such as the nature of baptism but more concerned with building
vibrant, worshiping communities. Also, their adaptation to the primal
religious worldview allows them to respond more adequately to popular
religiosity, which elitist approaches have largely ignored. Their emphases
on miracles, healing and exorcism coincide with the felt needs of many
NBBCs. In short, a Hindu believer in Christ is less likely to feel that he or

---

[185]Hoefer, *Churchless Christianity,* p. 246.

she has entered a totally strange culture when he or she goes into a Pentecostal church. At the same time, Pentecostal churches are less likely to compromise on what they regard as essential truths. They seek to establish contrast communities, such as the "faith homes" of the Ceylon Pentecostal Mission. They are quite prepared to break with whatever they perceive as un-Christian practices (for example, the caste system). It is noteworthy that in recent times the Catholic Church in Asia has been coming to see the value of Pentecostal adaptability and the challenges the movement poses.[186]

The family-based "local church" of Watchman Nee represents another indigenous response to this basic problem in a different social context, but his ecclesiology stands out as quite unusual in its sustained reflection that juxtaposes the universal and the local church. The result is an ecclesiology that is surprisingly traditional, perhaps closer to Catholicism and Orthodoxy than to Protestantism, but at the same time well-suited to a context where family life is highly valued.[187]

With regard to ancestral veneration it appears that the Japanese indigenous Christian movements' approach of providing an alternative set of rites based on the doctrine of the communion of saints offers one of the more viable solutions to a perennial problem for Asian Christians. While some may question the appropriateness of some of the JICM rites, its christologically grounded doctrine of the communion of saints, which provides the conceptual framework for these rites, appears to be basically sound. The rites of praying for the dead show that Christians are concerned about honoring their ancestors; at the same time the rites are sufficiently distinguished from Confucian and Taoist ancestral rites to be recognized by both Christians and non-Christians alike as Christian rites. They have also shown that where bold steps are taken to find appropriate Christian ritual expressions of ancestral veneration, fresh theological insights have emerged.

---

[186]"The Spirit at Work in Asia Today," FABC Paper no. 81, 1997, www.fabc.org/fabc%20pa pers/fabc_paper_81.pdf; John Mansford Prior, "Jesus Christ the Way to the Father," FABC Paper no. 119, 2006, www.fabc.org/fabc%20papers/fabc_paper_119.pdf.
[187]Chua Wee Hian, "Evangelization of Whole Families."

EPILOGUE

With the doctrine of the church as the communion of saints we reach the climax of the trinitarian story. God's eternal plan conceived before the creation of the world (Eph 1:4) and unfolded progressively in creation is finally fulfilled. The old creation is consummated in the new creation. The main plot of the story is worship of and communion with and in the triune God culminating in family reunion. I have not told the whole story but merely directed attention to some of its highlights. The full story from an Asian perspective remains to be told, but we offer a brief summary here.

The trinitarian family—Father, Son and Holy Spirit—purposed from eternity to enlarge the divine family by including humans so that the extended family could live in perfect communion. The trinitarian family is an ordered family, and humans being made in the divine image and likeness are to reflect that order in their families and ultimately in the ecclesial family. Sin disorders the filial relationship with God and fraternal relationship with other humans, turning family members into discrete individuals fighting for individual "rights" and "equality" and bringing dishonor to God and shame to the sinner. But at the appointed time the Father sent his Son and Spirit to realize his eternal plan. The Son's obedient response to the Father destroys the destroyer of the divine order of the universe at the cross and creates a reordered community, the ecclesial family, over which God established the Son as its head and big brother. Humans are set free to return to the divine family. Both God's and their honor are restored. The sending of the Spirit who is the bond of love actualizes the family bond, uniting all as one church in the communion of saints in heaven and on earth with the Father through Christ who continues his reconciling work in heaven as the ancestor-priest. The trinitarian work continues to the end of time when the marriage of the Lamb and the bride will be finally sealed and the grand reunion dinner will begin. The whole created order will participate in the eternal liturgy of glorifying God and enjoying him forever.[1]

This way of construing theology is not only closer to the Asian spirit at the grassroots level but also consistent with the larger Christian tradition. It is this correlation that validates its claim to universality. An authentic Asian theology is not just for the church in Asia but for the worldwide church.

---

[1]The Westminster Shorter Catechism Q. 1.

ACKNOWLEDGMENTS

I am grateful to Trinity Theological College for giving me a privilege that few seminary teachers in Asia have, namely, freedom from administrative duties and a reasonable teaching load. For this, I must thank the principal, Dr. Ngoei Foong Nghian, and dean, Dr. Tan Kim Huat. It means that my other brave colleagues have to shoulder some unwelcome burdens. To them, too, I owe an incalculable debt. It does give me a slight twinge of conscience sometimes. My longtime mentor and friend Joe Frary read parts of the manuscript and was enthusiastic about it. He had been a source of encouragement since the day I met him at his home as his first postgraduate student in 1978. Sadly, he did not live to read the rest—not that he would mind, since he no longer sees through a glass darkly. The assistance of our indefatigable librarian Michael Mukunthan and his staff is much appreciated. Finally, special thanks to my student Cathy Law for preparing the indexes under short notice.

AUTHOR INDEX

Abraham, K. C., 10, 22, 160

Acosta, Milton, 119

Afanasiev, Nicholas, 68, 187

Aikman, David, 63

Amaladoss, Michael, 132, 138

Anderson, Allan, 114, 172

Anderson, Norman, 66

Anselm, 44, 83, 113

Appasamy, A. J., 54, 104, 151, 153

Aquinas, Thomas, 53

Arevalo, C. G., 158

Athanasius, 51

Athyal, Saphir, 41-42

Au, Connie H. Y., 29

Augustine, Daniela, 125

Aulén, Gustav, 111

Bae Hyeon-Sung, 30

Barth, Karl, 19-20, 35-36, 38-40, 42, 44, 67-68, 70, 76, 80, 94, 191

Basinger, David, 79

Basinger, Randall, 79

Bays, Daniel, 96

Beasley-Murray, G. R., 134

Bediako, Kwame, 116

Benko, Stephen, 191

Bennett, Dennis, 106, 146

Berkhof, Louis, 71

Bevans, Stephen, 28

Bloesch, Donald, 174

Bobrinskoy, Boris, 135

Bong Rin Ro, 10, 60

Borg, Marcus, 31, 155

Boyd, Robin, 53, 92, 120

Breck, John, 14

Browning, Don, 74

Brunner, Emil, 170

Brusco, Elizabeth, 27, 41, 81-82

Bulatao, Jaime, 32, 60

Bulgakov, Sergius, 143-44

Burrell, David, 49

Byars, Ronald, 89

Calvin, John, 27, 42, 145

Carr, Dhyanchard, 55, 101

Cavary, Bahar, 88

Chan Kim-Kwong, 121

Chan, Simon, 18, 106, 131, 136-37, 197

Chen Cun-Fu, 63-64

Ching, Julia, 56, 80, 162, 174

Cho Yonggi, 30, 61, 146-47

Chua Wee Hian, 186, 202

Chuang Tsu-Kung, 56

Clammer, John, 59, 114

Clarke, Sathianathan, 56

Cooper, John, 71-72, 89

Cox, Harvey, 41

D'Ambrosio, Marcellino, 8

Dawn, Marva, 88

de Lubac, Henri, 182

DeSilva, David, 113

D'Costa, Gavin, 97, 106, 118, 138-41, 144, 146

DiNoia, J. A., 174, 196

Du Plessis, David, 146

Dubay, Thomas, 150

Dupuis, Jacques, 130

Edwards, Jonathan, 62, 151

Esther, Gulshan, 50, 92, 104-5

Ezeh, Uchenna, 72

Fabella, Virginia, 19, 22-23, 132, 160

Fackre, Gabriel, 42

Farhadian, Charles, 96, 189

Farley, Edward, 12

Farrow, Douglas, 136

Fekkes, Jan, III, 199

Fernandes, Walter, 122

Forsyth, P. T., 44

Frankl, Victor, 73

Fung, Raymond, 81

Gao Shining, 40-41, 60

George, Timothy, 48

Gnanadason, Aruna, 19

Gnanakan, Ken R., 43

Goh, Daniel, 32

Gosnell, Peter, 86, 88

Green, Joel, 71

Greene-McCreight, Kathryn, 19

Georges, Jayson, 81

Gregory of Nyssa, 80

Grenz, Stanley, 47

Groeschel, Benedict, 150

Guroian, Vigen, 17, 197

Hamrin, Carol, 21, 64

Han Chul-Ha, 10

Harvey, Thomas, 24, 176, 178

Hauerwas, Stanley, 15,

SCRIPTURE INDEX

Finding the Textbook You Need